RISK
ASSESSMENT
Theory, Controversy, and Emerging Strategies
OF YOUTH
WHO HAVE
SEXUALLY
ABUSED

Editor:

David Prescott, LICSW

Chapter Authors:

Janis Bremer, PhD   Douglas L. Epperson, PhD

Patricia Coffey, PhD   David Fowers, LCSW

John DeWitt, PhD   Kathleen S. Gore, MS

Dennis Doren, PhD   Christopher A. Ralston, MS

Published by:

Wood & Barnes Publishing
2717 NW 50th, Oklahoma City, OK 73112
(405) 942-6812

This publication is sold with the understanding that the publisher is not
engaged in rendering psychological, medical, or other professional services.

Cover Art by Blue Designs
Copyediting & Layout Design by Ramona Cunningham

Printed in the United States of America
Oklahoma City, Oklahoma
ISBN # 1-885473-83-4

Acknowledgments

For Louise, Owen, Keith,
and the families that preceded us.

This book would not have been possible without the persistence
of the many young people who have invited others and me
to understand them.

I am thankful for the support, encouragement, and patience of many
individuals throughout the years. These include the contributors to
this volume as well as Lloyd Sinclair, David Thornton, Gail Ryan,
Joann Schladale, Jan Hindman, David Burton, Robin Wilson, Sherri
Reynolds, Jim Grady, Ken Singer, Rob Longo, Jerry Thomas, Keith
Kaufman, Connie Isaac, and the members of ATSA and NAPN—too
numerous to mention—who provide continuous inspiration, thought,
and information to me and others.

I am also grateful to Louise Lloyd Prescott for her reviews of earlier
drafts and to the staff at Wood'N'Barnes who have continuously
supported and encouraged this project.

Contents

Introductory Notes

David Prescott

This book is the result of the frustrations experienced by professionals regarding risk assessment. Those working with sexually abusive youth are under increasing pressure to make statements and provide recommendations based on risk assessment, and yet no effective measure to this end currently exists. The chapters that follow are provided in the spirit of sharing resources with the recognition that the field has a long way to go before it can claim to understand this most diverse population. The contributors hope that this volume inspires further dialogue and inquiry at a time when there is no final word on this important topic.

A common theme in this book is the importance of using accurate and precise language. Like many, I believe in labeling behavior and not individuals. The term "sex offender" is problematic in many ways. It has taken on numerous pejorative connotations and implies that youth who have sexually abused are little more than younger versions of adult offenders. In many instances, the term is used to connote sleaziness and persistence. Given the increasingly stringent restrictions placed on youthful sexual abusers and the media emphasis on the grizzliest of sex crimes, the term "sex offender" is too easily misunderstood by an increasingly apprehensive public. Sex offender is also a legal term, and therefore inaccurate in many circumstances. English is truly a living language, and so the language of one era is unsuitable for another.

However, "sex offender" is common usage in research, where both adults and juveniles are often, in fact, offenders in the legal sense. To this end, the language throughout this book avoids the term "sex offender" except where it refers back to the research base from which many of the chapters are derived. My intention is not to edit the language of the researchers who intend for their work to be understood in a scientific context. The underlying guiding value in this book is to use terms such as "sexually abusive youth" when discussing human beings and "sex offender" when discussing legal and research contexts.

My hope is that the chapters in this volume are informative to those entering the field, and provide food for thought to those more experienced. The intention is to apply the current literature to diverse situations while maintaining a focus on who the evaluator is—both as a professional and as a human being.

Chapter one illustrates many of the flaws and controversies surrounding risk assessment and asks some basic questions. It illustrates the fact that although risk assessment is becoming increasingly important, our methods are by no means infallible. Chapters two and three highlight many of the available tools and outline a framework for understanding psychological factors that contribute to risk. In chapter four, Patricia Coffey discusses the role of the forensic evaluator of youth, and proposes new areas for inquiry (e.g., community notification, registration, and the effect of labeling) that will assist forensic evaluators in their recommendations. Dr. Coffey reminds us that forensic evaluators have a vital role in making recommendations that balance the long-term needs of the community and youth alike.

Janis Bremer looks at resilience and protective factors in chapter five. Dr. Bremer is one of a handful of researchers and practitioners who has turned the risk assessment process upside down and advocates evaluating and strengthening those factors that will mitigate risk. Her instrument in this endeavor, the *Protective Factors Scale*, is included in appendix B.

There is no question that civil commitment of juveniles is of concern from a number of perspectives (e.g., statistically, psychologically, legally, economically, and with respect to public policy). However, few professionals have entered the field seeking to make improvements within the immediate realities. While it is always easy to complain from a distance, Dennis Doren contributes to the solution by summarizing the current state of the science with respect to the civil commitment of juveniles in chapter six.

Pursuing a similar course, Douglas Epperson discusses the history, development, and current state of a promising new screening tool, the *Juvenile Sexual Offense Recidivism Risk Assessment Tool–II* (JSORRAT–II) in chapter seven. Professionals are quickly taking note of this instrument, whose construction has taken into account the current state of the literature. This volume concludes with ideas for putting these disparate elements into practice.

Despite the progress of recent years, risk assessment remains problematic. The meaning of the word "risk" can vary among professionals and across circumstances. The conceptualization of risk in this volume results from decades of thought and investigation by others. On its own, risk has been a course of study across many individuals' lives. In the end, however, risk is not the entire story; professionals still need to manage and reduce risk. Professionals should take care to understand and differentiate risk, need, responsivity, and readiness. For this reason, I argue that young people will benefit the most when professionals understand the many facets of this fascinating topic.

Why Be Concerned?

Current research suggests that juveniles commit 20% to 30% of reported rapes and 30% to 60% of child molestation (Hunter, 1999; Weinrott, 1996). Evidence exists that different pathways of sexual aggression may indicate different variations of risk in the short and long term (Doren, 2002; Hanson, 2000). However, it is important to note that typological studies of adolescents, such as those by Knight and Prentky (1993) and Hunter (2005), are only just beginning to explore this diverse population.

Retrospective studies of adult pedophiles show that 40% to 50% report a juvenile onset to their offending. Whether or not these individuals were ever detected or counseled is unknown in many instances. Further, same-sex pedophilia is associated with an earlier age of onset (Hunter, 1999). Ample evidence shows that boy-victim adult pedophiles are at an elevated risk for reoffense (e.g., Hanson & Bussiere, 1998). While existing evidence demonstrates that sexual interest and arousal is fluid and dynamic throughout adolescence (Hunter, 1999; Zolondek, Abel, Northey, & Jordan, 2001), clearly true sexual disorders can emerge in youth, although their course and factors influencing their remission are unknown.

Studies of juveniles who have assaulted same-age or older people suggest that this form of sexual aggression is less likely to persist into adulthood (e.g., Weinrott, 1996; Elliott, 1994). However, these youth may be at an increased risk for general and violent recidivism (Worling & Curwen, 2000; Hanson & Bussiere, 1998). In many instances, sexual aggression may only be part of an emerging pattern of diverse criminality (Hare, 1991; Forth & Mailloux, 2000).

One can't understand risk without understanding the base rates of sexual recidivism (Webster, Hucker, & Bloom, 2002; Serin & Brown, 2000; Webster, Ben-Aron, & Hucker, 1985; Monahan, 1981). However, gaining a sense of the overall base rate of adolescent sexual re-offense can be a frustrating experience. For example, Kenny, Keough, and Seidler (2001) observe that "between 3% and 70% of first-time apprehended juvenile sex offenders reoffend" (p. 131).

The recidivism rates of sexually abusive youth have been studied across diverse jurisdictions. The available studies often find lower re-offense rates than one might expect. In one meta-analysis with 1,025 juveniles, Alexander (1999) found recidivism rates of 5.8% for rapists, 2.1% for child molesters, and 7.5% for "unspecified" adolescent abusers. Although the length of follow-up varied across samples, she noticed that recidivism rates appeared to grow over time. Also of note, all were considered to have been treated, although this term was not defined.

In summary, when we undertake to assess sexually abusive youth, we must understand that it is statistically most likely that they will next come into contact with the legal system for some other kind of crime. In the language of research, "the youthful sexual recidivist is an outlier" in American studies. Because of the diversity of problematic outcomes, it might be most useful to frame assessments as how adults can best help youth become responsible adults.

References

Alexander, M. (1999). Sexual offender treatment efficacy revisited. *Sexual Abuse: A Journal of Research and Treatment, 11*, 101-116.

Doren, D.M. (2002). *Evaluating sex offenders: A manual for civil commitments and beyond.* Thousand Oaks, CA: Sage.

Elliott, D.S. (1994). *The developmental course of sexual and non-sexual violence: Results from a national longitudinal study.* Paper presented at the meeting of the Association for the Treatment of Sexual Abusers' 13th Annual Research and Treatment Conference, San Francisco.

Forth, A.E. & Mailloux, D.L. (2000). Psychopathy in youth: What do we know? In C.B. Gacono (Ed.), *The clinical and forensic assessment of psychopathy.* Mahwah, NJ: Lawrence Erlbaum Associates.

Hanson, R.K. (2000). *Risk assessment.* Beaverton, Oregon: Association for the Treatment of Sexual Abusers.

Hanson, R.K. & Bussiere, M.T. (1998). Predicting relapse: A meta-analysis of sexual offender recidivism studies. *Journal of Consulting and Clinical Psychology, 66(2),* 348-362. Available from www.psepc-sppcc.gc.ca/.

Hare, R.D. (1991). *The Hare psychopathy checklist—revised.* Toronto: Multi-Health Systems, Inc.

Henggeler, S.W., Schoenwald, S.K., Borduin, C.M., Rowland, M.D., & Cunningham, P.B. (1998). *Multisystemic treatment of antisocial behavior in children and adolescents*. New York: Guilford Press.

Hunter, J. (1999). *Understanding juvenile sexual offending behavior: Emerging research, treatment approaches, and management practices*. Center for Sex Offender Management. Available from www.csom.org.

Hunter, J. (2005, in press). *Understanding diversity in juvenile sex offenders: Implications for assessment, treatment, and legal management*. In R.E. Longo & D.S. Prescott (Eds.), *Current perspectives: Working with sexually aggressive youth and youth with sexual behavior problems*. Holyoke, MA: NEARI Press.

Kenny, D.T., Keough, T., & Seidler, K. (2001). Predictors of recidivism in Australian juvenile sex offenders: Implications for treatment. *Sexual Abuse: A Journal of Research and Treatment, 13*, 131-148.

Langstrom, N. & Grann, M. (2000). Risk for criminal recidivism among young sex offenders. *Journal of Interpersonal Violence, 15*, 855-871.

Knight, R.A. & Prentky, R. (1993). Exploring characteristics for classifying juvenile sex offenders. In H.E. Barbaree, W.L. Marshall, & S.M Hudson (Eds.), *The Juvenile Sex Offender* (pp.45-83). New York: Guilford.

Monahan, J. (1981/1995). *The clinical prediction of violent behavior*. Northvale, NJ: Jason Aronson Inc.

Prescott, D.S. (2005, in press). The current state of adolescent risk assessment. In B. Schwartz (Ed.), *The sex offender, Vol. 5*. Kingston, NJ: Civic Research Institute.

Serin, R.C. & Brown, S.L. (2000). The clinical use of the Hare psychopathy checklist–revised in contemporary risk assessment. In C.G. Gacono (Ed.), *The clinical and forensic assessment of psychopathy* (pp. 251-268). Mahwah, NJ: Lawrence Erlbaum Associates.

Weinrott, M.R. (1996). *Juvenile sexual aggression: A critical review.* Boulder, CO: Center for the Study and Prevention of Violence.

Webster, C.D., Ben-Aron, M.H., & Hucker, S.J. (1985). *Dangerousness: Probability and prediction, psychiatry and public policy*. Cambridge: Cambridge University Press.

Webster, C.D., Hucker, S.J., & Bloom, H. (2002). Transcending the actuarial versus clinical polemic in assessing risk for violence. *Criminal Justice and Behavior, 29*(5) 659-665.

Worling, J.R. & Curwen, T. (2000). Adolescent sexual offender recidivism: Success of specialized treatment and implications for risk prediction. *Child Abuse and Neglect, 24*, 965-982.

Zolondek, S.C., Abel, G.G., Northey, W.F., & Jordan, A.D. (2001). The self-reported behaviors of juvenile sex offenders. *Journal of Interpersonal Violence, 16*, 73-85.

Chapter One

Twelve Reasons to Avoid Risk Assessment

David Prescott

All too often the devastating effects of sexual abuse are only barely understood by practitioners, much less the public. Coming to terms with
the etiology of sexual abuse and the typologies of abusers is an ongoing struggle (Hunter, 2005; Ward & Beech, 2004). The impact of
sexual abuse on professionals has also been the subject of much recent investigation and discussion (Edmunds, 1999). Add to these factors the increasing public outcry around the management of sexual
abusers, and risk assessment becomes an ugly task indeed. Worse
still, young people are notorious for changing, developing, and growing
up. The simple fact that they leave home as young adults can make
long-term follow-up research difficult. This chapter explores a number
of factors that make our task of understanding risk in sexually abusive
youth problematic.

REASON #1: THE TERM "RISK ASSESSMENT" MAY BE MISLEADING.
WHAT ARE WE REALLY ASKING? HOW SHOULD WE ASK IT? HOW
EXACTLY DO WE ASK? "Risk assessment" has become well known,
even fashionable, in recent years. An Internet search quickly finds it
in diverse areas of human endeavor from financial sectors to human
services. More recently, "threat assessment" has also come into
vogue in the wake of numerous tragedies ranging from school
shootings to terrorism. One might ask, "Just what is it that we are
trying to assess? Is threat assessment about understanding the
threat, the young person who poses the threat, or is it something
else? If it's really all of these things, are we using the most precise
language by calling it "threat assessment"?

Likewise, it appears that "risk assessment" comes from simple and
innocent questions, such as is an individual going to do it again,
what is the likelihood they will do it again, and should we panic now?
While these are certainly worthwhile questions in their own right, they
may not capture the entirety of what is needed to reduce the likelihood of harm or make amends to those effected by the abuse. To
this end, a more worthwhile question might be "What do we need to

do to help this young person refrain from further harm?" This question addresses the specific needs, the tasks to be undertaken, and how these tasks can occur. To this end, it may actually be more productive to move past the term "risk assessment" to a more comprehensive understanding of a young person's development and ecology. After all, the term "risk assessment" seems to exclude assessment of the protective factors that mitigate risk.

Human beings' desperate attempts to predict the future provide an unfortunate backdrop for our work. From tea leaves to crystal balls, tossing bones and tarot cards, mankind's most creative efforts have yet to be validated, and often provide future generations with amusing anecdotes. One might wonder why we attempt to assess the likelihood of future events at all when so many of us engage in risky behaviors as individuals (e.g., speeding) and as societies (e.g., nuclear power). Only weather forecasters appear to have risen above the fray, although many of us have questioned their success. Whatever the case, meteorologists discover the outcome of their predictions (which are typically intuitive adjustments to computer-generated models) on a daily basis.

Many questions plague us as we undertake an assessment. Are we trying to assess a young person's willingness to repeat past behaviors? Are we taking stock of what a family and treatment team needs to do to make sure that this behavior doesn't happen again? If it is one thing to make a list of so-called "risk factors," are we able to explain how these factors interact or contribute to a reoffense process? Perhaps most important of all, are we able to communicate our assessment's findings in a way that is helpful to our audience?

Professionals are frequently asked to make judgments related to risk. While numerous problems are inherent in this task, it seems most beneficial to all if the professional looks past the immediate questions and the way they're asked ("What's his level of risk?") and develops a more complete understanding of what is being asked. What is the referral question, really?

REASON #2: NO EMPIRICALLY VALIDATED METHOD REMAINS FOR DETERMINING THE LIKELIHOOD OF A YOUNG PERSON TO ABUSE AGAIN. Although this simple fact can speak for itself, it is worthwhile to remember that even the most recently proposed methods of risk assessment (JSOAP–II and the ERASOR, described in chapter two) have yet to be validated, and their authors go to pains to describe their limitations and warn against their misuse.

REASON #3: RISK ASSESSMENT CAN CAUSE HARM. There is no shortage of stories of professionals' paperwork being misunderstood or misused. Often it is mistaken and our subjects misrepresented. In one instance, Worling (2001) described a finding of high risk that resulted in social service's becoming involved with a family 10 years after the finding. Despite laws around confidentiality and ethical practice, there is no way to predict where one's documentation will wind up or who will view it. No matter how one couches language around risk, it is still subject to misuse. The nearest thing to an antidote is to include a time limitation of 6 months to a year in any statement regarding risk.

REASON #4: YOUNG PEOPLE CHANGE. In our rush to classify individuals, it is easy to forget that adolescence is a time of dramatic change, with or without treatment interventions. In their introduction to the JSOAP–II, Prentky and Righthand (2003) observe that "No aspect of their development, including their cognitive development, is fixed or stable. In a very real sense, we are trying to assess the risk of 'moving targets.'" For this reason, they recommend that youth be reassessed every 6 months (p. i). Additionally, the factors that contribute to their behavior are subject to change. Further, "heterotypic continuity" (Kernberg, Weiner, & Bardenstein, 2000) describes how the expression of personality pathology can change across childhood. For example, an early proneness to boredom may lead to thrill seeking behavior later on. Vitacco, Rogers, Neumann, Harrison, and Vincent (in press) found evidence that affective aspects of psychopathy appeared to result from behavioral aspects. An assessor may therefore wish to consider whether an adolescent's sexual misconduct signals a trajectory of antisocial conduct, sexual disorder, or a willingness to engage in indiscriminate activities.

In a recent review of the general recidivism literature regarding juveniles, Quinsey, Skilling, Lalumiere, and Craig (2004) note that the best predictors of juvenile delinquency among general youth ages 6 through 11, include a prior history of offending, substance use, gender, low socioeconomic status, and having an antisocial parent. The best predictors for young people ages 12 to 14 are a lack of strong prosocial ties, antisocial peers, and prior delinquent offenses (p. 91). They observe that "theories to account for the patterns of these markers tend to focus on narrow domains. In the absence of a more general theory, the wealth of correlates of antisocial behavior that are themselves intercorrelated is something of an encumbrance rather than a benefit." The authors go on to describe three types of adolescent antisociality: "adolescence-limited delinquents, ... early-starting life-course-persistent antisocial individuals whose behaviors are associated with neuropathology resulting from prenatal, perinatal, and/or postnatal problems, sometimes in combination with family and neighborhood adversity," and "early-starting life-course-persistent antisocial individuals" without neurodevelopmental pathology. They note that this third category appears to comprise a distinct class of individual, or taxon, different from other antisocial individuals (p. 94).

REASON #5: AN EXCLUSIVE FOCUS ON "RISK" AND "RISK FACTORS" CAN LEAD PROFESSIONALS AWAY FROM OTHER IMPORTANT ASPECTS OF THE YOUTH'S FUNCTIONING. Understanding risk is best seen as one part of understanding the entire youth. The factors that led to a first instance of sexual abuse are not necessarily the same factors that will contribute to a future offense. Although professionals may be able to address aspects related to risk, this is not the same as addressing related but separate aspects such as readiness for treatment, learning style, factors that will interfere with treatment, family and community circumstances, etc. Likewise, a comprehensive assessment of all factors in a young person's life is not the same as an assessment focusing on a young person's capacity to persist.

Risk assessment should be viewed as separate from other forms of assessment; however, the stakes involved in young people's lives are too high for professionals to consider risk in a vacuum. Professionals making statements regarding the likelihood of a young person to persist in sexual abuse have an obligation to convey the limitations of their assessment and to place statements regarding risk in the context of steps that will mitigate that risk. As overwhelming as the work can become, practitioners are obliged to base assessment and treatment on the long-term needs of the youth who will someday be adults.

REASON #6: UNAIDED CLINICAL ASSESSMENTS HAVE NO EMPIRICAL SUPPORT. Many professionals are tempted to believe in their own assessment abilities. Many busy practitioners are forced into quick decisions based on thin information, while others are just plain wrong. Many take pride in their ability to observe and understand, but their ability to assess risk has gone largely untested.

Hanson and Bussiére (1998) found that typical clinical judgment yielded an average correlation not much better than chance (r=.10), while prior convictions on their own correlated at .20. Further complicating matters, some authors have observed that including too much information in the decision-making process can result in reduced accuracy of assessments (Monahan, 1981, p. 88; Quinsey, 2000). Quinsey, Harris, Rice, and Cormier (1998) observe that "more importantly, the amount of information available to the clinician was unrelated to accuracy but was highly related to the degree of confidence in the judgment," and that humans "are, in fact, most confident when making extreme judgments" (p. 56).

These findings are challenging. Accurate risk assessments should include only the critical information while a comprehensive assessment will include information vital to selecting treatment targets and strategies but is not necessarily predictive. How do we find the truth? One possibility is to seek out information related to risk as early in the assessment process as possible, and craft other aspects of the assessment process around it. Whatever the case, evidence suggests that risk assessments by treatment providers can become less effective the longer a professional is in contact with the subject (Williams, 1975; also see De Vogel & De Ruiter, 2004). Many (Doren, 2005) argue against treatment providers' engaging in risk assessment. Whatever the case, treatment providers should consider the ethics and nature of their therapeutic relationships before making statements about risk in most situations.

REASON #7: ELEMENTS THAT MIGHT SEEM IMPORTANT HAVE BEEN SHOWN TO HAVE NO EMPIRICAL BASIS. Put simply, much of what our field believed to be true has turned out to be unsupported. Nowhere is this more apparent than in the tenuous relationship between items that seem important but haven't been demonstrated in the literature.

Empathy is considered to be of fundamental importance in assessment and treatment, and yet its role in reoffense is not well established. However, its measurement and contribution to abusive behavior have been the source of much discussion and debate (Fernandez, 2002). In one study with adolescents (Curwen, 2000), the well-known Interpersonal Reactivity Index (which appears in Salter, 1988) did not tap victim empathy. Hanson (2003) has observed that some offenders genuinely do not understand the harm they have caused to others while others do understand but remain willing to abuse. Meanwhile, the human brain's pre-frontal cortex, where empathy is located, continues to develop well into adulthood (Stien & Kendall, 2004, p. 23). While how much of a youth's capacity for empathy remains to be developed into adulthood is open to speculation, this single element of adolescent development will give assessors of risk reason for caution.

For many years those working with sexual abusers assumed that *denial* was related to sexual reoffense risk. However, recent meta-analyses (Hanson & Morton-Bourgon, 2004; Hanson & Bussiére, 1998) found no correlation between denial and risk. There are many views on how this may be. Researchers could be measuring denial differently from practitioners. Denial may also be more closely related to readiness and motivation for treatment, or to the responsivity principle, so that its connection to reoffense is not as direct and "washes out" of research findings. It could also be as simple as denial indicating that the person is not ready to admit what s/he has done.

One may reasonably ask how people can engage in treatment for sexual aggression if they are not willing to admit the problem. Some practitioners believe that it is possible to engage in treatment that reduces the willingness to engage in harmful behaviors in general, including sexual aggression. Others may be willing to engage in abuse-specific treatment without fully divulging the extent of their abuse history. To the present, it seems that many individuals do not want to acknowledge high-stakes behaviors such as sexual aggression, and that some individuals take longer than others to fully disclose their actions in assessment and treatment situations. Denial may simply mean that professionals have not yet established an environment where the youth may safely disclose. Many things may drive a reoffense process, but just because a young person denies his actions does not mean he will do it again.

For many years, professionals have sought to "break down denial" before moving into more substantive aspects of treatment. For purposes of assessment, listening to denial and considering it a vehicle to understand a youth's attitudes may be more helpful. Many will offer pro-social protests as to why they would never do such a thing, and these protests in themselves can be illustrative and provide useful information. For example, "I wouldn't do that because my family would disown me" reflects different core attitudes from "I wouldn't waste my time on that whore." During an interview, a youth once stated, "Why bother? Once you've seen one naked woman you've seen them all."

Professionals entering the field of risk assessment are surprised to find that aspects of the youth's most recent offense (sometimes known as the "instant" or "index" offense) have not proved to be predictive (Marczyk, Heilbrun, Lander, & DeMatteo, 2003; Hanson & Thornton, 1999). Rather, the past history of sexual aggression is predictive. In other words, it is not the youth's willingness to abuse on one occasion that predicts, but rather the youth's persistence that can be predictive of future harm. Although professionals should not discount that the youth has, at least on one occasion, engaged in harmful behavior, there is no consensus in the literature that the referral offense in itself is predictive. Likewise, victim penetration has generally not proved to be associated with risk for sexual recidivism among youth, although it has been associated with elevated risk for violence (Langstrom & Grann, 2000). However, victim penetration has been associated with deviant sexual arousal patterns in the case of same-sex child molestation by adolescent males.

For years, considering aspects such as clinical presentation and psychological maladjustment (e.g., depression, anxiety) appeared as common sense. However, these too turn out to have very little long-term predictive validity on their own (Hanson & Bussiére, 1998; Hanson & Morton-Bourgon, 2004), and likely have more to do with an individual's ability to respond to treatment. They can also be useful in understanding the nature of an individual's decision to engage in harmful behavior in the shortterm. In other words, the fact that a young person is prone to anxiety is likely neither a risk nor a protective factor in the long run, although reducing anxiety is a worthwhile treatment goal in itself. However, anxiety may well contribute to or protect against future harm, depending on the individual.

REASON #8: THE UNCERTAINTY OF SEXUAL AROUSAL. There is little question that sexual arousal to children is a powerful predictor of sexual recidivism among adult abusers (Hanson & Bussiére, 1998; Hanson & Morton-Bourgon, 2004). However, the clarity appears to end there for risk assessment purposes. Arousal to rape among adults has not been shown to be predictive, although this may be due in part to the methods employed (ibid.). There is growing consensus, however, that sexual arousal in youth is more dynamic than once believed, that its changing nature prevents it from being an effective predictor, and that it is therefore less of a treatment target for youthful sexual abusers than their adult counterparts (Johnson, 2005; Rich, 2003). Hunter (1999) observes:

A minority of sexually abusive youth manifest paraphilic (deviant) sexual arousal and interest patterns. These arousal and interest patterns are recurrent and intense, and relate directly to the nature of the sexual behavior problem (e.g., sexual arousal to young children). Deviant sexual arousal is more clearly established as a motivator of adult sexual offending, particularly as it relates to pedophilia. A small subset of juveniles who sexually offend against children may represent cases of early onset pedophilia. Research has demonstrated that the highest levels of deviant sexual arousal are found in juveniles who exclusively target young male children, specifically when penetration is involved. In general, the sexual arousal patterns of sexually abusive youth appear more changeable than those of adult sex offenders, and relate less directly to their patterns of offending behavior (p. 3).

The sexual arousal patterns of youth have proved to be elusive targets for both assessment and treatment. Given that adolescence is by definition a time of accelerated development, it makes sense that sexual interest and arousal is subject to change. However, adolescence is also a time when antisocial behavior is common (Moffitt, 1993). Professionals working with youth must therefore ask fundamental questions: Is the current instance of sexual aggression the result of sexual interest or a willingness to engage in harmful behavior? Should professionals be more concerned about sexual deviance or antisociality? What is the most unacceptable element of this behavior?

Looking past the arousal patterns toward a more holistic understanding of the youth may make more sense (Prescott & Longo, 2005). Evidence demonstrates that youth are simply more willing to self-report behaviors that cause concern in adults (Zolondek et al., 2001). In many instances, youth may be reenacting their own abuse or situations they have witnessed (Schwartz, Cavanaugh, Prentky, & Pimental, 2005). Given the histories of abuse, neglect, and trauma among sexually abusive youth, harmful sexual behavior may not be deviant within the context of their experience. Finally, professionals are obligated to consider the effects of living in group care. Blasingame (2001), referring to individuals with developmental disabilities, makes a number of observations that are salient for out-of-home situations, as well as many in-home situations:

Some restrictive environments may place people with developmental disabilities in a facility that serves only same-gender persons. Such placement decreases the opportunities for pursuing healthy heterosexual relationships. By default, this may increase the likelihood of sexual conduct considered sexually offensive or inappropriate by care providers, including consenting homosexual activity.... But all human beings are sexual beings and prone to develop sexual attraction for whomever they socialize with regardless of gender. Without age-appropriate social and sexual outlets, people default to whomever they have access....

Learning, social environment, and personal experience further shape, train, and condition the behavior patterns of people.... When raised in an institutional setting, his/her behavior reflects the learning experiences and opportunities presented in that environment. Learning sexual scripts... is an informal process for most people, with or without developmental disabilities, but it has a long-term impact on behavior (pp. 14-15).

Professionals should be on guard for how our historical understanding of sexual deviance in adults can shape our concerns for youth. The most comprehensive report on practices and trends in sexual abuser management to date was conducted by the Safer Society Foundation (McGrath, Cumming, & Burchard, 2003). This survey included questions regarding sexual arousal reconditioning techniques, such as aversive behavioral rehearsal, covert sensitization, masturbatory satiation, odor aversion, and a technique called "minimal arousal conditioning," where the youth interrupts a fantasy as soon as it becomes arousing. The results of the programs that use one or more are as follows:

- Male adolescent residential: 56.4%
- Male adolescent outpatient: 49.4%
- Female adolescent residential: 48.5%
- Female adolescent outpatient: 37.2%

Research suggests, however, that youthful sexual abusers do not manifest sexual disorders in the same ways as adults. The evidence indicates that sexual arousal is fluid and dynamic across adolescence (Hunter & Becker, 1994). Although sexually abusive youth can engage in sexually deviant behavior, the majority of them appear not to experience persistent and entrenched sexual deviance. The inability to regulate, manage, or control sexually aggressive/inappropriate/

deviant thoughts or impulses may be a more effective and accurate treatment strategy.

Given the delicate state of adolescence, professionals involved in assessment may want to issue strong cautions around understanding and treating sexual interest in youth. The following are offered[1] as places to start:

Understand sexual arousal in the broader context of emotional and physiological development. Sexual arousal takes many different forms and changes across adolescence. In many instances, it is the capacity of the individuals to cope, self-soothe, regulate, and manage themselves that may be the most important treatment target. Traumatized individuals may also have intense difficulty managing all forms of arousal and be in a constant flight-fight-or-freeze mode.

Understand the context of the harmful sexual behavior. As noted above, many youthful sexual abusers come from settings where their behavior may be "normal" in keeping with their experiences and surroundings. Our focus should be on educating the individual on more healthy relational processes rather than on labeling his behavior as "deviant."

Understand the developmental history of the youth, including his harmful behaviors as well as his experiences with trauma (whether sexual, physical, or from neglect) or other developmental disruptions. Although we are often horrified by the actions of young people, it does them no good to understand behavior out of context. Although it may be easier to punish and target what we believe to be sexual deviance, these interventions can be short sighted and harmful to the youth's long-term development. There is certainly a place for short-term management strategies, but we should also actively consider long-term development in both evaluation and treatment.

Be careful with interventions targeting sexual deviance. It is likely more illusory than it seems in teenage years. Further, treatment that emphasizes "what's wrong" often overlooks "what's right" in the young person's life. While we might believe that we are holding youth accountable, it may make more sense to first teach what accountability is, and how to be responsible. By inviting the

---

[1] With thanks to Jim and Sherri Grady.

youth to become the person he wants to be (Schladale, 2002), we can set up goals to accomplish rather than goals based on avoidance. Although arousal reconditioning techniques can be useful in situations, in which individuals are motivated to reduce an entrenched pattern of arousal, these techniques present risks to a young person's development that are not at issue in the treatment of adults, where these interventions originated. Given that youth are still developing their own sense of values and identity, they may easily define themselves as little more than the sum of their harmful fantasies and behaviors. In this context, adults demanding accounts of sexual fantasies may appear as just another group of people who don't understand them.

Remember that all adolescents are sexual beings. It is easy to interpret evidence of adolescent sexuality as evidence of deviance. The willingness to tell a dirty joke at an inappropriate time may speak more to the individual's lack of social skills than to a propensity to abuse. Useful questions can be "Is this deviance or is this indiscriminate behavior? Might it simply be bad judgment or evidence of the lopsided nature of youth?"

REASON #9: RISK ASSESSMENT CAN REFLECT OR CONTRIBUTE TO POOR PUBLIC POLICY. There are many worthwhile reasons to consider the likelihood of a young person to engage in further harm. These include the establishment of treatment targets and plans, placement/reunification decisions, consideration of making amends to victims, etc. In many instances, however, risk assessment has been used to implement policies of unknown and/or questionable impact on youth. In one case, Poole, Leidecke, and Marbibi (2001), investigated Static-99 (Hanson & Thornton, 1999), an adult actuarial scale for use with adolescents. At that time, the Texas Youth Commission was interested in the use of this scale for registration and community notification purposes in accordance with Texas law SB 1650 and established a high-risk cutoff score of 4 rather than the authors' recommended score of 6. From the Executive Summary:

> In accordance with SB 1650, the Risk Assessment Review Committee chose the Static-99 as its assessment tool and altered the scoring procedure based on their data. All Texas sex offenders 18 years and older are subject to assessment using the Static-99. One concern of using the Static-99 was that all sex offenders 18 to 21 years of age received a score of one in the following categories: age at time of release and

marriage status. In order to obtain a high-risk level, an offender needs to score a four or more on the Static-99. Therefore, everyone in this population was automatically half way to being a high-risk sex offender. Research on juvenile sex offenders suggests that other characteristics may apply to offenders who were juvenile at the time their sex crime was committed....

This study found that Static-99 did assign a high-risk level to all juvenile offenders (four juveniles) who were arrested for another sex offense within the 4-year follow-up period. However, it also assigned to the high-risk category 17 juvenile offenders who did not recidivate sexually. This raises questions about the rate of false positives observed in this study and the sensitivity of the instrument with adults who committed their sex crimes as juveniles.... The high percentage of false positives is most likely attributable to the Risk Assessment Committee's decision to change the scoring system, making 4 or higher the high-risk cutoff point (pp.1-2).

The authors conclude with a recommendation to change the scoring system. Whatever side one comes down on with respect to policies such as notification and registration of sexually abusive youth or of changing scoring protocols, assessing risk in young people does not occur in a vacuum. Professionals will need to consult their personal and professional ethics before undertaking assessments of young people. If the purpose of an assessment is to identify treatment and management strategies, it may be best to forego the use of language such as "risk" and focus instead on ideas such as "predisposition to," "vulnerability toward," etc. in the context of a "sexual aggression assessment," "needs assessment," etc. and include the time limitations described earlier.

REASON #10: SEXUALLY ABUSIVE YOUTH ARE AT HIGHER RISK TO CAUSE OTHER KINDS OF HARM, AND SOME ARE MORE LIKELY THAN OTHERS. Many authors, such as Serin and Brown (2000) and Monahan (1981) have emphasized the importance of taking base rates of reoffense into account. However, studies of adolescent sexual recidivism have not been prolific and have yielded varying results across populations and jurisdictions (Worling & Curwen, 2000). Studies conducted outside North America appear to find higher base rates of reoffense (e.g., Nisbet, Wilson, & Smallbone, 2004; Langstrom & Grann, 2000). However, the available studies in North America often find lower reoffense rates than one might think. In one meta-analysis including 1,025 juveniles, Alexander (1999) found recidivism rates of 5.8% for rapists, 2.1% for child molesters, and 7.5% for "unspecified" adolescent abusers. While the length of follow-up varied across samples, Alexander noticed that recidivism rates appeared to grow over time. Also of note, all had been "treated." Any number of reasons could explain these discrepancies (including the presence of "status offenders" in North American samples), but none have been tested.

Langstrom and Grann (2000) found that among 46 adolescents ages 15 to 20, sexual recidivism was 20%, violent recidivism was 22%, and general recidivism (including violence) was 65% in a 6-year follow-up period. In contrast to Alexander's findings, the authors found that most of their recidivists did so within 1 to 2 years of follow-up. Maintaining caution is important in interpreting these numbers. This sample represents nearly all of the young sexual offenders who received court-ordered forensic psychiatric evaluations in Sweden across a number of years. One can easily infer that, given the small size and apparently unusual circumstances of their selection, these must have been considered particularly problematic young people. Worling and Curwen (2000) followed 148 Canadian youth for an average of 6 years. They found that those who received "abuse-specific" treatment had a 72% reduction in sexual recidivism. The untreated youth recidivated at 18% in the follow-up period, while the treated youth recidivated at a rate of 5%.

Clearly, all of these results must be interpreted with caution. First, ethical considerations have prevented the highest-quality randomized treatment/no-treatment comparisons. Even if these were possible, the specific "active ingredients" of treatment have yet to be determined, although *Multi-Systemic Treatment* (MST; Henggeler et al., 1998) appears particularly promising. Second, recidivism rates are susceptible to adults' ability to detect reoffense. One may argue that these rates are grossly underestimated given that victims often don't wish to report crimes. On the other hand, one might also argue that because youthful sexual abusers often have high rates of recidivism for nonsexual crimes, they are not particularly adept at evading detection. One might further argue that upon arrest for sexually abusive behavior, many youth have far fewer opportunities for reoffense due to increased supervision. Finally, some have argued that the measurement treatment effect is obscured by attrition.

An aspect of recidivism that often receives less attention is "time at risk" for various types of offenders, such as child molesters and rapists. Prentky, Harris, Frizzell, and Righthand (2000) found that among 75 youth studied, only 3 recidivated in a 1-year follow up. This was in the first study on which the *Juvenile Sex Offender Assessment Protocol* (JSOAP; Prentky, et al., 2000) was based. Of note, however, is that the 3 sexual recidivists all scored higher on the "impulsive, antisocial behavior" scale than on the "sexual drive/pre-occupation" scale. For total JSOAP scores, there was roughly a 6.5-point difference between the 8 recidivists (including three sexual recidivists) and the non-recidivists. Hecker, Scoular, Righthand, and Nagle (2002) found in a 10- to 12-year follow up that total JSOAP scores were not correlated with sexual recidivism, but that the sexual drive scale was strongly predictive. However, this represented only 6 recidivists (11%) in a sample of 54 male adolescents. The nonsexual recidivism in this sample was 37%.

Righthand, Knight, and Prentky (2002) found that higher scores on the sexual drive scale were associated with male victims and number of victims, while the antisocial behavior scale was associated with teenage and older victims. The numbers reported are low, but suggest beginning avenues for further inquiry in understanding these subscales. Hanson and Bussiére (1998) found that rapists and child molesters differed more in their time at risk than in their long-term recidivism rates. Many rapists were quick to reoffend, while child molesters appeared to reoffend at more uniform rates over time. For this reason, historical information related to sexual and antisocial aspects of sexual offending can contribute to decisions around treatment and supervision strategies over time.

The prudent assessor of risk will therefore wish to consider all forms of potentially harmful behavior, including sexual, violent, and general recidivism, as well as suicide risk.

REASON #11: BITTER DISAGREEMENT ABOUT THE BEST APPROACH OFTEN OCCURS. The diversity of thought regarding risk assessment challenges even the newcomer. Were the stakes not so high, it would make for an enthralling pastime. Considerable debate centers on the merits of clinical or mechanical methods of assessment. In a well-known statement, Quinsey et al. (1998) clarify their view on actuarial versus clinical assessment:

What we are advising is not the addition of actuarial methods to existing practice, but rather the complete replacement of existing practice with actuarial methods. This is a different view than we expressed in Webster, Harris, Rice, Cormier, and Quinsey (1994), where we advised the practice of adjusting actuarial estimates by up to 10% when there were compelling circumstances to do so.... Actuarial methods are too good and clinical judgment too poor to risk contaminating the former with the latter. The sorts of compelling circumstances that might tempt one to adjust an actuarial score are better considered separately in deciding on supervisory conditions, interventions designed to reduce risk, and so forth (p. 171).

In a review of recent research and meta-analyses, however, Hart, Kropp, and Laws (2004) dispute "the alleged superiority of actuarial risk assessment":

At present... the superiority of actuarial decision-making is an article of faith rather than a fact. Any claim of actuarial superiority is an inference based on evidence of questionable relevance and should be acknowledged as such. It is entirely reasonable for mental health professionals to conclude that current scientific evidence is not sufficient to support the use of or reliance on actuarial procedures; indeed, it is entirely reasonable to conclude that the weight of the scientific evidence is sufficient to reject altogether the use of or reliance on actuarial procedures (p.11).

These differences transcend academic debate. Referring to the use of the death penalty, Stone (1985) noted

Although the standard of future dangerousness in capital punishment makes sense in legal and moral discourse, and in the abstract is fair, it becomes, in its empirical application of particular cases, unfair. When the Supreme Court of the United States was presented with a legal brief making some of these points and arguing that a Texas death penalty statute with its dangerous standard should be rejected "because it is impossible to predict dangerous behavior," the Court stood its ground and wrote: "It is, of course, not easy to predict future behavior. The fact that such a determination is difficult, however, does not mean that it cannot be made. Indeed, prediction of future criminal conduct is an essential element in

many of the decisions rendered throughout our criminal justice system.... the task that a Texas jury must perform is thus
basically no different from the task performed each day
throughout the American system of criminal justice" (Jurek v.
Texas, 428 U.S. 262, 1976).

To an empiricist, the logic is baffling. Listening to a lot of irrelevant and perhaps false information does not improve
one's ability to make predictions. But to the legal mind a decision, even a predictive decision, made in good faith after all
the evidence has been weighed, has a kind of procedural validity even if it defies common sense and lacks moral substance. Lawyers may not all agree with this analysis, but it
seems to me a fair and not unsympathetic description of the
Supreme Court's current posture (pp. 20-21).

At a more practical level are differences in how people look at assessment in general. Rich (2000) describes risk assessment as a "clinical
process," while many of the best-studied adult actuarial measures are
in use by probation and parole officers. Many of those who work with
adolescents (e.g., Grady & Reynolds, 2003) have advocated looking
beyond risk assessment to holistic treatment. Others (e.g., Bremer,
2001) advocate investigation into protective factors and resilience
rather than risk. Beyond their idealistic appeal, these arguments clarify
areas for necessary further research.

Seeking to reconcile these extremes, Webster, Hucker, and Bloom
(2002) have made five recommendations, which may be summarized
as follows:

- Understand the applicable legal framework.
- Risk assessment must be **evidenced based**.
- Include an individualized statement of risk.
- Include steps to reduce risk.
- Compare the individual case with scientific data when
  possible.

However, even these are open to controversy, as one can easily note
that these guidelines have not been tested, and that the terms "individualized" and "risk" are not adequately defined. Further, one may
wonder whether an "individualized" statement of risk is not a de

facto comparison of an individual to a group of similar individuals, a process at the heart of actuarial assessment.

A final example is found in differing interpretations of a meta-analysis by Grove, Zald, Boyd, Lebow, Snitz, and Nelson (2001). This study concluded that "mechanical predictions of human behaviors are equal or superior to clinical prediction for a wide range of circumstances" (p. 19), and that "there seem, then to be no barriers to a general preference for mechanical prediction where an appropriate mechanical algorithm is available" (p. 26).

However, Hart et al. (2004, p. 11) take a different perspective in a section titled "The alleged superiority of actuarial risk assessment":

> Two things should be noted about the Grove et al. (2000) meta-analysis. First, most of the studies that directly compared the two decision-making approaches involved diagnosis or decisions about present state (for example, studies that compare the human versus mechanical interpretation of X-rays with respect to the diagnosis of lung cancer), rather than prognosis or predictions about the future. Second, only a handful of studies compared actuarial versus clinical predictions of violence, and none examined predictions of sexual violence. In fact a more recent review of the literature on violence found only eight studies that purported to compare actuarial versus clinical predictions of violence; and just one of the eight studies examined sexual offenders. There was no clear evidence supporting the superiority of either method of decision-making (Litwack, 2001).

It is worthwhile to remember that even John Monahan, who has strongly argued against unguided clinical judgment in predicting violent behavior (1981) has more recently stated: "This reliance on clinical judgment—aided by empirical understanding of risk factors for violence and their interactions—reflects, and in our view should reflect, the standard of care at this juncture in the field's development" (Monahan et al., 2001, pp. 134-135). Also noteworthy is that many leaders in the field have reviewed and refined their outlooks throughout the evolution of their work (Greenland, 1985).

REASON #12: AN EXCLUSIVE FOCUS ON REDUCING RISK CAN STEER OUR FIELD'S ATTENTION AWAY FROM VICTIM-CENTERED TREATMENT. Hindman (2005) observes that it is all too easy for those treating sexual abusers to forget the well-being of those most impacted by sexual abuse. Although treatment that reduces risk for future harm clearly benefits abuser and community alike, we may easily to place less emphasis on the emotionally challenging task of making amends to those who experienced the abuse. To a very real extent, our field's understanding of risk and victimization remain mutually exclusive. Hindman (2005) states

> There is a major difference in favor and power between the two groups [victim advocates and sexual abuser specialists]. High profile cases of child abduction, rape, and murder may represent only about 1% of sex offenders, but those cases garner perhaps 90% of the media coverage. With this limited information, the marketing plan for the victim advocates is clear, intentional, and powerful. The victim advocate's train is driven by outrage and retribution (rightly so for what they know) and the offender folks strive forward claiming success of treatment through correlations and percentages about efficacy, but usually preaching to their own choir. And the sad reality is that offender folks are actually victim advocates—they are just disguised... as sex offender therapists and that is what makes the efforts of both factions so far apart and why a marriage of the two efforts seems so remote....
>
> Even if the data within the field of sex offender treatment and management continues its positive spiral—even if the contribution to a safer society is clear within the field—all could be for naught. What will it matter how astute the risk assessment and treatment outcome studies reveal themselves if the success is not and cannot be sold (yes marketed) to an outraged public, still with tender tears for Amber, Megan, Polly, and Jacob? (p. 3)

Professionals are urged to take these observations into account when working to assess sexual abuse risk. Behind the statistics cited throughout this book is a very clear human toll. Risk management plans that do not account for the long-term needs of the victim will miss their mark.

Conclusion

Professionals entering the field of youthful sexual aggression have many reasons to be cautious in their understanding of youth and predictions of what they might do. Young people have long been considered fundamentally unpredictable, and the notion that we can reasonably predict behaviors that thrive on secrecy is testimony to both our profession's optimism and desperation. However, despite the lack of empirically validated means by which to assess the risk of young sexual abusers to persist, professionals face strong pressure to make statements about risk, as well as obligations to the community and those affected by sexual abuse. Given the impact of current public policy on youth, and the high visibility of sex crimes, the stakes have gotten higher in the last decade. This becomes increasingly complicated as we realize that those affected by sexual abuse often include these young abusers themselves. Despite the research into adult and adolescent abusers, no research describes an individual's inherent willingness to persist in causing sexual harm. While many indicators of this willingness are described in the following chapters (e.g., sexual deviance and antisociality), the field of sexual abuser management and treatment remains in its own sort of adolescence, marked by strong emotions and contentious debate.

References

Alexander, M. (1999). Sexual offender treatment efficacy revisited. *Sexual Abuse: A Journal of Research and Treatment, 11*, 101-116.

Blasingame, G. D. (2001). *Developmentally disabled persons with sexual behavior problems: Treatment, management, supervision.* Oklahoma City: Wood'N'Barnes.

Curwen, T. (2000, May 29). *Utility of the Interpersonal Reactivity Index (IRI) as a measure of empathy in male adolescent sex offenders.* Paper presented at the 6th International Conference on the Treatment of Sexual Offenders, Toronto, Ontario, Canada.

de Vogel, V. & de Ruiter, C. (2004). Differences between clinicians and researchers in assessing risk of violence in forensic psychiatric patients. *The Journal of Forensic Psychiatry and Psychology, 15(1)*, 145-164.

Edmunds, S. B. (Ed.). (1999). *Impact: Working with sexual abusers.* Brandon, VT: Safer Society Press.

Fernandez, Y. (Ed.). (2002). *In their shoes: Examining the role of empathy and its place in the treatment of offenders.* Oklahoma City: Wood'N'Barnes.

Grady, J. & Reynolds, S. (2003, October). *Holistic assessment and treatment of sexually abusive youth.* Presented at the Annual Meeting of the Association for the Treatment of Sexual Abusers, Montreal, Quebec, Canada.

Greenland, C. (1985). Dangerousness, mental disorder, and politics. In C.D. Webster, M. H. Ben-Aron, & S. J. Hucker (Eds.), *Dangerousness: Probability and prediction, psychiatry and public policy* (pp. 25-40). Cambridge, UK: Cambridge University Press.

Grove, W. M., Zald, D. H., Boyd, S., Lebow, S., Snitz, B. E., & Nelson, C. (2001). Clinical versus mechanical prediction. *Psychological Assessment, 12(1)* 19-30.

Hanson, R. K. (2003). Empathy deficits of sexual offenders: A conceptual model. *Journal of Sexual Aggression, 9*, 13-23.

Hanson, R. K. & Bussiére, M. T. (1998). Predicting relapse: A meta-analysis of sexual offender recidivism studies. *Journal of Consulting and Clinical Psychology, 66*(2), 348-362. Available from www.psepc-sppcc.gc.ca/.

Hanson, R. K. & Morton-Bourgon, K. E. (2004). *Predictors of sexual recidivism: An updated meta-analysis.* Available from www.psepc.gc.ca/publications/ corrections/pdf/200402_e.pdf.

Hanson, R. K. & Thornton, D. (1999). *Static-99: Improving actuarial risk assessments for sex offenders (User Report 1999-02).* Ottawa: Department of the Solicitor General of Canada. Available from www.sgc.gc.ca.

Hart, S. D., Kropp, P. R., & Laws, R. L. (2004). *The risk for sexual violence protocol (RSVP).* Burnaby, BC: Mental Health, Law, and Policy Institute, Simon Fraser University.

Hecker, J., Scoular, J., Righthand, S., & Nangle, D. (2002, October). *Predictive validity of the J-SOAP over 10-plus years: Implications for risk assessment.* Paper presented at the Annual Meeting of the Association for the Treatment of Sexual Abusers, Montreal, Quebec, Canada.

Henggeler, S. W., Schoenwald, S. K., Borduin, C. M., Rowland, M. D., & Cunningham, P.B. (1998). *Multisystemic treatment of antisocial behavior in children and adolescents.* New York: Guilford Press.

Hunter, J. (1999). *Understanding juvenile sexual offending behavior: Emerging research, treatment approaches, and management practices.* Center for Sex Offender Management. Available from www.csom.org.

Hunter, J. (2005). Understanding diversity in juvenile sexual offenders: Implications for assessment, treatment, and legal management. In R. E. Longo & D. S. Prescott (Eds.), *Current perspectives: Working with sexually aggressive youth and youth with sexual behavior problems.* Holyoke, MA: NEARI Press.

Hunter, J. A. & Becker, J. V. (1994). The role of deviant sexual arousal in juvenile sexual offending: Etiology, evaluation, and treatment. *Criminal Justice and Behavior 21,* 132-149.

Johnson, B. R. (2005). Comorbid diagnosis of sexually abusive youth. In R. E. Longo & D. S. Prescott (Eds.), *Current perspectives: Working with sexually aggressive youth and youth with sexual behavior problems.* Holyoke, MA: NEARI Press.

Kernberg, P. F., Weiner, A. S., & Bardenstein (2000). *Personality disorders in children and adolescents.* New York: Basic Books.

Langstrom, N., & Grann, M. (2000). Risk for criminal recidivism among young sex offenders. *Journal of Interpersonal Violence, 15,* 855-871.

Litwack, T. R. (2001). Actuarial versus clinical assessments of dangerousness. *Psychology, Public Policy, and Law, 7*(2), 409-443.

Marczyk, G. R., Heilbrun, K., Lander, T., & DeMatteo, D. (2003). Predicting juvenile recidivism with the PCL:YV, MAYSI, and YLS/CMI. *International Journal of Forensic Mental Health, 2,* 7-18. Available from www.iafmhs.org/files/Marczyk.pdf.

McGrath, R. J., Cumming, G. F., & Burchard, B. L. (2003). *Current practices and trends in sexual abuser management: The Safer Society 2002 nationwide survey.* Brandon, VT: Safer Society Foundation.

Moffitt, T. E. (1993). Adolescence-limited and life-course-persistent antisocial behavior: A developmental taxonomy. *Psychological Bulletin, 100,* 674-701.

Monahan, J. (1981/1995). *The clinical prediction of violent behavior.* Northvale, NJ: Jason Aronson Inc.

Monahan, J., Steadman, H. J. Silver, E., Applebaum, P. S., Robbins, P. C., Mulvey, E. P. et al. (2001). *Rethinking risk assessment: The Macarthur study of violence and mental disorder.* New York: Oxford University Press.

Nisbet, I. A., Wilson, P. H., & Smallbone, S. W. (2004). A prospective longitudinal study of sexual recidivism among adolescent sex offenders. *Sexual Abuse: A Journal of Research and Treatment, 16*, 223-234.

Poole, D., Liedecke, D., & Marbibi, M. (2001). *Risk assessment and recidivism in juvenile sex offenders: A validation study of the Static-99.* Austin, TX: Texas Youth Commission.

Prentky, R., Harris, B., Frizzell, K., & Righthand, S. (2000). An actuarial procedure for assessing risk with juvenile sex offenders. *Sexual Abuse: A Journal of Research and Treatment, 12*, 71-94.

Prentky, R. & Righthand, S. (2003). *Juvenile Sex Offender Assessment Protocol–II (JSOAP–II)*. Available from Center for Sex Offender Management at www.csom.org.

Prescott, D. S. & Longo, R. E. (2005). Current perspectives. In R. E. Longo & D. S. Prescott (Eds.). *Current perspectives: Working with sexually aggressive youth and youth with sexual behavior problems.* Holyoke, MA: NEARI Press.

Quinsey, V. L. (2000, March). *The violence risk appraisal guide.* Presented at Sinclair Seminars' Sex Offender Re-Offense Risk Prediction Symposium, Madison, WI. Available from www.sinclairseminars.com.

Quinsey, V. L., Skilling, T. A., Lalumiere, M. L., & Craig, W. M. (2004). *Juvenile delinquency: Understanding the origins of individual differences.* Washington, DC: American Psychological Association.

Quinsey, V. L., Harris, G. T., Rice, M. E., & Cormier, C. A. (1998). *Violent offenders: Managing and appraising risk.* Washington DC: American Psychological Association.

Rich, P. (2000). *Juvenile risk assessment tool.* Barre, Massachusetts: Stetson School.

Rich, P. (2003). *Understanding, assessing and rehabilitating juvenile sex offenders.* Hoboken, NJ: John Wiley and Sons.

Righthand, S., Knight, R., & Prentky, R. (2002, October). *A path analytic investigation of proximal antecedents of JSOAP risk domains.* Paper presented at the Annual Meeting of the Association for the Treatment of Sexual Abusers, Montreal, Quebec, Canada.

Salter, A. C. (1988). *Treating child sex offenders and victims.* Newbury Park, CA: Sage Publications.

Schladale, J. (2002). *The T.O.P. (Trauma Outcome Process) workbook for taming violence and sexual aggression.* Freeport, ME: Self-published. Available from www.resourcesforresolvingviolence.com.

Schwartz, B., Cavanaugh, D., Prentky, R., & Pimental, A. (2005). Family violence and severe maltreatment in families of sexually reactive children and adolescents. In R. E. Longo & D. S. Prescott (Eds.), *Current perspectives: Working with sexually aggressive youth and youth with sexual behavior problems.* Holyoke, MA: NEARI Press.

Serin, R. C. & Brown, S. L. (2000). The clinical use of the Hare Psychopathy Checklist–Revised in contemporary risk assessment. In C. G. Gacono (Ed.), *The clinical and forensic assessment of psychopathy* (pp. 251-268). Mahwah, NJ: Lawrence Erlbaum Associates.

Stien, P. T. & Kendall, J. (2004). *Psychological trauma and the developing brain: Neurologically based interventions for troubled children.* Binghamton, NY: Haworth Press.

Stone, A. A. (1985). The new legal standard of dangerousness. In C. D. Webster, M. H. Ben-Aron, & S. J. Hucker (Eds.), *Dangerousness: Probability and prediction, psychiatry and public policy* (pp. 13-24). Cambridge, UK: Cambridge University Press.

Vitacco, M. J., Rogers, R., Neumann, C. S., Harrison, K. H., & Vincent (2005, in press). A comparison of factor models on the PCL-R with mentally disordered offenders: The development of a four-factor model. *Criminal Justice and Behavior*.

Webster, C. D., Hucker, S. J., & Bloom, H. (2002). Transcending the actuarial versus clinical polemic in assessing risk for violence. *Criminal Justice and Behavior, 29* (5) 659-665.

Williams, M. (1975). Aspects of the psychology of imprisonment. In S. McConville (Ed.), *The use of imprisonment: Essays in the changing state of English penal policy* (pp. 32-42). London: Routledge & Kegan Paul Ltd.

Worling, J. (2001, May 7). *Estimate of risk of adolescent sex offender recidivism.* Plenary address at the 16th annual conference of the National Adolescent Perpetration Network, Kansas City, MO.

Worling, J. R. & Curwen, T. (2000). Adolescent sexual offender recidivism: Success of specialized treatment and implications for risk prediction. *Child Abuse and Neglect, 24*, 965-982.

Zolondek, S. C., Abel, G. G., Northey, W. F., & Jordan, A. D. (2001). The self-reported behaviors of juvenile sex offenders. *Journal of Interpersonal Violence, 16*, 73-85.

Chapter Two

Terms and Tools

David Prescott

In light of the dilemmas and controversies described in the first chapter, professionals need to be clear about what they are being asked and what they are asking. This includes an often-overlooked first step: accurate and precise use of language. The impact of sexual abuse not only affects our senses, but also our ability to communicate. It becomes easy to overstate or understate one's case in a report, just as it becomes easy to speak in vague but emotionally charged language. Often, practitioners appear to be at highest risk for one extreme or another when they do not have a complete understanding of the situation or the vocabulary to communicate what they observe. Suggestions for communicating findings are discussed in later chapters, while attention is paid here to the basics.

Helpful Principles

Place too much information under the umbrella of risk assessment is a mistake. For example, although learning disabilities can easily compromise one's ability to profit from treatment that aims to reduce risk, they are not in themselves risk factors. Many factors may lead to reoffense. Learning disabilities may certainly contribute, but they do not drive a reoffense process on their own. This is an important distinction. Individuals experiencing learning disabilities and their attendant problems (e.g., poor school performance, less access to a satisfying peer group, difficulties at home due to conflicts around homework, decreased self-esteem, etc.) may develop core beliefs about their ability to function as sexual beings. They may go on to seek out someone who they perceive as an equivalent but who is actually younger and more vulnerable. If they are poorly supervised by an antisocial parent, then the chances of opportunity and willingness to engage in rule breaking becomes even stronger, and individuals who may otherwise have decided against manipulating a younger person into sexual contact will be less discouraged from doing so. In this context, viewing learning disabilities as one risk factor among a "laundry list," with no consideration for its context, does no service to the young persons or their families. To this end, considering a number of frameworks to guide understanding can be useful.

Risk, Need, and Responsivity

As explained in chapter one, not all sexual aggression is the result of sexual deviance. For most young people, whose sexual scripts and erotic templates remain unformed, sexual aggression may best be understood in the context of a general willingness to break rules. Looking closer at the elements of criminal behavior and treatment, Andrews and Bonta (2003) describe three principles: *risk, need,* and *responsivity.*

THE RISK PRINCIPLE states that interventions should be matched to the risk the abuser poses. In this context, it is best to consider "risk" as a long-term underlying vulnerability or predisposition to engage in a constellation of behaviors. Certain factors may temporarily mitigate or aggravate that predisposition. To some degree we are all "at risk" to engage in various behavior. Persons who spend more time listening to music than others may be "at risk" to play a musical instrument, and vice versa. Underneath each is a propensity to enjoy music. Infants and toddlers are "at risk" to explore their surroundings, and safety-conscious adults are aware that electrical outlets create a hazard under these conditions. The underlying propensity in this situation is exploration and not self-harm. In this case, adult intervention and the child's own development protect against this risk's turning into a bad experience.

Sadly, our profession does not yet have a means by which to measure this underlying vulnerability toward sexual aggression. At present, the best indicators or "markers" of this predisposition exist in elements that are established in an individual's history, such as the number of pre-convictions or the absence of long-term relationships with a partner. Based on the axiom that "the best predictor of future behavior is past behavior," actuarially derived scales such as *Rapic Risk Assessment of Sexual Offense Recidivism* (RRASOR; Hanson, 1997) and Static-99 are based entirely on these elements which are fixed in the abuser's past. However, even these are not the entire picture. Zamble and Quinsey (1999) describe these historical (or "static") markers as proxies for underlying dynamic processes. Ward and Beech (2004) argue that static risk factors "can be viewed as historical markers of the same underlying psychological dispositions measured by stable dynamic risk factors ... [and] acute risk factors ... should be defined as the state expression of traits triggered by triggering/contextual risk factors" (p. 271).

More important to Andrews and Bonta's (2003) conception of risk, however, is that the most effective interventions for high-risk youth will be misplaced with low-risk youth and vice versa. They cite as examples the failure of programs such as D.A.R.E., Scared Straight, and boot camps. Although the latter can offer much to troubled youth, and many who have completed them report a positive experience, they do not address the problem of underlying willingness to engage in problem behavior in the environments to which these youth return. Among adults, Smith, Goggin, and Gendreau (2002) found that prison and community-based sanctions not only had no effect on eventual recidivism, but they were associated with slightly higher recidivism rates among the lower-risk offenders!

Developmental and contextual factors (Ryan & Lane, 1997) can increase and reduce risk in the shorter term. While understanding these factors as they exist in the life of the young person is important, it is also necessary to understand that inherent risk differs from one person to the next. Research has identified only a few indicators of risk in young people:

- Early onset is a pattern of behavior and not just the fact that a prepubertal individual engaged in harmful sexual behavior. Many children engage in sexual behaviors that produce anxiety in adults, but this is not the same thing as an established willingness to persist in harmful behavior. Typically, the available research uses the age of 12 as a cutoff point in determining early onset.

- Persistence refers to harmful sexual behavior's persisting despite detection, despite sanction, and despite treatment. Persistence is not the same thing as having numerous victims before the first instance of detection. Useful questions include, To what extent has this behavior persisted and under what circumstances? The youth who persists despite family awareness, arrest, involvement with the legal system, and while under the supervision of staff in a residential treatment center may well represent a greater cause for concern than the young person who persists despite parental admonition alone.

- Clearly established deviant sexual preferences are important to understand. Central to this is that youth must show a clear preference for behavior that is likely to bring them into contact with the law. However, proper exploration is critical. For example, take the case of a young man who steals underwear from his neighbor's clothesline. What is the most problematic aspect of this behavior? Is it that he masturbated with the underwear? If so, this is not common among young men. Is it that he stole the underwear? If so, this may be more related to a willingness to engage in generally illegal behavior than illegal sexual behavior. Is the greatest concern that he prefers masturbating with the underwear to seeking out appropriate peer-age relationships? This could indicate a sexual behavior problem, although it is important to recall that the sexual arousal patterns of youth are more subject to change than those of their adult counterparts. Many, if not most, youth will find their interests move from the underwear to the underwear's owner by the time they reach maturity. Very often youth are willing to self-disclose these kinds of interests.

THE NEED PRINCIPLE states that interventions should specifically target areas related to criminal behavior. In other words, while developing assertiveness skills is a worthwhile goal for many individuals, it may not necessarily reflect the abuse-related treatment needs of the individual. Individuals with psychopathic traits can be notoriously assertive, and training around these skills could well make them more dangerous. On the other hand, increased healthy assertion could prevent both violent rape and child molestation by providing increased interpersonal competence.

The need principle can appear to stand in direct contradiction to the axiom of "meet the client where they are." After all, few ever seek out treatment in order to reduce their callous and exploitative disregard for the rights and welfare of others. Andrews and Bonta (2003) describe as "criminogenic needs" those areas where intervention in the present can prevent problematic behavior from emerging in the future. Most young people who come to the attention of professionals assessing sexual abuse will likely be more concerned about staying out of trouble. With patience and skill, presenting problems and criminogenic needs needn't be mutually exclusive. Because youth are more likely to recidivate with nonsexual crimes, concerned adults should take all forms of misconduct into account, including self-harm.

The need principle overlaps with the risk principle to the extent that the point of treatment is to reduce risk. Where a truly high-risk individual has a strong predisposition toward persisting in sexual harm, interventions that target areas such as sexual scripts and identity, core beliefs, interpersonal relationships, and one's ability to manage his/her behavior and solve problems as they arise can be successful. Because these areas can change dramatically over time in young people, they are often referred to as "dynamic risk factors." They are discussed in greater detail in the following chapter.

THE RESPONSIVITY PRINCIPLE states that interventions should match the characteristics of the offender. For example, developmentally disabled individuals will respond better to treatment that accommodates their needs. The responsivity principle may account for many of the factors that seem to be predictive but aren't. While categorical denial, minimization, and empathy deficits may not correlate to recidivism in the research, they certainly can make efforts to reduce the likelihood of recidivism more difficult.

The distinctions among these principles are critical to accurate assessment. The novice may equate treatment needs with level of risk. This would be confusing inherent predisposition with other aspects of an individual's functioning. A low-risk youth who has difficulty responding to treatment that is poorly matched to his needs and abilities might appear more worrisome to those around him, and therefore at higher risk than he really is. For example, a low-functioning incest abuser who does not comply with treatment targeting sexual deviance may appear more problematic than he is. Assuming that he is truly low risk (e.g., no prior history of sexual aggression, no attitudes tolerant of sexual abuse, etc.), these interventions may be less effective than education and restorative treatment tailored to his abilities and targeting interpersonal deficits. In this case, an assessment of risk, need, and responsivity would be more helpful to others than simply making a statement about "high risk" or "low risk."

Given the dynamic nature of youthful development, readiness to change is another area worthy of consideration. Although not directly related to risk, readiness contributes indirectly via the individual's ability to participate meaningfully in treatment and collaborate with the supportive adults in his life. Ward, Day, Howells, and Birgden (2004) have added to these principles the idea of "readiness." They write:

> We argue that there has been little attempt in the literature to distinguish between three distinct, although related, constructs: treatment motivation, responsivity, and readiness. Motivation involves assessing whether or not someone really

wants to enter treatment and therefore is willing to change his or her behavior in some respect (e.g., cease to behave aggressively). Typical clinical criteria for deciding that offenders are motivated to enter treatment include expressions of regret for their offenses, a desire to change, and sounding enthusiastic about the treatments available. In one important respect, the judgment that an offender is motivated for therapy is essentially a prediction that he or she will engage in, and complete, therapy. In current practice, it is widely accepted that offender motivation constitutes an important requirement for selection into rehabilitation programs, and therapists are expected to have the skills to initiate, enhance, and sustain motivation in reluctant individuals. Ironically, despite a plethora of literature on motivational interviewing and related interventions, there has been comparatively little attention paid to clarifying the relevant underlying mechanisms or consideration of the relationship between motivational states and other aspects of treatment preparedness (p. 646).

The authors also differentiate between readiness and the responsivity principle:

Within the broad responsivity principle lays an invitation to attend to an offender's motivation to engage in therapy and to commit to change. Responsivity, as usually understood in the rehabilitation literature, is primarily concerned with therapist and therapy features, and is therefore essentially concerned with adjusting treatment delivery in a way that maximizes learning. The major problem with the way the responsivity principle has been formulated is that there has been relatively little attention paid to the underlying constructs or an account of how the different processes and structures impacting on responsivity are interrelated. In our view, there has been a failure to realize that the ability to capitalize on therapeutic opportunities also involves the dynamic interaction between person, therapy, and contextual factors (p. 647).

The authors go on to distinguish between internal and external readiness, and provide simple ideas for motivating the "low-readiness" client. These are useful because they can help professionals consider how best to communicate an understanding of the young person:

- INTERNAL READINESS:
  1. Cognitive
  2. Affective
  3. Behavioral
  4. Volitional
  5. Personal identity

- EXTERNAL READINESS:
  1. Circumstance
  2. Location
  3. Opportunity
  4. Resource
  5. Support (including family and extended family)
  6. Program/Timing

- MOTIVATION OF LOW READINESS:
  1. Modify the client
  2. Modify the therapy
  3. Modify the setting

To summarize up to this point, key questions include:

- What is known about this person's underlying willingness to continue in harmful behaviors?

- What kinds of treatment needs relate to this person's engaging in harmful or illegal behaviors?

- How exactly are these needs related to sexual aggression, and how might they drive or contribute to sexual aggression in the future?

- What factors do adults need to understand to properly tailor services to help this person benefit from treatment?

- What psychological factors should treatment providers and supervisory adults know about to best meet this young person's needs?

Classifying Factors

The classification of risk factors into *static* (those elements solidly fixed in a person's history, such as gender or number of convictions) and *dynamic* (elements that are subject to change) has gained appeal in recent years. While useful for differentiating factors, these factors become less useful outside of a framework for understanding them. Of the dynamic variables, Hanson (2000) has differentiated between those that remain relatively *stable* across time, such as personality disorder or self-regulation style, and those that are *acute* and subject to rapid change or escalation. Examples of acute factors include substance abuse, anger, or other negative moods. These distinctions are important. Hanson and Bussiére (1998) found that substance abuse did not distinguish recidivists from non-recidivists in long-term studies of adult sex offenders, while Hanson and Harris (2000) found it to be a useful indicator of imminence.

Methods

CLINICAL ASSESSMENTS are made by a clinician, typically in the absence of objective measures. As noted earlier, unguided clinical risk assessments have not been supported in the literature. Purely clinical assessments can be highly subjective, difficult (if not impossible) to defend or challenge, and often take the form of an appeal to one's authority or experience ("based upon my 22 years of experience, I believe this young man to be among the most dangerous I have met"). Clinical risk assessments often rely upon information not supported by the literature (e.g., fire setting). Some tools are essentially lists of aspects to consider based upon common sense factors that are not necessarily empirically supported (see Gray & Wallace, 1992). Often, however, these are little more than lists, in that they do not provide guidance as to weighing, understanding, or combining factors.

EMPIRICALLY GUIDED ASSESSMENT follows an established structure or protocol. A number of examples of empirically guided assessment methods are described in later sections. Advantages of empirically guided methods include their reliance on the research literature, their coverage of areas that unguided professionals might forget to consider, and their provision of common language across evaluators. Disadvantages can include their questionable psychometric properties (including inter-rater reliability) and questionable application to individual situations. Empirically guided methods often do not use research-based cutoff scores or provide discrete categories for decision making. While the current empirically guided methods show promise, they require further study before they can be used in more than an exploratory fashion.

ACTUARIAL ASSESSMENT is, in its purest sense, an explicit and fixed method for arriving at a conclusion. For purposes of assessing sexual abusers, actuarial methods weigh specific factors and serve to compare an individual to one or more samples of others. Actuarial scales do not provide an absolute statement of an individual's likelihood for reoffense. A high score on a scale means that a sexual abuser's score is in the same range as a group of abusers whose known reoffense rate was at a specific percentage.

Actuarial scales can be very easy to use, are optimized for situations (such as sexual abuse) where recidivism can be statistically unusual, and a number have been demonstrated to have moderate predictive validity. However, they are currently limited in their ability to provide other forms of information useful for applications to individuals (e.g., risk reduction strategies) and their contribution to understanding an individual can be quite limited.

CLINICALLY ADJUSTED ACTUARIAL ASSESSMENT is the use of additional information to tailor one's estimate of risk for reoffense. For example, the lower-risk abuser who states an intention to reoffend is likely at higher risk than his actuarially derived score suggests. Individuals who display high levels of psychological factors whose relationship with sexual recidivism has been demonstrated may also be at higher risk than their scores suggest (Thornton, 2000, 2002).

The Basics

Even the most effective methods are only as good as the diligent rigor of the professional. In a recent examination of the differences between treatment professionals and researchers in assessing risk using a structured instrument, De Vogel and De Ruiter (2004) found that "clinicians usually relied on their personal experiences with the patient and made almost no use of file information" (p. 157). Although the authors note that the researchers didn't know the patients as well as the clinicians who worked with them, this study outlined a fundamental problem faced by clinicians: It is easy to over-rely on clinical impression and the belief that one "knows" the individual. Many professionals have had the experience of returning to the file and finding forgotten information. Even worse, much of the information one sees in daily interactions with individuals is not predictive of their long-term functioning (Hanson & Bussiére, 1998).

Another aspect that is often forgotten is ensuring that the assessment environment is conducive to building trust, gaining honesty, and encouraging self-disclosure. This includes both office space and interpersonal style. It is useful to remember that many youthful sexual abusers have themselves been victimized, traumatized, and neglected. Although their harmful behaviors can be horrific, appearing punitive, impatient, or demanding does not help a comprehensive assessment. Further, by coming into an assessment, the youth is likely already aware that he is about to have a challenging experience. While this can be useful, the youth may easily view adults as punitive as well.

Professionals will therefore wish to anticipate resistance and consider it a normal part of the assessment and treatment experience. Even the most normal adolescents may appear aloof and unwilling to share personal information. Professionals may lose sight of the fact that most well-adjusted adults find it difficult to be completely open and honest, particularly with respect to private details related to embarrassing material. In some cases, sexually abusive youth feel that a fundamental fairness is lacking when they were caught while others who have harmed them were not. Whether or not this is true, engaging in even small arguments in these areas can hinder further dialogue. Professionals may wish to recall the military axiom of "winning the battle but losing the war" and asking themselves whether "this is the hill they want to die on."

Emerging Scales

The field of assessing and treating sexually abusive youth has seen many tools become available in the last 2 decades. There is no shortage of measures, especially self-report forms, that lack psychometric properties. No empirically validated method remains for accurate classification of risk, although a number of scales, including the JSORRAT–II (this volume), the *Protective Factors Scale* (PFS; this volume), the JSOAP–II (Prentky & Righthand, 2003) and the ERASOR (Worling & Curwen, 2001) show promise. Professionals are urged to keep current with the research in this area, as many older tools still in use have no empirical support. The following is an overview of some tools, in varying stages of development, that may be of use to professionals assessing sexually abusive youth.

All scales are subject to misuse, and professionals must ensure that they familiarize themselves both with the scales and with the authors' recommendations for use. In the case of the JSORRAT–II (Epperson, this volume), JSOAP–II (Prentky & Righthand, 2003), and the ERASOR (Worling & Curwen, 2001), the authors go to pains to discuss limitations. Further, risk scales for adolescents contain numerous problems with respect to their total score. Among the scales discussed in this book, only the JSORRAT–II is intended solely for risk classification purposes, and even then it is intended to be used as a screening instrument (and currently only on an exploratory basis). Monahan et al. (2001) reviewed the *Hare Psychopathy Checklist: Screening Version* (PCL:SV; Hart, Cox, & Hare, 1995), and found that although PCL:SV scores were the most robust predictor of violence in their study, the items related to past behavior were the most predictive. Of note, the Hare psychopathy scales were developed to measure a construct ("psychopathy") commonly associated with persistent criminality, and not the likelihood of future criminality itself.

More recently, Marczyk et al. (2003) found that the most predictive aspects of several scales were not their total scores, but the subscales related to past behavior, suicidal thoughts, anger, fighting, and anxiety. These scales included the *Psychopathy Checklist: Youth Version* (PCL:YV; Forth, Kosson, & Hare, 2003) and *Youth Level of Service/ Case Management Inventory* (YLS/CMI; Hoge & Andrews, 2003). Of particular interest, the authors found that the referring offenses that brought youth to the attention of the authorities were not in themselves predictive. They concluded that the use of these tools for prediction "may not be a straightforward process" (p. 15). Although other studies have shown more promise, such as Catchpole and Gretton's (2003) retrospective examination of the PCL:YV, YLS/CMI, and the *Structured Assessment of Violence Risk in Youth* (SAVRY; Borum, Bartel, & Forth, 2002) on 74 young criminal offenders, the current state of the science suggests that professionals are not yet positioned to rely on total scores of the existing scales.

Questions therefore remain around the best use of the instruments currently available for sexually abusive youth. What does a total score tell us? The authors of the JSOAP–II and ERASOR note that these are less important than the empirical grounding of the process itself. To what extent can one use the existing scales to gain a greater understanding of the youth? Can we look past the scores and develop an understanding from the items? Unfortunately, no proven method exists for combining clusters of risk factors among youth, although studying the nature of the items can inform assessment. No assessment scheme speaks to every referral question, practice context, or legal application. Further, the more one strays from the scales' intended use, the less likely one is to be accurate and reliable. However, there may be some guidelines by which professionals can gather information from the existing scales and place them in a context of what the current research reveals. Serin & Brown (2000) have proposed a "10 Commandments of Risk Assessment." These are:

1. Thou shalt know thy base-rate.

2. Thou shalt use multi-method assessment strategies.

3. Thou shalt not confuse shared method variance with increased validity (i.e., more information does not necessarily increase accuracy).

4. Thou shalt be wary of clinical overrides.

5. Thou shalt heed statistical estimates.

6. Thou shalt not covet thy neighbor's data.

7. Thou shalt know the limits of thy prediction.

8. Thou shalt know thy false positive and false negative rates for specific cutoffs.

9. Thou shalt provide conditional predictions.

10. Thou shalt follow an *aide-mémoire*.

To these ends, one should begin any risk assessment with an acknowledgment of the inherent problems of such a task, and provide conditions for its use (including a strict time limitation). Professionals should ground themselves in the available base rates with the caution that one researcher's remarkably low- or high-risk population may not reflect one's own population. Groups of adolescents in residential centers can appear unbelievably disturbed and seemingly high risk, and yet the fact remains that not all of them go on to reoffend. Conversely, those exposed to the media learn quickly that some of the most dangerous individuals in history appear as solid citizens in every other aspect.

The cautious professional should then be aware of his/her own biases and backgrounds, and take for granted that interesting clinical data (e.g., fire setting, a family history of exotic illnesses, unusual statements or behavior) do not necessarily add to an understanding of an individual's predisposition to persist in future harm. Although many fascinating and worthwhile areas await further inquiry regarding the well-being of the youth, his community, and those affected by sexual abuse, one must always guard against indiscriminate use of information in considering risk.

Armed with a good understanding of the base rates and static factors associated with sexual reoffense, the professional will be better prepared to place the existing scales in a useful context and examine areas of dynamic risk, described in further detail in the following chapter.

Because young people, on average, are at greater risk for generally delinquent crimes, measures that look at the risks and needs of adolescent offenders in general can be helpful. One such tool is the *Youth Level of Service/Case Management Inventory*. According to its authors, the YLS/CMI (Hoge & Andrews, 2003) "is designed to aid professionals in assessing adolescent male and female offenders. Probation officers, youth workers, psychologists, and social workers are among those who might make use of this instrument. YLS/CMI is a checklist that produces a detailed survey of the risk and need factors of the youth. It provides a linkage between these factors and the development of a case plan" (p. 1). The YLS/CMI is essentially a youth version adapted from the *Level of Service Inventory–Revised* (Andrews & Bonta, 1995). The YLS/CMI reflects a theory of risk and need described throughout its manual. Scores in eight categories contribute to estimates of risk based upon a sample of 314 young offenders ages 12 to 17 (p. 6). The YLS/CMI is available to a wide range of professionals and can be helpful in case formulation.

The JSOAP–II and the ERASOR: Key Assessment Methods Specific to Sexually Abusive Youth

THE JUVENILE SEX OFFENDER ASSESSMENT PROTOCOL–II[1] (JSOAP–II; Prentky & Righthand, 2003) is regarded by many as an actuarial scale in that it contains fixed and explicit rules for scoring and weighting items. However, it has not yet been cross-validated and was developed on a small sample of 76 youth including 3 recidivists at a 1-year follow up. According to its authors, the JSOAP–II "is a checklist that aids in the systematic review of risk factors that have been identified in the professional literature as being associated with

---

[1] JSOAP-II is currently available from the Web site of the Center for Sex Offender Management at www.csom.org.

sexual *and criminal* offending (emphasis added, p. i))." Second, given that total scores on this instrument have yet to demonstrate significant predictive validity, one must use extreme caution in interpreting its results. The scales themselves may better address areas of need than the total score. Rather than viewing the JSOAP–II as a scale that predicts reoffense, professionals may do better to consider it as a method for addressing treatment needs and their severity.

Of the four scales, the second ("Impulsive, Antisocial Behavior") constellation correlated the most highly with recidivism in the small research sample. Of note, the authors modeled this scale on the *Child and Adolescent Taxon Scale* (Quinsey et al., 1998). Also known by its acronym, the CATS was developed as a substitute for *Psychopathy Checklist–Revised*, (PCL-R; Hare, 1991) scores in the *Violence Risk Appraisal Guide* (VRAG; Quinsey et al., 1998). In this case, the CATS proved to be effective and easy to score from file review and/or self-report, and for many applications can be more cost-effective than the PCL-R. More recently, the CATS was used to provide evidence of an underlying antisociality taxon among children (Skilling, Quinsey, & Craig, 2001).

The "Sexual Drive/Preoccupation" scale correlated less with recidivism in the development sample. Its authors have since observed that in its original form it "performs suboptimally" (Righthand et al., 2005). Reasons for this are not known. It may be speculated that the nature of the youths' sexual crimes, fantasies, and drives result in many of the more dangerous youths not being released from institutions and therefore being unavailable for follow-up. The small sample sizes and brief follow-up periods in various studies also may have played a role. Hanson and Bussiére (1998) found that, on average, rapists recidivated more rapidly than child molesters. Hecker et al. (2002) found in a 10- to 12-year follow-up that total JSOAP scores were not correlated with sexual recidivism, but that scale one ("Sexual Drive") was very strongly predictive, albeit with a sample of only 6 recidivists (11%) in a sample of 54 male adolescents. However, Righthand et al. (2002) found that higher scores on the sexual drive scale were associated with male victims and number of victims, while the Antisocial Behavior scale was associated with teenage and older victims. Clearly, the numbers reported are astronomically low. However, they do suggest beginning avenues for further inquiry in understanding these scales.

The JSOAP–II can be an effective aid to those assessing risk among youth. Clinical items such as remorse, guilt, and cognitive distortions are included but not weighted heavily when compared to historical items. Unfortunately, the specific role of these clinical items is not discussed fully. Many evaluators have met youth who freely admit their offenses out of pride and the arousal associated with recalling them. Other evaluators are familiar with the fact that strongly expressed remorse in a clinical interview does not mean that the same remorse will prevent future offenses (see the item description for remorse in Hare, 1991). Similarly, an internal motivation for change can change all of us with time.

The JSOAP–II is relatively easy to score and contains many items associated with juvenile recidivism in the literature. It has become widely used in understanding sexually abusive youth in many quarters. Like the SVR-20 and HCR-20, it can contribute to a common expression of findings and methods of treatment planning among groups of clinicians and other service providers.

Items in the *Juvenile Sex Offender Assessment Protocol–II* (JSOAP–II):

These items cannot properly be scored without the instructions that are available from the original articles.

FACTOR 1: SEXUAL DRIVE/PREOCCUPATION
- Prior legally charged sex offenses
- Number of sexual abuse victims
- Male child victim
- Duration of sex offense history
- Degree of planning in sex offenses
- Sexualized aggression
- Sexual drive and preoccupation
- Sexual victimization history

FACTOR 2: IMPULSIVE, ANTISOCIAL BEHAVIOR
- Caregiver instability
- Pervasive anger
- School behavior problems

- History of Conduct Disorder
- Juvenile antisocial behavior
- Ever charged/arrested before age 16
- Multiple types of offenses
- Physical assault history and/or exposure to family violence

FACTOR 3: INTERVENTION
- Accepting responsibility for offenses
- Internal motivation for change
- Understanding risk factors
- Remorse and guilt
- Cognitive distortions
- Quality of peer relationships

FACTOR 4: COMMUNITY STABILITY/ADJUSTMENT (past 6 months)
- Management of sexual urges and desire
- Management of anger
- Stability of current living situation
- Stability in school
- Evidence of support systems

Figure 1.A

THE ESTIMATE OF RISK OF ADOLESCENT SEX OFFENDER RECIDIVISM[2] (ERASOR; Worling & Curwen, 2001) clearly states in its introduction that it "is designed to assist evaluators to estimate the risk of a sexual reoffense ONLY for individuals ages 12 to 18 who have previously committed a sexual assault." Modeled on scales such as the PCL-R, HCR-20, and SVR-20, where items are scored as present, absent, and partially/possibly present, the ERASOR is an example of an empirically grounded structured risk assessment method. Although the items may appear easy to score, many require a great deal of consideration.

---

[2] This tool is available from its principle author, James Worling, The Safe-T Program, Thistletown Regional Centre, 51 Panorama Court, Toronto, Ontario, Canada, M9V 4L8. E-mail: jworling@ican.net.

The ERASOR is constructed so that the total score is not the primary consideration. As its authors point out, the presence of only one risk factor, under certain circumstances, may be enough to warrant a determination of high risk. Although it is designed specifically to assess risk of sexual reoffense, a recent study (Bourgon, 2002) concluded that while the ERASOR assesses static factors related to sexual aggression, its dynamic factors are related to general delinquency. A large-scale study of the ERASOR's predictive validity has not been conducted.

Advantages of the ERASOR include the ability to consider a wide range of information in forming impressions and recommendations. It can be used for evaluation, treatment planning, and service delivery. Like other structured assessment methods, it enables the use of a common language among groups of clinicians. Many of the items have the potential to be used for evaluating treatment outcomes.

Perhaps the greatest advantage of the ERASOR is its manual and the item descriptions themselves, which provide an extensive overview of the literature as well as the difficulties inherent in adolescent sexual abuser risk assessment. In its present form, it represents the current state of the art.

Items from Estimate of Risk of Adolescent Sex Offender Recidivism (ERASOR)

The item descriptions are of primary importance. The items below are included only to give the reader a rough idea of areas to be assessed in the ERASOR.

- Deviant sexual interest (younger children, violence, or both)
- "Obsessive" sexual interests/preoccupation with sexual thoughts
- Attitudes supportive of sexual offending
- Unwillingness to alter deviant sexual interests/attitudes
- Assaulted two or more victims
- Assaulted same victim two or more times
- Prior adult sanctions for sexual assault(s)
- Threats of, or use of, violence/weapons during sexual offense
- Sexually assaulted a child
- Sexually assaulted a stranger

- Indiscriminate choice of victims
- Sexually assaulted a male victim (male offenders only)
- Diverse sexual-assault behaviors
- Antisocial interpersonal orientation
- Lack of intimate peer relationships/social isolation
- Negative peer associations and influences
- Interpersonal aggression
- Recent escalation in anger or negative affect
- Poor self-regulation of affect and behavior (impulsivity)
- High-stress family environment
- Problematic parent-offender relationships/parental rejection
- Parent(s) not supporting sexual-offense-specific assessment/ treatment
- Environment supporting opportunity to offend
- No development or practice of realistic prevention plans/ strategies
- Incomplete offense-specific treatment

Figure 1.B

The items in the ERASOR reflect several possible pathways to reoffense. In keeping with current research, these can include pathways reflective of an emerging sexual disorder, antisociality, or chronic detachment (Roberts, Doren, & Thornton, 2002). It includes both static and dynamic factors as well as those that are relatively stable over time (e.g., incomplete offense-specific treatment) and those that can change acutely and rapidly (e.g., recent escalation in anger or negative affect). The manual provides a comprehensive yet succinct set of descriptions of the individual items.

Other Helpful Instruments: Beyond Those Tools Designed for Use with Sexually Abusive Youth

THE STRUCTURED ASSESSMENT OF VIOLENCE RISK IN YOUTH[3] (SAVRY; Borum, Bartel, & Forth, 2002) is an empirically grounded

---

[3] The SAVRY is available from www.specializedtraining.com and from http:// fmhi.usf.edu.

method for assessing violence risk (including sexual violence) in adolescents. Its structure is similar to the ERASOR in that it contains items established in the literature as being associated with violence, each of which is scored as present, absent, or partially/possibly present. Preliminary psychometric data are provided. Like the ERASOR, it is intended as a guide for professionals, and not to provide a total score with cutoffs for risk classification. It contains:

- Ten *historical* items (related to age of onset, history of violence, failure to comply with supervision, etc.)

- Six *contextual* items (such as the presence or absence of parental support, quality of peer relationships, ability to cope, etc.)

- Eight *individual* items (presence of ADHD, low remorse or empathy, low commitment to school, etc.)

- Six *protective* items (e.g. strong social supports, resilient personality, positive attitude toward intervention, etc.)

THE HARE PSYCHOPATHY CHECKLIST: YOUTH VERSION[4] (PCL: YV). A full description of psychopathy and its measurement is beyond the scope of this chapter. Although originally intended as a measure of the construct of psychopathy, scores on the *Hare Psychopathy Checklist–Revised* (Hare, 1991) have been found to be predictive of violence, criminality, and when combined with sexual deviance, sexual recidivism in adult populations. However, one study (Gretton, McBride, Hare, O'Shaughnessy, & Kumka, 2001) found no correlation to sexual recidivism among youth with psychopathic traits who measured high on indices of sexual deviance. There was great anticipation of the release of the PCL:YV (Forth et al., 2003).

Among adults, psychopathy can be a powerful predictor of harmful behavior. However, extending this construct to youth can be problematic. Many have taken note that even normal adolescents can display psychopathic traits. Ultimately, youth can change in ways that adults can't predict. The seemingly psychopathic 16-year-old can look remarkably better even a year later. Ethical issues with the construct

---

[4] The PCL: YV is a psychological test that requires special qualifications to administer. Those unable to purchase and administer it should still develop knowledge of the construct and make referrals for assessment as needed. It is published by Multi-Health systems, and available at www.mhs.com or www.parinc.com.

and even use of the word "psychopath" can convince a professional to avoid consideration of it altogether. Were it not for the importance of the construct, this might even be advisable. Ultimately, those attempting to understand adolescent sexual aggression are obligated to have some knowledge of the construct. *Robert Hare's Page for the Study of Psychopaths, "Sociopaths," Violent Offenders, Serial Killers ...* (www.hare.org) maintains a list of upcoming workshops, as well as a bibliography related to psychopathy.

VIEWING TIME[5] is not a risk assessment method but deserves mention for those assessing youth. The use of phallometry (i.e. the penile plethysmograph) with adolescents has seen a decline in recent years. This decline may be due to concerns about its intrusiveness and the ethics of exposing youth to sexually oriented material. The dynamic nature of sexual arousal across adolescence has also led many professionals to question its benefits in relationship to its costs. While there is no doubt a time and place for phallometry with adolescents, there are numerous situations in which its use is inappropriate (Letourneau & Prescott, 2005).

Viewing time measures examine, among other things, how long a subject looks at an image on a screen. The underlying theory is that people look at things they are attracted to longer than those they are not. The most widely distributed, and first commercially available viewing time measure, is the Abel Screen, also known as the *Abel Assessment of Sexual Interest.* Notice the term "interest" as viewing time purports to measure interest and not physical arousal.

While neither viewing time nor phallometry can measure an individuals willingness to engage in harmful sexual behavior or help determine guilt or innocence, viewing time such as the Abel Screen can provide useful information for assessment and treatment purposes within the parameters in which they have been established. Critics of viewing time assert that it is built on too many inferences to be used in forensic settings, and note that the language involved (e.g., "probability values") can be misleading. Critics note that the data involved in its construction have not been shared to any great extent with other researchers. Proponents note that when used appropriately, viewing time can be helpful and significantly less intrusive than

---

[5] For more information, readers can visit www.abelscreen.com.

phallometry. They also note that it can be used in numerous applications where the plethysmograph cannot, such as screening those working with youth in high-sensitivity situations.

Other Assessments

In many situations, assessing the youth exclusively will miss other useful avenues. Family assessments can yield important information for getting youth and family back on track (Schladale, 2005). Although there is less research into the impact of family life on sexual aggression (e.g., exposure to pornography), the role of the family in the young person's life is of clear importance. Thomas and Viar (2005, in press) observe:

> If we do not involve parents, parental figures, and/or entire families in the treatment process, who will provide the support needed by a child—or adult for that matter—in what is a painful and difficult process? Who will help families to understand what has happened or teach them how to regain control of their lives? How will the family heal from the tremendous impact of victimization? And where will they learn the information needed in order to develop an environment that provides barriers to sexually abusive behavior and that supports non-offending, non-abusive behavior?

Many professionals have worked with families who appear to have turned a blind eye to the aggression of their children, or even encouraged it. Under these circumstances it can be easy to focus on the individual youth and not on promoting health for the family. Ample research describes the failure of such interventions as boot camps and residential treatment to support change (Rutter, Giller, & Hagell, 1998).

Conclusions

A number of researchers and practitioners have put enormous energy into the development of scales to assess risk, need, and mitigating factors. Although these contributions are significant in their own right, they are not in themselves the entire assessments. Professionals will want to enter an assessment with a firm understanding of the base rates of sexual, violent, and general criminality for their population, taking into account the limitations on understanding both the population and the assessment process itself. The professional can then use the principles of risk, need, responsivity, and readiness to differentiate the various findings they make through a painstaking file review and clinical interview. Attempts to understand an individual's underlying propensity toward sexual aggression should be anchored in the historical factors that signal early onset and, most of all, persistence. The professional's focus should then turn to the dynamic factors described earlier and in the next chapter.

References

Andrews, D. A. & Bonta, J. L. (1995). *Manual for the level of service inventory–revised.* Toronto: Multi-Health Systems, Inc.

Andrews, D. A. & Bonta, J. L. (2003). *The psychology of criminal conduct, 3rd ed.* Cincinnati, OH: Anderson Publishing.

Borum, R., Bartel, P., & Forth, A. E. (2002). *Manual for the structured assessment of violence risk in youth.* Tampa, FL: University of South Florida. Available from http://fmhi.usf.edu/.

Bourgon, G. (2002). *The Estimate of Risk of Adolescent Sex Offender Recidivism (ERASOR): Evaluating its psychometric properties.* Paper presented at the Annual Meeting of the Association for the Treatment of Sexual Abusers, Montreal, Quebec, Canada.

Bremer, J. F. (2001, May 7). *The Protective Factors Scale: Assessing youth with sexual concerns.* Plenary address at the 16th annual conference of the National Adolescent Perpetration Network, Kansas City, MO.

Briere, J. (1996). *The trauma symptom checklist for children.* Lutz, FL: Psychological Assessment Resources.

Catchpole, R. E. H. & Gretton, H. M. (2003). The predictive validity of risk assessment with violent young offenders: A 1-year examination of criminal outcome. *Criminal Justice and Behavior, 30,* 68-708.

de Vogel, V. & de Ruiter, C. (2004). Differences between clinicians and researchers in assessing risk of violence in forensic psychiatric patients. *The Journal of Forensic Psychiatry and Psychology, 15(1),* 145-164.

Doren, D. M. (2002). *Evaluating sex offenders: A manual for civil commitments and beyond.* Thousand Oaks, CA: Sage.

Fernandez, Y. (2002). *In their shoes: Examining empathy and its place in the treatment of offenders.* Oklahoma City: Wood'N'Barnes.

Forth, A. E., Kosson, D. S., & Hare, R. D. (2003). *Psychopathy checklist: Youth version.* Toronto, Ontario, Canada: Multi-Health Systems.

Gray, A. S. & Wallace, R. (1992). *Adolescent sex offender packet.* Brandon, VT: Safer Society Press.

Gretton, H. M., McBride, M., Hare, R. D., O'Shaughnessy, R., & Kumka, G., (2001). Psychopathy and recidivism in adolescent sex offenders. *Criminal Justice and Behavior, 28,* 402-426.

Hanson, R. K. (2000). *Risk assessment.* Beaverton, OR: Association for the Treatment of Sexual Abusers.

Hanson, R. K. & Bussiére, M. T. (1998). Predicting relapse: A meta-analysis of sexual offender recidivism studies. *Journal of Consulting and Clinical Psychology, 66(2),* 348-362. Available from www.psepc-sppcc.gc.ca/.

Hanson, R. K. & Harris, A. J. R. (2001). A structured approach to evaluating change among sexual offenders. *Sexual Abuse: A Journal of Research and Treatment, 13*, 105-122.

Hare, R. D. (1991). *The Hare psychopathy checklist-revised.* Toronto, Ontario, Canada: Multi-Health Systems, Inc.

Hare, R. D. (2003). *The Hare psychopathy checklist-revised II.* Toronto, Ontario, Canada: Multi-Health Systems, Inc.

Hart, S. D., Cox, D. N., & Hare, R. D. (1995). *The Hare PCL-SV.* Toronto, Ontario, Canada: Multi-Health Systems, Inc.

Hecker, J., Scoular, J., Righthand, S., & Nangle, D. (2002, October). *Predictive validity of the JSOAP over 10-plus years: Implications for risk assessment.* Paper presented at the Annual Meeting of the Association for the Treatment of Sexual Abusers, Montreal, Quebec, Canada.

Hindman, J. (2005). The best of times, the worst of times: Sex offender therapists and their costumes. *The ATSA Forum.* Newsletter of the Association for the Treatment of Sexual Abusers.

Hoge, R. D. & Andrews, D. A. (2003). *Youth Level of Service/Case Management Inventory.* Toronto, Ontario, Canada: Multi-Health Systems, Inc.

Hunter, J. (1999). *Understanding juvenile sexual offending behavior: Emerging research, treatment approaches, and management practices.* Center for Sex Offender Management. Available from www.csom.org.

Hunter, J. A. & Becker, J. V. (1994). The role of deviant sexual arousal in juvenile sexual offending: Etiology, evaluation, and treatment. *Criminal Justice and Behavior 21,* 132-149.

Jesness, C. (2004). *Jesness Behavior Checklist.* Toronto, Ontario, Canada: Multi-Health Systems, Inc.

Keenan, T. & Ward, T. (2003). Developmental antecedents in sexual offending. In T. Ward, D. R. Laws, & S. M. Hudson (Eds.), *Sexual deviance: Issues and controversies* (pp. 119-134). Thousand Oaks, CA: Sage.

Lambie, I. & Robson, M. (2005, in press). Words from the heart: The process of change with sexually abusive youth. In R. E. Longo & D. S. Prescott (Eds.), *Current perspectives: Working with sexually aggressive youth and youth with sexual behavior problems.* Holyoke, MA: NEARI Press.

Letourneau, E. J. & Prescott, D. S. (2005, in press). Ethical issues in sex offender assessments. In S. W. Cooper, A. P. Giardano, V. I. Vieth, & N. D. Kellogg (Eds.), *Medical and legal aspects of child sexual exploitation: A comprehensive review of child pornography, child prostitution, and internet crimes against children.* St. Louis, MO: G.W. Medical Publishing.

Marczyk, G. R., Heilbrun, K., Lander, T., & DeMatteo, D. (2003). Predicting juvenile recidivism with the PCL:YV, MAYSI, and YLS/CMI. *International Journal of Forensic Mental Health, 2,* 7-18. Available from www.iafmhs.org/files/Marczyk.pdf.

Marshall, W. L., Fernandez, Y. M., Serran, G., Mulloy, R., Thornton, D., Mann, R. E. et al. (2003). Process variables in the treatment of sexual offenders: A review of the relevant literature. *Aggression and Violent Behavior, 8,* 205-234.

Miller, W. R., & Rollnick, S. (2002). *Motivational interviewing: Preparing people for change.* New York: Guilford.

Monahan, J., Steadman, H. J., Silver, E., Applebaum, P. S., Robbins, P. C., Mulvey, E. P. et al. (2001). *Rethinking risk assessment: The Macarthur study of violence and mental disorder.* New York: Oxford University Press.

Prentky, R. & Righthand, S. (2003). *Juvenile Sex Offender Assessment Protocol–II (JSOAP–II).* Available from Center for Sex Offender Management at www.csom.org.

Prescott, D. S. (2005). Emerging strategies for assessing risk: Theory, controversy, and practice. In R. Geffner, K. C. Franey, T. G. Arnold, & R. Falconer (Eds.), *Identifying and treating youth who sexually offend: Current approaches, techniques, and research.* Binghamton, NY: Haworth Press.

Prescott, D. S. (in press). The current state of adolescent risk assessment. In B. Schwartz (Ed.), *The sex offender, Vol. 5.* New York: Civic Research Institute.

Quinsey, V. L., Harris, G. T., Rice, M. E., & Cormier, C. A. (1998). *Violent offenders: Managing and appraising risk.* Washington DC: American Psychological Association.

Righthand, S., Knight, R., & Prentky, R. (2002, October). *A path analytic investigation of proximal antecedents of JSOAP risk domains.* Paper presented at the Annual Meeting of the Association for the Treatment of Sexual Abusers, Montreal, Quebec, Canada.

Righthand, S., Prentky, R., Knight, R., Carpenter, E., Hecker, J. E., & Nangle, D. (2005). Factor structure and validation of the Juvenile Sex Offender Protocol (JSOAP). *Sexual Abuse: A Journal of Research and Treatment, 17,* 13-30.

Roberts, C. F., Doren, D. M., & Thornton, D. (2002). Dimensions associated with sex offender recidivism risk. *Criminal Justice and Behavior, 29,* 569-589.

Rutter, M., Giller, H., & Hagell, A. (1998). *Antisocial behavior by young people.* Cambridge, UK: Cambridege University Press.

Ryan, G. & Lane, S. (1997). *Juvenile sexual offending: Causes, consequences, and correction.* San Francisco: Jossey-Bass.

Schladale, J. (2005, in press). Family matters: The importance of engaging families in treatment with sexually aggressive youth. In R. E. Longo & D. S. Prescott (Eds.), *Current perspectives: Working with sexually aggressive youth and youth with sexual behavior problems.* Holyoke, MA: NEARI Press.

Serin, R. C. & Brown, S. L. (2000). The clinical use of the Hare Psychopathy Checklist–Revised in contemporary risk assessment. In C. G. Gacono (Ed.), *The clinical and forensic assessment of psychopathy* (pp. 251-268). Mahwah, NJ: Lawrence Erlbaum Associates.

Siegel, D. J. (1999). *The developing mind: Toward a neurobiology of interpersonal experience.* New York: Guilford Press.

Skilling, T. A., Quinsey, V. L., & Craig, W. M. (2001). Evidence of a taxon underlying serious antisocial behavior in boys. *Criminal Justice and Behavior, 28,* 450-470.

Smith, P., Goggin, C., & Gendreau, P. (2002). *The effects of prison sentences and intermediate sanctions on recidivism: General effects and individual differences (User Report 2002-04).* Ottawa: Department of the Solicitor General of Canada.

Strunk, W. & White, E. B. (2000). *The elements of style, 4th ed.* Boston: Allyn and Bacon.

Thomas, J. & Viar, W. (2005, in press). From family research to practice. In R. E. Longo & D. S. Prescott (Eds.), *Current perspectives: Working with sexually aggressive youth and youth with sexual behavior problems.* Holyoke, MA: NEARI Press.

Thornton, D. (2000, March). *Structured risk assessment,* Presented at Sinclair Seminars' Sex Offender Re-Offense Risk Prediction Symposium, Madison, WI. Available from www.sinclairseminars.com.

Thornton, D. (2002). Constructing and testing a framework for dynamic risk assessment. *Sexual Abuse: A Journal of Research and Treatment, 14,* 139-154.

Thornton, D. (2004, April 27). *Psychological factors underlying offending.* Workshop at Sand Ridge Secure Treatment Center, Mauston, WI.

Thornton, D. & Prescott, D.S. (2001). *Structured risk assessment: Youth version.* Unpublished manuscript.

Ward, T. & Beech, A. R. (2004). The etiology of risk: A preliminary model. *Sexual Abuse: A Journal of Research and Treatment, 16,* 271-284.

Ward, T., Day, A., Howells, K., & Birgden, A. (2004). The multifactor offender readiness model. *Aggression and Violent Behavior, 9*, 645-673.

Weinrott, M. R. (1996). *Juvenile sexual aggression: A critical review.* Boulder, CO: Center for the Study and Prevention of Violence.

Worling, J. R. & Curwen, T. (2001). *Estimate of Risk of Adolescent Sexual Offense Recidivism (ERASOR). Version 2.0.* Toronto, Canada: Safe-T Program, Thistletown Regional Centre for Children and Adolescents, Ontario Ministry of Community and Social Services.

Zamble, E. & Quinsey, V. L. (1997). *The criminal recidivism process.* New York: Cambridge University Press.

Chapter Three

Dynamic Variables

David Prescott

Chapter Introduction

Establishing a list of risk factors is of little use without developing an understanding of how those factors may interact and contribute to a potential reoffense process. The dynamic factors (those areas of functioning that can change over time) described in this chapter should be considered a framework for understanding youthful sexual abusers that can help in assessment, treatment planning, critical incident review, and communication. It is vital to understand that these factors are not the complete picture of risk assessment and management, but they represent an approach that professionals can use for organizing information. Its five domains ensure that those working with youthful sexual abusers have an easily memorized framework for use in diverse situations. It is intended to be used in the context of the caveats noted throughout this book. Although this framework has origins in research with adults as a way of managing clinical data among adults, it should be understood in the rapidly changing context of adolescent development, and the fact that adolescents are inherently more dependent upon their environment than adults.

Hanson (2000) describes dynamic factors as being either stable (those that are relatively persistent across time, such as personality structures) and acute (those that can change rapidly, such as anger and substance abuse). This chapter first considers stable dynamic factors, and includes discussion of acute factors. Case examples are provided.

Dynamic Risk

Understanding dynamic factors is critical to constructing effective treatment and intervention strategies. As noted earlier, many of the elements apparent in an interview (e.g., denial, remorse, empathy) have turned out to have little contribution to risk, but can provide information about motivation and readiness for treatment. Evidence of dynamic risk, however, can seem to flourish in a clinical interview, whereas evidence of the same factors may be lacking in the file. When interviewers are observing denial and the absence of guilt or remorse, they can learn much information about dynamic factors. The following framework will assist professionals with their formulations and those at the front lines to understand situations as they unfold. Rather than being a simple list, these factors may interact with each other and provide insight into "implicit theories" that the young person has about the world (Keenan & Ward, 2003).

This framework is empirically grounded for use with adolescents. It is a modification of the "Initial Deviance Assessment," a portion of *Structured Risk Assessment* (SRA), developed by David Thornton, PhD at Her Majesty's Prison Service in the United Kingdom and in continuing development at Sand Ridge Treatment Center in Mauston, Wisconsin, where Dr. Thornton currently serves as Treatment Director.

The SRA is a multistage assessment process that considers both static and dynamic risk factors (Andrews & Bonta, 2003) empirically related to sexual recidivism among adult offenders (e.g., Hanson & Bussiére, 1998; Hanson & Harris, 1998, 2001). The first stage in the SRA process is a measure of static risk variables in an offender's history that do not change over time. The static measure currently used is the Static-99 (Hanson & Thornton, 2000). Scores on this actuarial scale have been associated with accurate classification of low, medium, and high risk.

The second stage of the SRA is an Initial Deviance Assessment (IDA). In this instance, deviance refers to the range and intensity of factors driving an adolescent's harmful sexual behavior. This can include elements of the youth's functioning that

- are markedly unusual when compared to non-abusive adolescents,
- contribute to harmful behaviors, and
- bring him into conflict with themselves, others, society, and the law.

The IDA has contributed to the further refining of risk classification in a number of British studies. For example, offenders who receive a low-risk classification on static variables but display psychological characteristics common among high-risk offenders can have treatment and supervision interventions tailored more effectively. Offenders whose static variables indicate a moderate risk but who display lower dynamic risk factors may benefit from different interventions. By identifying those factors that are subject to change, the SRA process serves to assist in the selection of appropriate treatment targets. In the third step of the SRA, carefully defined treatment progress is associated with decreased levels of overall risk. Indications of increased risk can include delinquent behavior while in the prison or hospital, deterioration in treatment, and beginning a sex offender program but failing to complete it.

As described in the first chapters of this book, accounting for sexual recidivism among adolescents has remained problematic (Alexander, 1999; Prentky et al., 2000; Worling & Curwen, 2000). Difficulties in establishing risk assessment schemes include

- The often-low base rates of adolescent sexual recidivism (e.g., Alexander, 1999; Worling, 1999; Langstrom & Grann, 2000).

- Measurement problems in studying recidivism in adolescents (Prentky, 2001).

- The difficulties inherent in long-term follow-up of adolescents.

- The uncertain role of physical and emotional development in adolescent sexual recidivism.

- Etiological factors in sexual abuse by adolescents are not necessarily the same as those factors that predict recidivism (see Ryan & Lane, 1997; Hanson & Bussiére, 1998).

- The fluidity of sexual arousal in adolescence (Hunter, 1999).

- The uncertain role of treatment effect on recidivism in adolescents (Alexander, 1999; Worling, 1999) when compared to adults.

- The relatively minor number of investigations of mitigating factors (see Bremer, 2001; Gilgun, Klein, & Pranis, 2000), particularly when compared to adults.

- The fundamental difference in the significance of external factors (such as peer groups, educational circumstances) between adults and juveniles.

- The uncertain role of empathy development in adolescence.

- Uncertainty around how much weight to assign social and developmental factors.

- Uncertainty around how much weight to assign the combination of static and dynamic factors.

Despite these limitations, adults frequently need to make decisions regarding the level of risk presented by youth. Although many questions remain unanswered, enough research into recidivism validates its consideration when clinicians are making decisions around treatment targets and risk-management strategies.

Although research indicating static risk factors that contribute to criminality among adolescents is available, static risk factors do not lend themselves to treatment. However, recent research suggests that accurate risk assessment should rely heavily on these items (Hanson & Bussiére, 1998). Static variables shown to be predictive among adolescents include

- An early age of onset (Loeber & Farrington, 1998).

- A prior history of sexually abusive behavior (Prentky et al., 2000; Langstrom & Grann, 2000).

- A history of prior treatment failure (Hunter, 1999).

- The selection of stranger victims (Langstrom, in press; Langstrom & Grann, 2000).

- High scores on appropriate measures of psychopathy (Forth & Burke, 1998; Hart et al., 1995).

Other static factors related to sexual recidivism among adolescents are noted in such scales as the J-SORRAT–II (Epperson, this volume), *Juvenile Sex Offender Assessment Protocol* or JSOAP–II (Prentky et al., 2000) and the *Estimate of Risk of Adolescent Sex Offender Recidivism* or ERASOR (Worling & Curwen, 2001).

This framework can

- Contribute to refining an understanding of factors contributing to recidivism.

- Assist in selecting treatment targets.

- Assist in measuring treatment gain.

- Assist in identifying risk-management strategies.

- Assist in making conditional recommendations (Serin & Brown, 2000).

- Assist in allocating resources for treatment and risk-management strategies.

- Assist in understanding incidents of abusive behavior and the context in which they occur.

- Serve as an *aide-mémoire* in overall risk assessment (Serin & Brown, 2000).

- Contribute to an understanding of the risk, need, and responsivity of an adolescent (Andrews & Bonta, 1998).

While elements such as denial have been difficult for researchers to properly associate with recidivism (Hanson & Bussiére, 1998; Lund, 2000), many of the attitudes underlying denial may be more effective in risk classification (Bremer, 1998). Similarly, elements such as empathy have had an unknown contribution to recidivism. Lane described empathy as a fundamental element in preventing sexual abuse (Ryan & Lane, 1997), while Hanson and Bussiére (1998) found little correlation between victim empathy and recidivism. Marshall and his colleagues (1999) noted the difficulty of researchers to adequately define and measure empathy. As a result, specific measurement of adolescent empathy is not included in this framework, although indications of the interpersonal and behavioral expressions of empathy (and its absence) are included among the domains.

Thornton (2000, 2002) and Ward and Beech (2004) have described a framework of dynamic risk that includes

1. Sexual deviance
2. Distorted attitudes
3. Socio-affective functioning
4. Self-management

Given the importance of family and peer groupings on adolescents, a fifth domain should also be included:

5. Influential others

Useful questions for each of these domains include

- How much has this factor played a role in the young person's sexual aggression?

- If you took this factor out of the youth's aggression, would it have been less likely to occur? Would it have happened at all?

- To what extent does this factor have a role in the youth's general functioning?

A description of these domains follows, adapted from Thornton (2000, 2004) and Thornton and Prescott (2001):

1. SEXUAL DEVIANCE. Professionals should consider this domain only with great caution, as discussed in chapter one. The role of sexual interest in sexual abuse by adolescents has attracted considerable discussion and controversy. Barbaree and Cortoni (1993) observed that 50% of adult sex offenders reported sexually deviant behavior in adolescence. Hanson and Bussiére (1998) found phallometrically measured attraction to children to be the most robust predictor of sexual recidivism among adults.

However, the sexual arousal patterns of adolescents are more fluid and dynamic than those of adults (Hunter & Becker, 1994; Hunter, 1999). Further, given that adolescence is a time when sex and sexuality are salient themes for all adolescents, adults can easily over estimate their role in the long term. Interestingly, Kenny et al. (2001) observed that among a sample of adolescents in Australia, deviant sexual fantasy did not differentiate recidivists from non-recidivists, but that deviant sexual fantasy combined with cognitive distortions did. In one study, Zolondek and her colleagues (2001) noted that adolescents were more likely to acknowledge paraphilic behaviors than their adult counterparts. Prentky et al. (2000) pointed out that recidivists did not appear to differ significantly from non-recidivists in their sexual interest. Reasons for this remain unknown. The brief follow-up (1 year) and unwillingness by adults to release those sexually abusive youth who display deviant interests from residential treatment may both have a role (Prentky, 2001). In summary, the contribution of sexual interest to sexual recidivism is an area in need of further study.

What may appear as sexually deviant may simply be a willingness to break rules, expressed through harmful sexual behavior. This is not intended to downplay the impact of sexual abuse on its victims, but to underscore the importance of differentiating the elements that contribute to sexual aggression. While true sexual preoccupation is clearly important to understand, it is easy to overestimate in youth, for whom a level of preoccupation is normative. Finally, professionals should assess sexual interest carefully to differentiate it from the willingness to engage in indiscriminate sex.

Key questions to ask are

- What is the direction of the young person's sexual interest?
- How narrowly is that interest defined?
- What is the intensity of that interest?
- Given the transitory nature of adolescent sexual interest and arousal, what evidence exists that the youth's current interest is firmly established?

Professionals can consider three forms of sexual deviance:

- *Sexual preference for children* refers to a stronger response to those significantly younger (by 4 or 5 years).
- *Sexualized violence* refers to either a preference for coerced sex or a strong sexual response to the victim's pain, suffering, or fear.
- *Sexual preoccupation* refers to the intensity of the youth's sexual interest. How much time do they spend thinking about sex? Do they think about sex to such an extent that it becomes uncomfortable or has caused them concern? Do they engage in frequent indiscriminate and diverse sexual behaviors? Do they regularly masturbate several times a day? Do they regularly use or collect pornography over and above what would be considered normal for a teenager? How difficult is it to let go of a sexual idea once it has occurred? While none of these in themselves defines preoccupation, the guiding principle is that it is over and above what one would expect to find in an adolescent.

2. DISTORTED ATTITUDES/CONTRIBUTORY ATTITUDES. This refers to the permission-giving self-statements that precede sexual aggression. It is important to note that this includes the attitudes *before* the incidents of sexual aggression, and not the defensive statements made afterwards ("I didn't think I'd get caught"). These require caution because, although they can be easy to treat, they can also be easy to hide.

The role of distorted attitudes and beliefs has been shown to contribute to sexual recidivism in adult populations (Hanson & Harris, 1998,

2001). Hunter and Becker (1999) have reviewed the role of positive and negative attitudes in adolescent sexual aggression and found mitigating and aggravating effects respectively. Kahn and Chambers (1991) found that those adolescents who blamed their victim were significantly more likely to recidivate sexually. More recently, Kenny et al. (2001) described the contribution of cognitive distortions to sexual reoffense among adolescents. Other authors have noted the contribution of thought processes to ongoing criminality (e.g., Yochelson & Samenow, 1985).

The core features of this domain are those attitudes that tolerate assault and harmful sexual behavior. They are the attitudes, values, and beliefs that the youth experienced prior to his abusive behavior. They should not be confused with the denial, minimization, or the impression management that many youth engage in after detection. A youth who perceives anger as a more socially acceptable excuse for sexual assault than loneliness may blame his poor anger control for his offense. On the other hand, many clinicians have observed youth who blame loneliness and abandonment by others for what are clearly hostile acts. Although these examples of impression management can be interesting on their own, they are not central to this domain.

Examples include

- *Sexual entitlement.* The belief that having a sexual desire entitles one to gratify it can be common in sexually abusive youth, as is the belief that their sex drive is stronger than others' (e.g., "You don't understand: I'm a very sexual person"). Central to entitlement is the belief that one has a right to satisfy their sexual urges.

- *Child-abuse supportive beliefs.* This involves seeing much younger children as peers, and the belief that children can consent to sex. In some cases the youth may believe that his actions are of benefit to the child or that the child is interested in sex.

- *Rape minimization.* This includes the idea that others enjoy or want to be raped.

- *Rape justification.* This includes the belief that others deserve to be raped, especially when they behave badly. This belief is sometimes seemingly absent in normal functioning but activated when the young person is upset, angry, or anxious.

- *Seeing others as deceitful* can correspond with a worldview that others are deceitful or manipulative and that the youth has to fight back to gain the respect and safety s/he deserves. It can also correspond to a worldview that the world is cold, hostile, or out of control.

3. INTERPERSONAL/SOCIO-AFFECTIVE FUNCTIONING is essentially the relationship of the young person to the world around him, himself, and his future. Marshall, Hudson, and Hodkinson (1993) have addressed the importance of attachment in the etiology of sexual abuse by adolescents. Although negative emotional states such as loneliness, anger, hostility, frustration, and stress have not been found to be predictive of long-term risk among adult sex offenders (Hanson & Bussiére, 1998), they have been found to contribute to short-term risk, as have intimacy deficits (Hanson & Harris, 1998, 2001). Paul Frick (1998) has documented callous and unemotional traits associated with an increased severity of Conduct Disorder. Indeed, the Callous/Unemotional cluster is best scored by clinicians trained in the use of the appropriate Hare Psychopathy Checklist scales (Hart et al., 1995; Forth et al., 2003).

This domain includes both relationships to others and perceptions of one's self within the context of these relationships:

- *Dysfunctional evaluation of self-worth* includes an emotionally painful or negative view of one's identity and ongoing functioning. Conversely it can be an ongoing sense of pride based on antisocial characteristics. It can also include a narcissistic self-image that combines an explicit, conscious evaluation of one's self that is arrogant or grandiose but fragile, unstable, vulnerable to injury. When threatened, a negative self-appraisal can be activated quickly.

- *Dysfunctional evaluation of self-efficacy* includes inaccurate perceptions of controlling current or future behavior, and a belief that other individuals and situations are responsible for one's actions. It can result in passive behaviors and viewing self as helpless.

- *Lack of emotionally intimate relationships* includes the inability, for a variety of reasons, to establish healthy and stable peer relationships or dating relationships.

- *Emotional congruence with younger children* involves feeling that it is easier to engage in relationships with those who are much younger.

- *Callousness/shallow emotions* include callous and ruthless behaviors toward others in the absence of any strong emotions. While many youth do not appear to demonstrate guilt, remorse, or empathy in clinical interviews, a key feature of this is its duration across time and situations. Youths for whom this factor is prominent often fail to accept responsibility for their actions and demonstrate a lack of concern for the rights and welfare of others to an extent that is unusual even among other sexually abusive youth. This is the equivalent of the affective facet in Hare's (2003) four-facet model of psychopathy.

- *Grievance thinking* involves both an active belief that one is a victim and a persistent scanning of one's environment in search of potential threats. It can provide a sense of justification for harming others. It can often motivate behavior that leads to high-risk situations.

4. SELF-MANAGEMENT refers to the ability to manage one's behavior in a way that reflects long-term goals rather than short-term gratification. The contribution of self-management to antisocial behavior across the life span has been well documented (Hare, 1991; Hare, Forth, & Strachan, 1992; Andrews & Bonta, 1998). Hanson and Harris (1998, 2001) found that poor self-management contributes to sexual recidivism in adult populations. For purposes of assessing youth, it consists of

- *Lifestyle impulsivity* includes behavior patterns that do not reflect healthy self-regulation. Impulsivity can range from failure to manage impulses (e.g., blurting out the answers in class) to an ongoing pervasive failure to consider the effects of one's actions on others and self. It also refers to reckless and irresponsible behavior as described in factor two of the *Psychopathy Checklist: Youth Version* (Forth et al., 2003).

- *Dysfunctional coping* refers to recurrent difficulties in dealing with stress or other problems. It might include overreliance on only a handful of coping skills that become ineffective over time. It can include overreliance on sexual behavior as a coping mechanism. Dysfunctional coping can include

- poor cognitive problem solving;

- poor problem anticipation;

- continued engagement in problem behavior despite obvious consequences;

- affective dysregulation, including irritability or other easily triggered negative affect;

- emotional rumination, where the youth copes with stress by persistently ruminating upon it in a negative way; and/or

- avoidant coping, where the youth attempts to manage stress by avoiding it.

- *Poor executive functioning.* In some cases, prefrontal cortex disturbances or deficits can contribute to poor self-management.

5. INFLUENTIAL OTHERS. Key questions are whether peers or family members actively support sexual aggression, or whether they might tacitly support sexual aggression by ignoring risk situations or treatment recommendations. Research by Ageton and her colleagues (1983) showed that "Involvement with Delinquent Peers" correctly classified 76% of recidivists. Relationships with peers and family are important factors in the *Juvenile Sex Offender Assessment Protocol–II* (Prentky & Righthand, 2003). Worling and Curwen (2001) have noted that deviant peer groups have consistently been a robust predictor of subsequent general recidivism among juveniles. Negative peer groups have also played a part in the development of the *Protective Factor Scale* (Bremer, 2000, in press). Recently, Dishion, McCord, and Poulin (1999) described the potential iatrogenic effects of peer group interventions among adolescents.

The key feature of this item is obvious: Poor supervision and attitudes toward sexual assault among family and other adults are clear pathways to relapse among sexually abusive adolescents. The role of deviant peer groups in supporting sexual assault and general criminality is important to consider in treatment and case-management decisions.

Schemas

A key aspect of each of these factors is that in combination they can speak to an individual's life experience. Underneath the circumstances and attitudes that contributed to a sexual crime reside the worldviews that help make meaning of circumstances and contribute to the thought processes that support destructive behaviors. Ward, Hudson, Johnson, and Marshall (1997) define "schema" (known in the plural as "schemata," and more recently, "schemas") as the "implicit theories" an abuser has about his world.

The dynamic risk/need factors described above can be useful in understanding these schemas and their origins. A young person experiencing a true emerging sexual disorder is less likely to act upon that interest without the attitudes that make sexual misconduct appear permissible. As is often the case, if the youth feels lonely and isolated from others, he may well develop a worldview that life is disappointing, that he will never be close to his peers, and that despite the best efforts of adults, he is always going to be in trouble. He might just as well attempt to be intimate with younger, more vulnerable individuals even though he knows he will likely get in trouble. A full description of schemas and schema therapy is beyond the scope of this book, but consideration of the above domains can be useful in understanding the theories a young person has about the world around him.

Mann and Beech (2003, p. 137) summarize a number of schemas in adults that can often be found in younger people. The dangerous world and uncontrollable schemas can be particularly apparent among traumatized individuals who have gone on to abuse others. These schemas are based on the work of Neidigh and Krop (1992):

> *Children as sexual beings.* An implicit theory that perceives children as able to and wanting to engage in sexual activity and able to consent to, and not be harmed by, any sexual contact.... Here the offender has the idea that the existence of sexual desires is "natural, benign, and harmless."

> *Entitlement.* The nature of this implicit theory is the belief that one is superior and more important than others. The offender sees himself as being entitled to have sex when he wants from those who are less powerful/less important than he is.

> *Nature of harm.* The main aspect of this theory is that sexual activity does not cause harm and may in fact be beneficial to the child (in terms of teaching the child about sex). The offender will also tell himself that there are degrees of harm and that provided the offender doesn't inflict any serious damage, then little harm is caused.

Dangerous world. Here the content of the implicit theory is that the world is a dangerous place and that others are abusive and rejecting. Therefore the offender will tell himself that it is important both to fight back and to achieve control over others.

Uncontrollable. This implicit theory may have its roots in the offender's being abused as a child or being exposed to other traumatic events. Hence, the offender perceives the world as uncontrollable. Distortions that arise out of this implicit theory relate to offenses that the offender sees as beyond his control.

It is worth noting again that the theories that young people have about the world differ from those held by adults, and these examples are provided for purposes of producing thought and not for classifying youthful sexual abusers. It is important to remember, however, that many of the families from which these youth emerge will have held similar theories about the world. Mann and Beech (2003, p. 140) mention seven schemas proposed by Beck (1999). They relate more toward nonsexual violence:

- Authorities are controlling and punitive.
- Spouses are deceitful.
- Outsiders are hostile.
- Nobody can be trusted.
- I need to fight back.
- Physical force gets respect.
- If you don't get even, people will walk all over you.

As above, these can be the hallmarks of the families of young sexual abusers (and others who engage in seriously problematic behaviors) as well as examples of core attitudes that make young people more vulnerable to circumstances that trigger harmful behavior.

A noteworthy element of the domains described earlier is that many of them are easier to change in adolescents than in adults (although they can be easy to hide by individuals of all ages). The contributory attitudes described above are by definition less established in younger people than in adults. Similarly, the drive toward peer relationships and pair-bonding is one of the central hallmarks of adolescence. Given the uncertain nature of sexual arousal and impulsivity over time, professionals assessing and treating youth should place strong emphasis on interpersonal functioning. Emerging research suggests that treatment based on developing healthy relationships should be central to any therapeutic program (Prescott, 2001; Longo & Prescott, 2005; Caldwell & Van Rybroek, 2005).

Acute Factors

It is useful to separate the longer-term factors described above from those acute factors which can act as triggering events. An individual with a long history of impulsivity and frequent perceptions of being wronged by others could easily become more willing to cause harm when engaging in substance abuse. Conversely, many individuals do not need to engage in substance abuse in order to give themselves permission to abuse others.

A key component of assessment is not in listing the possible risk factors, but considering their potential interactions. Substance abuse has not been as predictive in the literature (e.g., Hanson & Bussiére, 1998) but could play an obvious role with specific individuals. Given that acute factors such as substance abuse and escalation of affect are not proved in the literature, it may be best to consider acute factors in the development of risk management strategies rather than as indicators of risk itself.

Young people can be surprisingly helpful in discussing acute factors. Simply asking "What are the warning signs that things aren't going well for you and that you're about to get in trouble?" and "What would you look like to others just before you get into trouble?" can produce helpful information. Some young people become agitated and giddy, while others become sullen and withdrawn. Providing a simple list of these factors can remind the adults in these young people's lives to pay attention.

Of course, young people will not share some "warning signs," often because it doesn't occur to them or because they do not yet possess enough insight. For example, medication noncompliance may signal a chain of events that can lead to destructive behavior through multiple pathways. On the one hand, the medications may be helping the young person's thought patterns or impulsivity. Without medication, these could become more vulnerable to triggering events. On the other hand, refusal to take medication could reflect a broader emerging pattern of willingness to contravene past commitments, or an escalation of irresponsible thought and behavior.

Another possible indicator to consider is making complaints about others, whether justified or not (Quinsey et al., 1998). Young people may have any number of very legitimate reasons to complain, and certainly these should be taken care of on their own merits. However, making complaints may also coincide with an emerging sense of entitlement, whether for revenge or to engage in other destructive acts. For example, the young person who perceives himself as insulted by treatment providers may then dismiss treatment itself as unnecessary and meaningless, and may feel justified in engaging in further antisocial acts. Clearly, every situation is different, but escalation can be easy to miss when it exists behind a complaint.

Other potential indicators include, but are by no means limited to increases in antisocial attitudes and values and threats made towards others. Statements of intent to engage in harmful behavior clearly should be taken seriously in even the lowest-risk individuals. In any event, those considering risk are obliged to consider internal states, developmental stages, and contextual factors when defining risk-management strategies.

Organization, Immersion, and Imminence

At times, risk assessment occurs in the context of critical incident review or considerations of short-term situations such as home visits. In some cases, this "risk assessment" may better be considered as safety planning, but in other situations the operative question may be "Should we panic now?"

In addition to the indicators of imminence mentioned above, it can be useful to consider organization and immersion in both the shorter and longer terms. In the absence of problems in the self-management domain, how organized is this individual generally, and what was their level of organization at the time of their sexually abusive acts? While it is true that impulsive people can also plan harmful behaviors for long periods of time, well-organized adolescents can avoid the attention of those who are supposed to supervise them.

Beyond organization, is there any indication that a young person is immersed in sexual or nonsexual violence? Beyond sexual preoccupation, is there any indication that aggression is important to them, as evidenced by a fascination with violent or sexual media above and beyond what one might expect? Is there a sense that they are immersed to such an extent that it seems virtually a part of their culture? While most teenagers are highly interested in sexuality, many are simply more open to discuss it or lack the sense that they should keep it private. Is there evidence that the youth is immersed more than this? And if so, what specific evidence is there?

Beyond immersion, is there any sense of the direction of the immersion? Is it toward one person, a group of people, or a class of people? This can help identify level of concern and inform management strategy. Beyond the direction of the immersion, is there any sense of whether they perceive violence or sexual aggression as imperative? And whether they feel it's imperative to do soon?[1]

As an example, consider the young man who is typically well organized and develops a strong crush on a staff member in his group home. He does not typically display behavior problems such as opposition, defiance, or disruption, so when he states that he wants to have sex with this staff member, the staff member sets a limit on this behavior. The next day, the young person attempts to sexually assault her. Although many young people in placements make ridiculous statements (and many sexual assaults are not preceded by statements of intent), it is a mistake not to consider whether there is a genuine sense of the imperative behind this statement.

Related to the action and time imperatives, is there any evidence that the youth is not just immersed in sexual aggression and/or violence, but that they have persistent ideation and immersion in a specific sequence of events? Mohandie (2000) describes the role of immersion in both theme and sequence in threat assessment for violence in schools. In some instances, young people will describe sequential fantasies that can serve as rehearsals for sexual aggression. One young man reported that he didn't just want to have sex with his sister. He specifically wanted to handcuff her, take her down the hall into a room, hold her down, turn out the light, and rape her. Obviously this kind of sequential statement can signal imminent risk and present the need for a Tarasoff warning. While it may not reflect a long-term underlying predisposition toward sexual violence, it is certainly of concern in the short term and should not be ignored.

---

[1] See Mohandie (2000) for further discussion of time and action imperatives, as well as sequential immersion.

Examples

The following examples are provided in the hopes that they are useful for illustration. It is important to note that these vignettes are fictitious and based on common scenarios seen in diverse settings.

> *Example #1[2]: Timmy's mother was concerned because she found him in possession of women's underwear. Although he was not known to have committed sexual harm, she was concerned that he might escalate toward sexual violence. What was his risk?*
>
> *Closer inspection revealed that Timmy and his family had experienced a number of problems, including the father's absence from their lives, moving across the country (and away from friends and extended family), and economic hardship. Timmy's mother had been understandably preoccupied with her work and relocation.*
>
> *It was learned that one day, Timmy, his mother, and sister went to the laundromat. It was a rare occasion when all three of the family members had time together. Although Timmy's mother was unaware, it was one of those days when he felt closer to her than ever. In his mind they were at least connecting and enjoying each other's company even if they were otherwise broke and miserable. While washing their clothes, they had reason to return home for a while. However, all of Timmy's clothes were still wet. His mother gave him a pair of his sister's silk panties, which he wore for a few hours until his clothes were finished. Although his mother and sister teased him about this, he could never remember a time when he had felt so connected to them. At last, he could talk and feel heard. While walking home he remembered how good the silk felt. When he later experienced puberty and began to masturbate, the thought of the comfort and attention he experienced on that one day was never far from his mind. While adolescent sexuality in the rest of the world seemed to be about conquest and mastery, he couldn't forget the warmth of his previous experience.*

What is the most unacceptable element of this young man's stealing underwear? How should we further assess the crime of stealing underwear? If we know that theft is common among adolescents, and that sexual arousal and interest change rapidly across these tumultu-

---

[2] With thanks to Joann Schladale

ous years, should we emphasize the importance of this young man's ability to feel connected to others, or should we make a plan to ward off "relapse" with a plan for dealing with high-risk situations such as clotheslines? Given the range of sexual experiences this young man has had, should our referral question reflect risk for harm or treatment need and responsivity related to healthy relationships that will reduce any interest in harming others?

Example #2: Tom was nearly 16 when the juvenile justice system referred him to residential placement. He had been locked up awaiting placement for 8 months. Psychological testing indicated that he was prone to experiencing paranoia and might have sadistic "tendencies." Tom acknowledged making some mistakes with his sexuality but hotly denied that it was a current concern. Several programs felt that Tom was too risky for admission, based on his denial. Tom's first month in the program was marked by a wide-eyed but suspicious stare. He hardly said a word....

Tom asked for extra time with his clinician. He asked whether it was too late for him to become somebody else. He explained that after his parents' divorce some years back, he sexually abused younger children from his neighborhood and within his family on a nearly daily basis, using threats and coercion. He verified earlier reports that this happened whenever adults left him alone. He also verified earlier reports that he had been sexually abused over the course of several years by an uncle with whom he no longer had any contact, but who possibly still lived in another part of the state. Above all, Tom missed his father, a seemingly nice man who was now married to a woman who wanted to forget about the past several years, and didn't want Tom to visit. In treatment Tom expressed a desperate hope that it was not too late to reunite with his father.

While in placement, Tom's behavior was very stable. He experienced no problems and was able to respond to challenging situations appropriately. When other residents offered to engage in a range of problematic behaviors, Tom was able to abstain. Tom's only problem was in response to direct threats, to which he responded with threats, apparent disorganization, and anxiety. Tom has a speech dysfluency, which caused him to isolate himself at times.

It became clear that Tom had an extensive history of sexually aggressive behavior. However, this history was not reflected in his statements or actions while in placement. He appeared to use therapy effectively and was able to discuss his sexual fantasies. An overarching focus, however, was Tom's strong desire to be a kind, gentle, and benevolent young man.

On balance, Tom's sexual interests appeared to be very much in flux. While in treatment his statements and behaviors were entirely pro-social and reflected no attitudes supportive of aggression except when experiencing a direct threat. Tom had a long and pronounced history of problems in forming healthy relationships with others. This was reflected by a long history of neglect as well as his speech impediment. While in treatment Tom made considerable progress. Tom quickly learned self-care skills and had few, if any, problems in the self-management domain.

One day, Tom ran from the program and threw many of his belongings into the irrigation ditch of a nearby farm. The question that others asked was whether his risk had increased, and how should they understand this incident. Was he getting worse?

Although Tom's history of sexual aggression was of great concern, he did not hold attitudes that supported a reoffense process. He had no history of reoffense after detection, sanction, or treatment. In fact, he used treatment effectively to address his past behavior, relationship issues, and how to become the person he wants to be. He had no history of impulsivity, although he could react very strongly to perceived threats.

Understanding these domains, then, the staff concluded that his current problem was purely situational. It was an impulsive act following his father's canceling a visit. Although Tom had numerous problems in the interpersonal domain, this problem had been triggered by his father, and Tom's greatest challenge was in coping with the disappointment. In the end, the staff determined that as long as Tom experienced a supportive environment he had little interest in abusing others. Tom would eventually be discharged to a foster home close to his father, where he lived without further incident into adulthood.

Example #3: Ricky lived with his aunt in another country for the first several years of his life. He returned to his mother at the age of four, although she was essentially a stranger to him at that time. While with his aunt, Ricky was exposed to extreme neglect.

Ricky became increasingly involved in fetish burglary, stealing items such as jewelry and underwear from young, attractive neighborhood women. Although the police were notified on several occasions, Ricky's mother and stepfather consistently convinced the authorities to refrain from prosecution and sent him to various counselors and psychiatrists. Ricky, however, persisted in stalking, stealing, and spying on neighborhood women. He would later state that if he owned their belongings, this was like owning them outright. He spied on his mother, sister, and several neighbors while they showered. When younger, he told family members they were "hot," and seemed to enjoy their unhappy responses. At an early age, Ricky had an unusual skin condition which remitted. Ricky was very invested in his appearance after that time.

Ricky's adjustment to placement and treatment was marked by an apparent ability to follow rules and routines. However, he frequently lied to clinical staff about his personal history and behaviors. Ricky could be quite arrogant and seemed to enjoy sharing some aspects of his past behavior with staff. He told a number of anecdotes about how easy it was to break into houses. Through various conversations, a picture emerged of normal development gone badly awry through neglect.

Although he had both athletic and musical abilities, Ricky could not form appropriate relationships with peers, and spent much of his childhood feeling inadequate and isolated from others. As he entered puberty, Ricky became interested in the opposite sex but was frequently rebuffed. Having never formed a deep attachment to others, Ricky became used to keeping his own counsel and rarely talked to others. His only sense of mastery was in being able to keep secrets and manage his rich fantasy life, which became increasingly organized over time. Ricky's solution to feeling emotionally, socially, and sexually isolated from others was to steal from and stalk attractive women. In this way, he perceived a sense of ownership without having to risk being hurt and abandoned. Privately, Ricky congratulated himself on his smooth ability to keep track of neighborhood women while his peers were involved in the dating mishaps that mark adolescents.

Ricky gradually became able to discuss much of his life history with his clinical team. He appeared to be making progress for a period of time. However, his placement outside his home resulted in his feeling even more estranged from others in his hometown. The adults in his community had not forgotten his *misconduct, while his peers continued to view him as an out-sider. Ricky made a conscious decision that he no longer be-longed anywhere and committed himself more fully to his fantasy life. Believing fully that potential sex partners say no when they mean yes and vice versa, Ricky decided that the best way to feel productive in relationships was to keep them at some distance and have unwilling and unknowing partners. Ricky was able to find out extensive personal information about staff mem-bers and others in the nearby community. He kept this informa-tion secured in a series of journals which he secreted in various locations around his living area.*

Ricky smuggled a book on a famous serial murderer back into the program and later mentioned to others that he looked up to this individual and thought he was "cool." He acknowledged that the killer's victims wouldn't feel the same way, but that there was certain elegance to his organizational skills and ability to do so much harm while seeming to function well in the com-munity. Ricky was referred to another program whose admis-sions process involved clinical interviews but only a light file review and no collateral interviews. After a seemingly positive adjustment, Ricky was later arrested for attempting to rape a staff member.

Ricky was a classic example of a young person who could be ignored in a group-care setting while busy staff were attending to the more impulsive and disruptive adolescents. Ricky had grown up with a rich fantasy life—a response to neglect and family disruption. His emerg-ing sexuality, skin condition, lack of impulsivity, and imagination combined to create a dangerous mix. The same problems with inter-personal relationships (at both the skill and affective levels) fueled both a possible emerging sexual disorder and a reluctance to engage in the treatment that could help him experience greater interpersonal competence. While others might have simply avoided contact with potential sources of hurt, Ricky sought it out at a distance with little regard for the rights and welfare of his "partners." He persisted de-spite numerous instances of detection, light sanction, and treatment experiences. Not only was he immersed in sexual aggression, but he was also immersed in the details of sexual aggression (collecting per-sonal information and belongings of victims).

Ricky's rape of a staff member was the direct result of the second group home's forming opinions based primarily on clinical interview.

Clinicians who view themselves as being able to detect deception and form an accurate risk assessment without adequate file review embody the axiom that "pride cometh before a fall."

Ricky clearly had difficulties in the sexual interest, contributory attitudes, and interpersonal domains noted above. Of particular concern was that he rarely, if ever, showed any kind of warning sign prior to engaging in harmful behavior. He was able to hide the fact that he was continuously preparing for his next opportunity. This was missed by the staff who were more accustomed to impulsivity preceding escalation into aggression. Ricky was immersed in both the theme and details of sexual aggression.

> *Example #4: Billy was 12 years old when he held down a girl, threatened her with a sharp object, and attempted to force intercourse on her. He had a long history of disruptive behavior in school and at home. Billy was sent to a juvenile detention center where he was diagnosed with pedophilia, due to his victim's being 11, and ADHD. The evaluator expressed concern that Billy admitted to experiencing erections on a daily basis. Billy's mother harassed everyone involved in his case. It was quickly decided that she was little more than a saboteur resistant to change. Billy was placed in a residential treatment center at a great distance from his mother. He expressed surprise at his conviction, apparently with the genuine belief that his victim had been quite open to having sex with him in the past.*
>
> *Billy quickly adjusted to his placement and got along well with staff and peers. Although he did not seem to take treatment seriously at first, he later used individual therapy to express his newfound realization of the harm he had done. Billy was not involved in any major incidents during the course of his placement. His mother became supportive of his progress, although she also wanted him home quickly. Billy was discharged to his mother with strong recommendations regarding treatment involving his mother. Billy went on to win a number of academic and athletic awards at his school.*

Although incorrectly diagnosed with pedophilia at the age of 12 (with an essentially same-age victim), Billy had no prior history of sexual misconduct for which he had been sanctioned or treated. He held no attitudes in his daily life or offense chain that supported sexual aggression, and he experienced little difficulty getting along with others.

Although he had a history of impulsivity, this was managed as part of his psychiatric treatment for ADHD.

Billy was a classic example of how an egregious referral offense does not equal high risk. There was no persistence of problematic behavior beyond those associated with ADHD. With attention being given to other aspects of his life (e.g., in the interpersonal domain), Billy was able to understand this incident, make decisions about who he wanted to become, and take adequate steps over time to get there. Of particular importance were the steps taken to engage his mother in the treatment process. Had professionals only attended to his "offense cycle" without including the most important person in his world, all of his progress could have deteriorated.

Summary

Attending to dynamic risk and treatment need requires not just understanding research findings, but studying the problems in creating this research. The fact that the field of sexual abuse has had such difficulty defining and studying denial and empathy in adults should be of great concern to professionals (Hanson & Bussiére, 1998; Hanson & Morton, 2004; Fernandez, 2002). In any of the vignettes above, considering such aspects as denial, empathy, remorse, or clinical presentation may have gotten a careless professional off the track of understanding and treating the youth. By understanding the young person's life history as well as offenses, rather than establishing a list of problematic behaviors, professionals can better separate issues of risk, need, responsivity, and readiness while keeping track of historical and dynamic indicators of elevated and lowered risk. This will then pave the way toward a better understanding of the factors that can protect the youth from future reoffense.

References

Ageton, S. S. (1983). *Sexual assault among adolescents*. Lexington, MA: Lexington Books.

Alexander, M. (1999). Sexual offender treatment efficacy revisited. *Sexual Abuse: A Journal of Research and Treatment, 11*(2). New York: Plenum Press.

Andrews, D. A. & Bonta, J. L. (1998). *The psychology of criminal conduct, 3rd ed.* Cincinnati: Anderson Publishing.

Barbaree, H. & Cortoni, F. A. (1993). Treatment of the juvenile sex offender within the criminal justice and mental health systems. In H. Barbaree, W. L. Marshall, & S. M. Hudson (Eds.), *The juvenile sex offender* (pp. 243-263). New York: Guilford Press.

Barbaree, H., Marshall, W., & Hudson, S. (1993). *The juvenile sex offender.* New York: Guilford Press.

Beck, A. T. (1999). *Prisoners of hate: The cognitive basis of anger, hostility, and violence.* New York: Harper Collins.

Boer, D. P., Hart, S. D., Kropp, P. R., & Webster, C. D. (1997). *Sexual Violence Risk-20: Professional guidelines for assessing risk of sexual violence.* Burnaby, British Columbia, Canada: The Mental Health, Law, and Policy Institute of Simon Fraser University.

Bonta, J. (1999). *Approaches to offender risk assessment: Static versus dynamic (User Report 1999-02).* Ottawa, Ontario, Canada: Department of the Solicitor General of Canada. Available from www.psepc.gc.ca/publications/corrections.

Bremer, J. F. (1998). Challenges in the assessment and treatment of sexually abusive adolescents. *The Irish Journal of Psychology, 19* (1).

Bremer, J. F. (2001, May 7). *The Protective Factors Scale: Assessing youth with sexual concerns.* Plenary address at the 16th annual conference of the National Adolescent Perpetration Network, Kansas City, MO.

Caldwell, M. & Van Rybroek, M. (2005, May). *Data from psychopathy and treatment outcome.* Presented at a conference of the Wisconsin Association for the Treatment of Sexual Abusers, Madison, WI.

Cooke, D. J., Forth, A. E. & Hare, R. D. (1998). *Psychopathy: Theory, research, and implications for society.* Dordrecht, Netherlands: Kluwer Press.

Cooke, D. J. & Michie, C. (1997). An Item Response Theory analysis of the Hare Psychopathy Checklist. *Psychological Assessment, 9,* 3-14.

Dishion, T. J., McCord, J., & Poulin, F. (1999). When interventions harm: Peer groups and problem behavior. *American Psychologist, 54,* 755-764.

Doren, D. M.(1998). Recidivism base rates, predictions of sex offender recidivism, and the "sexual predator" commitment laws. *Behavioral Sciences and the Law, 16,* 97-114.

Fernandez, Y. (2002). *In their shoes: Examining the role of empathy and its place in the treatment of offenders.* Oklahoma City: Wood'N'Barnes.

Forth, A. E. & Burke, H. (1998). Psychopathy in adolescence: Assessment, violence, and developmental precursors. In D.J. Cooke, A.E. Forth, & R.D. Hare (Eds.), *Psychopathy: Theory, research, and implications for society* (pp. 205-229). Dordrecht, The Netherlands: Kluwer Academic Publishers.

Forth, A. E., Kosson, D. S. & Hare, R. D. (2003). *Psychopathy Checklist: Youth Version.* Toronto, Ontario, Canada: Multi-Health Systems.

Frick, P. (1998). *Conduct disorder and severe antisocial behavior.* New York: Plenum Press.

Gacono, C. B. (2000). *The clinical and forensic assessment of psychopathy.* Mahwah, NJ: Lawrence Erlbaum Associates.

Gilgun, J. F., Klein, C., & Pranis, K. (2000). The significance of resources in models of risk. *Journal of Interpersonal Violence, 15,* 621-650.

Grisso, T. (1998). *Forensic evaluation of juveniles.* Sarasota, FL: Professional Resource Press.

Grove, W. M., Zald, D. H., Lebow, B. S., Snitz, B. E., & Nelson, C. (2000). Clinical versus mechanical prediction: A meta-analysis. *Psychological Assessment 12*(1) 19-30.

Gendreau, P., Little, T., & Goggin, C. (1996). A meta-analysis of the predictors of adult offender recidivism: What works! *Criminology, 34,* 401-433.

Hanson, R. K. (1997). *The development of a brief actuarial risk scale for sexual offense recidivism.* Ottawa, Ontario, Canada: Department of the Solicitor General of Canada. Available from www.psepc.gc.ca/publications/corrections/.

Hanson, R. K. & Bussiére, M. T. (1998). Predicting relapse: A meta-analysis of sexual offender recidivism studies. *Journal of Consulting and Clinical Psychology, 66,* 348-362.

Hanson, R. K. & Harris, A. (1998). *Dynamic predictors of sexual recidivism. (User Report 1998-01)* Ottawa, Ontario, Canada: Department of the Solicitor General of Canada. Available from www.psepc.gc.ca/publications/corrections.

Hanson, R. K. & Harris, A. J. R. (2001). A structured approach to evaluating change among sexual offenders. *Sexual Abuse: A Journal of Research and Treatment, 13,* 105-122.

Hanson, R. K. (1998). *Characteristics of abusive men (User Report 1998-05)*. Ottawa, Ontario, Canada: Department of the Solicitor General of Canada. Available from www.psepc.gc.ca/publications/corrections.

Hanson, R. K. (1999). *Static 99: Improving Actuarial Risk Assessments for Sex Offenders (User Report 1999-02)*. Ottawa, Ontario, Canada: Department of the Solicitor General of Canada. Available from www.psepc.gc.ca/publications/corrections.

Hanson, R. K. (2000). *Risk assessment.* Beaverton, OR: Association for the Treatment of Sexual Abusers.

Hanson, R. K. & Morton-Bourgon, K. E. (2004). *Predictors of sexual recidivism: An updated meta-analysis.* Available from www.psepc.gc.ca/publications/corrections.

Hanson, R. K. & Thornton, D. (2000). Improving actuarial risk assessments for sex offenders. *Law and Human Behavior, 24,* 119-136.

Hare, R. D. (1991). *The Hare Psychopathy Checklist–Revised.* Toronto, Ontario, Canada: Multi-Health Systems, Inc.

Hare, R. D. (2003). *The Hare Psychopathy Checklist–Revised–II.* Toronto, Ontario, Canada: Multi-Health Systems, Inc.

Hare, R. D., Forth, A. E., & Strachan, K.E. (1992). Psychopathy and crime across the life span. In R. D. Peters, R. J. McMahon, & V. L. Quinsey, *Aggression and violence throughout the life span* (pp.285-300). Newbury Park, CA: Sage Publications.

Hare, R. D. & Hart, S. D. (1997). *Psychopathy and the Hare PCL-R* (Audio tape and audio tape handbook). Toronto, Ontario, Canada: Multi-Health Systems.

Hart, S. D., Cox, D. N., & Hare, R. D. (1995). *The Hare Psychopathy Checklist–Screening Version.* Toronto, Ontario, Canada: Multi-Health Systems.

Hunter, J. (1999). *Understanding juvenile sexual offending behavior: Emerging research, treatment approaches, and management practices.* Center for Sex Offender Management. Available from www.csom.org.

Hunter, J. A. & Becker, J. V. (1994). The role of deviant sexual arousal in juvenile sexual offending: Etiology, evaluation, and treatment. *Criminal Justice and Behavior, 21,* 132-149.

Hunter, J. A. & Becker, J. V. (1999). Motivators of adolescent sex offenders and treatment perspectives. In J. Shaw (Ed.), *Sexual aggression.* Washington, DC: American Psychiatric Press.

Kahn, T. J. & Chambers, H. J. (1991). Assessing reoffense risk with juvenile sex offenders. *Child Welfare, 70,* 333-345.

Keenan, T. & Ward, T. (2003). Developmental antecedents of sex offending. In T. Ward, R. D. Laws, & S. M. Hudson (Eds.), *Sexual deviance: Issues and controversies* (pp. 119-134). Thousand Oaks, CA: Sage.

Kenny, D. T., Keough, T., & Seidler, K. (2001). Predictors of recidivism in Australian juvenile sex offenders. *Sexual Abuse: A Journal of Research and Treatment, 13(2),* 131-148.

Langstrom, N. & Grann, M. (2000). Risk for criminal recidivism among young sex offenders. *Journal of Interpersonal Violence, 15,* 855-871.

Laws, D. R. & O'Donohue, W. (1997). *Sexual deviance: Theory, assessment, and treatment.* New York: Guilford Press.

Loeber, R. & Farrington, D. P. (1998). *Serious and violent juvenile offenders.* London: Sage Publishing.

Longo, R. E. & Prescott, D. S. (2005). *Current perspectives: Working with sexually aggressive youth and youth with sexual behavior problems.* Holyoke, MA: NEARI Press.

Lund, C. A. (2000). Predictors of sexual recidivism: Did meta-analysis clarify the role and relevance of denial? *Sexual Abuse: A Journal of Research and Treatment, 12,* 275-288.

Lynam, D. R. (1996). The early identification of chronic offenders: Who is the fledgling psychopath? *Psychological Bulletin, 120,* 209-234.

Lynam, D. R. (1997). Pursuing the psychopath: Capturing the fledgling psychopath in a nomological net. *Journal of Abnormal Psychology, 106,* 425-438.

Lynam, D. R. (1998). Early identification of the fledgling psychopath: Locating the psychopathic child in the current nomenclature. *Journal of Abnormal Psychology, 4,* 566-575.

Mann, R. E. & Beech, A. R. (2003). Cognitive distortions, schemas, and implicit theories. In T. Ward, R. D. Laws, & S. M. Hudson (Eds.), *Sexual deviance: Issues and controversies* (pp. 135-153). Thousand Oaks, CA: Sage.

Marshall, W. L., Anderson, D., & Fernandez, Y. (1999). *Cognitive behavioural treatment of sexual offenders.* Chichester, UK: Wiley.

Marshall, W. L., Hudson, S. M., & Hodkinson, S. (1993). The importance of attachment bonds in the development of juvenile sex offending. In H. Barbaree, W. L. Marshall, & S. M. Hudson (Eds.), *The juvenile sex offender* (pp. 164-181). New York: Guilford Press.

Meloy, J. R. (2000). *Violence risk and threat assessment.* San Diego, CA: Specialized Training Services.

Monahan, J. & Steadman, H. J. (1994). *Violence and mental disorder: Developments in risk assessment.* Chicago: University of Chicago Press.

Monahan, J. (1981/1995). *The clinical prediction of violent behavior.* Northvale, NJ: Jason Aronson Inc.

Neidigh, L. & Krop, H. (1992). Cognitive distortions among child sexual offenders. *Journal of Sex Education and Therapy, 18,* 208-215.

Prentky, R., Harris, B., Frizzell, K., & Righthand, S. (2000). An actuarial procedure for assessing risk with juvenile sex offenders. *Sexual Abuse: A Journal of Research and Treatment, 12,* 71-94.

Prentky, R. (2000, March). *Juvenile Sex Offender Assessment Protocol (JSOAP).* Paper presented at Sinclair Seminars' Sex Offender Re-Offense Risk Prediction Symposium, Madison, WI.

Prentky, R. (2001, May) *J-SOAP: Structured assessment of risk for sexually abusive youth.* Plenary address at the 16th annual conference of the National Adolescent Perpetration Network, Kansas City, MO.

Prentky, R. & Righthand, S. (2003). *Juvenile Sex Offender Assessment Protocol–II (JSOAP–II).* Available from Center for Sex Offender Management at www.csom.org.

Prescott, D. S. (2001). Collaborative treatment for sexual behavior problems in an adolescent residential treatment center. In M. H. Miner & E. Coleman (Eds.), *Sex offender treatment: Accomplishments, challenges, and future directions* (pp. 43-58). Binghamton, NY: Haworth Press.

Quinsey, V. L., Harris, G. T., Rice, M., & Cormier, C. (1998). *Violent offenders: Managing and appraising risk.* Washington DC: American Psychological Association.

Rasmussen, L. A. (1999). Factors related to recidivism among juvenile sexual offenders. *Sexual Abuse: A Journal of Research and Treatment, 11,* 69-86.

Ryan, G. & Lane, S. (1997). *Juvenile sexual offending: Causes, consequences, and correction.* San Francisco: Jossey-Bass.

Serin, R. C. & Brown, S. L. (2000). The clinical use of the Hare Psychopathy Checklist– Revised in contemporary risk assessment. In C. G. Gacono (Ed.), *The clinical and forensic assessment of psychopathy* (pp. 251-268). Mahwah, NJ: Lawrence Erlbaum Associates.

Thornton, D. (2000, March). *Structured risk assessment.* Presented at Sinclair Seminars' Sex Offender Re-Offense Risk Prediction Symposium, Madison, WI. Available from www.sinclairseminars.com.

Thornton, D. (2002). Constructing and testing a framework for dynamic risk assessment. *Sexual Abuse: A Journal of Research and Treatment, 14,* 139-154.

Thornton, D. (2004, April 27). *Psychological factors underlying offending.* Workshop at Sand Ridge Secure Treatment Center, Mauston, WI.

Thornton, D. & Prescott, D. S. (2001). *Structured Risk Assessment: Youth Version.* Unpublished manuscript.

Ward, T. & Beech, A. R. (2004). The etiology of risk: A preliminary model. *Sexual Abuse: A Journal of Research and Treatment, 16,* 271-284.

Ward, T., Hudson, S. M., Johnston, L., & Marshall, W. L. (1997). Cognitive distortions in sex offenders: An integrative review. *Clinical Psychology Review, 17,* 479-507.

Webster, C. D. & Jackson, M. A. (1997). *Impulsivity: Theory, assessment, and treatment.* New York: Guilford Press.

Webster, C. D., Douglas, K. S., Eaves, D., & Hart, S. D. (1997). *HCR-20: Assessing Risk for Violence.* Burnaby, British Columbia, Canada: The Mental Health, Law, and Policy Institute of Simon Fraser University.

Weinrott, M. R. (1996). *Juvenile sexual aggression: A critical review.* Boulder, CO: Center for the Study and Prevention of Violence.

Worling, J. R. (1999, Sept). *Beyond the looking glass: Predicting adolescent sex offender recidivism from the results of a 10-year treatment study.* Paper presented at the 18th Annual Research and Treatment Conference, Association for the Treatment of Sexual Abusers, Lake Buena Vista, FL.

Worling, J. R. & Curwen, T. (2001). *Estimate of Risk of Adolescent Sexual Offense Recidivism (ERASOR). Version 2.0.* Toronto, Ontario, Canada: Safe-T Program, Thistletown Regional Centre for Children and Adolescents, Ontario Ministry of Community and Social Services.

Yochelson, S. & Samenow, S. E. (1985). *The criminal personality, Vol. 2: The change process.* Northvale, NJ: Jason Aronson, Inc.

Zolondek, S. C., Abel, G. G., Northey, W. F., & Jordan, A. D. (2001). The self-reported behaviors of juvenile sex offenders. *Journal of Interpersonal Violence, 16,* 73-85.

Chapter Four

Forensic Issues in Evaluating Juvenile Sexual Offenders

Patricia Coffey

Courts increasingly rely on mental health professionals for evaluations that can help guide decision making regarding juvenile sexual offenders. Forensic evaluations are designed for the specific purpose of informing the court or providers in the legal system. These evaluations differ from treatment-related assessments. Forensic psychological assessment can be defined as psychological assessment for the purpose of assisting the legal fact finder (Otto & Heilbrun, 2002). This type of assessment has been increasingly recognized as a unique form of assessment and specialty guidelines for forensic psychological evaluations have been developed (American Psychological Association [APA], 1992; Heibrun, DeMatteo, & Marczyk, 2004; Hecker & Steinberg, 2002). The forensic evaluator is objective and does not have a treatment relationship with the juvenile. A forensic evaluation of a juvenile is likely to be helpful to a treatment provider, but the purpose is to assist the legal system in the decision-making process.

Beyond the risk-assessment components discussed in depth in previous chapters, forensic evaluators can provide important information for the court in making risk-management, community-notification, placement, and treatment decisions. The risk assessment is most helpful when it is placed in the broader context of individualized risk-management strategies. The forensic evaluator has a unique opportunity to inform the court of the story of this juvenile's life, environmental influences on a family and peer level, the developmental issues present, and the steps necessary to move this juvenile toward a positive adult lifestyle.

This chapter provides a format for structuring the information presented in these evaluations, presents information to consider when making placement decisions, and focuses on the unique issues to consider in making a community-notification recommendation.

A Comprehensive Psychosexual Evaluation for the Court

An evaluation for the court should help provide information regarding the juvenile's life and functioning in a manner that allows the court to understand the individual's offending behavior and the factors that need to be addressed to reduce risk. Through the process of reading the evaluation, the court and various parties in the legal system should be able to develop an independent understanding of the relevant issues in the case. An evaluator should present the information in a transparent manner with quotes from the juvenile and examples that demonstrate the points being presented. Psychological jargon and speculation should be avoided. The conclusions and recommendations should follow naturally from the information already presented. The forensic evaluation should not present an opinion without sufficient information for the court to form an independent conclusion from the data presented. It is important to recognize that information is being presented for consideration by the court. A forensic evaluation should provide information in a transparent and objective manner, while recognizing that the court will make the final decision in each case.

The evaluation report can be effectively organized into the following sections:

- Review of Background Information/History
- Prior Non-Sexual Offense History
- Prior Sexual Offense History
- Current Offense Situation
- Offender's Version of Events Regarding Offenses
- Sex Offending Dynamics Associated With Offense
- Sexual History/Deviance
- General Psychological Functioning
- Environmental Issues (Family, Peers, Community)
- Risk to Reoffend Sexually
- Conclusions/Recommendations

The psychosexual evaluation should conclude with a section that provides concrete recommendations regarding placement, supervision, treatment needs, sexual offender registry issues, and other risk-management concerns. This section should include the evaluator's opinion regarding the level of risk present for the individual. The primary focus of the recommendation section is related to risk management. Three areas need to be addressed within subsections of the conclusion section: Placement, Supervision, and Treatment Needs. Within each category, the focus needs to remain on specific steps to reduce risk and facilitate positive growth. It is also important to note if any variation within a category (i.e., placement at home versus foster home) impacts on the juvenile's risk to reoffend. A juvenile returning to a home environment with minimal supervision and easy access to children may be at higher risk than the same juvenile placed in a treatment foster-home setting. The environment of a juvenile is important in risk management, and the court needs to understand the context of the risk assessment information. In addition, a time limit must be placed on the opinions provided considering the rapid development that occurs in adolescence.

The criminal justice system increasingly focuses on the concept of therapeutic jurisprudence (Winick, 1998). This concept focuses on how the law can enhance, rather than reduce, the psychological well-being of individuals involved in the legal system. This concept can be applied to the interactions that sexual offenders experience in the legal system (Winick, 1998; Birgden & Ward, 2003). A forensic evaluator has the opportunity to interact with the juvenile and family in a manner that may facilitate their involvement in the legal system in a positive manner. While the results of the evaluation may not be desirable to the juvenile or their family, a respectful interaction and well-considered evaluation can create a situation in which the juvenile has had an opportunity to express his perspective and have his unique situation considered. The evaluation process itself has the potential to positively impact the next step, which is likely to include treatment.

Recommendations should also consider the strength-based approach advocated by Ward & Stewart (2003) that focuses not just on risk management, but also on the "good lives model," which includes a focus on creating positive lives beyond simply managing risk.

Diagnostic Considerations

Applying any paraphilia diagnosis to an adolescent requires caution due to the significant developmental changes that occur during this time. The same behavior demonstrated in adulthood may indicate a paraphilia disorder is present, but in a juvenile sexual offender, this behavior may not be firmly entrenched or repeated in adulthood. The mental health field recognizes that paraphilia diagnoses should be cautiously applied with juvenile offenders. The DSM-IV recognizes the need for caution in applying the diagnosis of pedophilia (APA, 1994). A diagnosis of pedophilia requires that the person is a least 16 years of age and at least 5 years older than the child or children about whom they are having sexual fantasies, urges, or behaviors. The manual specifically states that this diagnostic category should not include an individual in late adolescence involved in an ongoing sexual relationship with a 12- or 13-year-old. A paraphilia diagnosis is considered a lifelong condition and is inappropriately applied if it has not been found to exist into the late teen and adult years.

An interesting finding regarding the distinction between adolescents and adults in this area is found in the research by Gretton et al. (2001). Research on adult sexual offenders (Rice and Harris, 1997) has found a high rate of sexual recidivism for adults presenting with a combination of a high degree of psychopathy (>25) and deviant sexual preferences as measured by the penile plethysmograph (PPG). The theory explaining this finding is that the individual is both sexually deviant and does not care about how they may harm others by acting on these interests. It would seem likely that this relationship would hold for juvenile offenders as well. Surprisingly, research by Gretton et al. (2001) does not support this conclusion. They studied 220 adolescent males to assess the relationship between a high score on the youth version of *Hare Psychopathy Checklist* and deviant sexual preferences on the PPG. This research measured actual *preferences* for deviant stimuli over non-deviant stimuli and these preferences needed to be demonstrated on the PPG. This research did not find a relationship between the combination of high psychopathy and deviant sexual preferences and sexual recidivism. In fact, a deviant preference on a PPG was not related to sexual recidivism. The combination was related to a high risk for general and violent reoffending. This finding supports the concept that deviant sexual arousal, even to the point of a preference, is not a firmly entrenched trait for a juvenile that extends into adulthood.

Placement Decisions

Placement decisions are often the most complicated component of the forensic evaluation. This decision is the most important decision in balancing the risk to reoffend and the need to help the juvenile develop in a manner that increases the likelihood of a positive adult lifestyle. Leaving a juvenile in a placement where he can reoffend is detrimental to the community and the juvenile. Placing the juvenile in an overly restrictive and unnatural environment is detrimental to the juvenile. While some might conclude that is not the concern of the community, ultimately, these juveniles return to our communities. We are all harmed if their risk has not been addressed or, worse yet, has increased due to the placement.

Considerable efforts have been made to keep juveniles in the community. In light of the research on the negative impact of residential placements, this is a positive trend. Research suggests that exposure to negative peer groups is detrimental to juveniles. Exposure to a negative peer group is a component of any residential treatment or correctional facility. Dishion et al. (1999) present longitudinal evidence that peer-group interventions can increase problem behavior and negative life outcomes. They conclude that placing juveniles with antisocial peers may be harmful. Juvenile offenders are generally more focused on peer relationships than adult offenders are. In normal adolescent development, peers have a major influence. Rejection by nondelinquent peers is associated with increased risk for future antisocial behavior. Evidence shows that relationships with delinquent peers are important in escalating delinquent behavior (Shortt, Capaldi, Dishion, Bank, & Owen, 2003). The court must understand this concept of "delinquency training" within a peer group when placement decisions are made (Dishion et al.; Poulin, Dishion, & Burraston, 2001).

In light of the risk to do harm in placing a juvenile in an institution or group home, it is important to explore and establish other options for juveniles whose risk can be safely managed in the community. Research by Chamberlain & Reid (1998) demonstrates that a treatment foster-care model resulted in lower recidivism compared to a group-care placement. This finding is consistent with research on the potentially negative impact of antisocial peers. A treatment foster home often provides the most normalized environment for juveniles to successfully progress through the developmental tasks of adolescence.

Placing a child in the community does not necessarily mean keeping them in the family home. Some families are unable and/or unwilling to supervise the juvenile appropriately. In addition, some families have abused the juvenile or are continuing to engage in abusive or antisocial behavior. Prioritizing the needs of the juvenile is important in placement decisions, despite often significant family and financial pressure to return the juvenile to the family home.

There are reasons to be concerned about the home environments of some juvenile sexual offenders. Treatment and supervision are not likely to be effective in situations where the juvenile is living in a traumatic home environment. Juvenile child molesters are more likely to have been sexually victimized themselves than juvenile rapists. Juvenile sexual offenders are more likely to have higher levels of being physically and sexually abused than other conduct-disordered youth. Juvenile sexual offenders are more likely to be exposed to hard-core pornography (and at an earlier age) than nonsexual juvenile offenders (Ford & Linney, 1995). Domestic violence is also an issue. Research shows that recent exposure to violence in the home can be a significant predictor of violent behavior for children and teenagers (Edelson, 1999).

A home placement should be considered when the following characteristics are present:

1. It is in everyone's best interests.
2. The juvenile is a relatively low-risk offender.
3. The juvenile is likely to comply with supervision.
4. Treatment services are in place.
5. The family home situation is appropriate.
6. Risk-management strategies are in place.
7. It is not considered detrimental to the victim.

A home placement should *not* be considered when the following characteristics are present:

1. A history of severe abuse in the home by offender or others.
2. The family is unwilling or unable to monitor risk.
3. A history of repetitive assaults in the home despite prior interventions.
4. A high risk of reoffending and potential victims in the home or neighborhood.
5. Signs of sexual deviance and access to victim type in the home.

6. It would be detrimental to a victim in the home.

7. Substance abuse by the offender or others.

8. Other factors that clearly indicate that risk cannot be managed in the environment.

While placing a juvenile sexual offender in their home can sometimes be inappropriate, the option of partial integration into the home environment is an important consideration. This does not need to be an "all or nothing" decision. The juvenile and his family are less likely to resist an out-of-home placement if they are allowed contact and time together as a family. The juvenile will likely have contact with family once s/he is off supervision. Contact during the course of supervision provides an opportunity for treatment interventions to address family issues. A partial-integration approach allows the juvenile to spend time in the home environment during highly monitored and low-risk times (i.e., after school and during dinner, but not overnight when parents are asleep). Families often feel betrayed by the system, but we are all best served by families working cooperatively with the social service system. In addition, contact with the family can be important for the well-being and formation of healthy attachments for the juvenile. This may help to lower risk by stabilizing the offender in the community.

Community Notification and Registry of Juvenile Sexual Offenders

An important role of the forensic evaluator is to help the court decide the necessary steps for helping the juvenile make a successful transition into a non-offending adult lifestyle, while minimizing the risk to the community. This focus in our legal system on balancing the need for rehabilitation of the juvenile offender and community safety is undergoing a change. A significant philosophical change has occurred over time in society's approach to juvenile sexual offenders. This is evident both in increasingly severe penalties for juveniles and the current trend toward placing juveniles on a sexual offender registry and including in the community-notification process sexual offenders whose only known offenses were as juveniles. The sealed juvenile record of the past, designed to allow the youth to make positive changes, is no longer a core philosophy in the juvenile justice system.

By 2001, over half of the states in the U.S. required juveniles adjudicated for a sexual offense to register (Trivits & Repucci, 2002). Due to concerns regarding the trend away from protecting the juvenile's potential for rehabilitation, the Association for the Treatment of Sexual Abuse (ATSA, 2000) has published an opinion regarding community notification procedures for juveniles. This organization's position on this issue states:

> The Association for the Treatment of Sexual Abusers believes that juveniles should be subject to community notification procedures in only the most extreme cases.... Despite the questionable public safety benefits of community notification with juveniles, it is likely to stigmatize the adolescent, fostering peer rejection, isolation, increased anger, and consequences for the juvenile's family members. Until research has demonstrated the protective efficacy of notification with juveniles and explored the impact of notification on the youth, their families and the community, notification—if imposed at all for juveniles—should be done conscientiously, cautiously, and selectively.

Wisconsin is just one state that recently established a juvenile sexual offender registration law that significantly limits the confidentiality of this juvenile information (Assembly Bill 99, Wisconsin State Legislature, May 2005). While juveniles have already been required to register, this new law allows the community to be notified about the juvenile's sexual offense history. Law enforcement officials are the designated individuals to decide if the risk requires community notification. Unfortunately, law enforcement officials are not typically trained in making these types of assessments. Judges still have the option not to place a juvenile on the register in the disposition process, but this process has passed for the majority of the offenders on the list. The goal behind these laws is to provide information to the community with the hope that this will help protect the public from dangerous sexual offenders. Unfortunately, there is reason to be concerned that this public exposure for juvenile behavior may make it more difficult for the juvenile to establish a non-offending adult lifestyle.

In a recent review article regarding the application of community notification laws to juveniles, Trivits & Reppucci (2002) summarize the potential negative impact of this trend. Traditionally, juvenile courts have had a rehabilitative, rather than punitive, focus due to the general belief that juveniles are less culpable than adults due to their stage of development. Community notification has not been demonstrated to reduce risk to the community, but has the potential to negatively impact on the potential for rehabilitation. There is no research data directly addressing the affect of this law on juveniles.

Placement on a potentially open registry creates a permanent and public label due to adolescent behavior. This is particularly problematic considering research indicating that the majority of juvenile sexual offenders will not reoffend.

As we increase our knowledge in the field of juvenile sexual offending, it is important to recognize that general psychological research is also relevant. Research has already demonstrated the powerful effect of labels. Beyond the importance of recognizing that labeling a juvenile as a "sexual offender" or "sexual predator" is not likely to accurately characterize who they are as adults, labels also have the potential to be harmful. Evidence suggests that one person's expectations for another person can become a self-fulfilling prophecy (Rosenthal, 2002). This self-fulfilling-prophecy theory has been well documented in a variety of settings. The basic premise of this theory is that the "The behavior expected actually came to pass because the expecter expected it" (Rosenthal, 2002, p. 847).

A well-published social psychology research study from 1973, commonly referred to as the *Stanford Prison Experiment* (Haney & Zimbardo, 1998), provided important insights into the impact of labels. This study involved randomly assigning college students to guard or prisoner roles. This study needed to be stopped after 6 days due to the extreme distress the "prisoners" experienced in their role and the abusive and dehumanizing behavior exhibited by the "guards." This study provides important insights into the role of institutions on behavior, as well as into how a simple label can shape how a person is treated and behaves, the ultimate result being that the individual acted in a manner consistent with the label he had been randomly assigned.

Once a label is applied to an individual, the tendency is to engage in what researchers describe as a "confirmatory bias" (Festinger, 1957; Frey, 1986; Jonas, Schulz-Hardt, Frey, & Thelen, 2001). We have a strong tendency to fail to consider information that disconfirms a theory, and seek out and overvalue information that confirms it. Once someone has a negative label, the tendency is to pay attention to information that confirms this label, and discount signs of change. The impact of notifying teachers, neighbors, and an entire community that a juvenile-only sexual offender is a sexual offender has not been studied. Although no research suggests that this reduces risk, research in the broader psychological literature suggests that this labeling may have a significant negative impact.

Evaluating the Need for Placement on the Registry: A Helpful Component to any Forensic Psychosexual Evaluation

Considering the changing nature of community notification, and the increasing trend toward making juvenile registry lists public, the forensic evaluator should specifically address this issue in evaluations for the court. In providing information to the courts regarding risk and registry, it is important for a forensic examiner to remember that, regardless of his opinion regarding this social policy, his role is to provide information for the court to make the ultimate determination. The ethical responsibility of a forensic evaluator is to answer the question in front of the court, with all the caveats to his opinion clearly stated.

In making recommendations regarding placement on the registry, forensic evaluators can be of assistance to the court by providing the following information:

- The base rate of juvenile sexual recidivism.

- An individualized risk assessment.

- An assessment regarding risk management strategies, including consideration of whether or not community notification would decrease the offender's risk.

- A consideration of the individual dynamics in this case. Addressing whether or not the risk to public will be reduced by placement on registry.

  > Consider whether the offender has an established victim group that would benefit from being warned. For example, a 16-year-old repetitive offender against children may not be appropriate for work with children as an adult. It is possible that an open record regarding his history could prevent future victims. Learning that a 16-year-old who had sexual contact with his 14-year-old girlfriend has been convicted of sexual assault may result in little increase in public safety.

- Information regarding the potential to increase the offender's risk to reoffend sexually.

- Information regarding the negative impact of labeling and difficulty establishing a non-offending adult lifestyle.

- The nature/severity of potential risk, and the pattern of behavior.

- Consideration of victims being traumatized.

  Many victims are family members who may suffer if the family address is placed on the registry.

- Recommendation of periodic reviews of registration requirements due to the often unpredictable ability of adolescents to change.

In sum, the forensic evaluation can help address this important issue to assist the court in making juvenile registration issues in a well-informed manner.

Conclusions/Summary

A carefully developed plan for one stage of adolescence will need to be adapted to changing internal and external conditions for the youth. The challenge of conducting an evaluation of juvenile sexual offenders is their rapid development, but this is also the hope for this population. As discussed in other chapters, the hope for this population grows out of the fact that the vast majority of juveniles are not firmly entrenched in a long-term pattern of sexual offending behavior. In providing information to courts and others working with juveniles, it is crucial that we educate others about the possibilities for change, while establishing plans that prevent further sex-offending behavior. A delicate balance exists between managing risks and allowing for the growth that can reduce future risk. The forensic evaluation is an important step to guiding the decisions that will influence the adolescent throughout their lifetime.

References

American Psychological Association (1992). Ethical principles of psychologists and code of conduct. *American Psychologist, 47*, 1597-1611.

American Psychiatric Association (1994). *Diagnostic and statistical manual of mental disorders, 4th ed.* Washington, DC: American Psychiatric Association.

Association for the Treatment of Sexual Abusers (2000). *The effective legal management of juvenile sexual offenders.*

Birgden, A. & Ward, T. (2003). Pragmatic psychology through a therapeutic jurisprudence lens: Psycholegal soft spots in the criminal justice system. *Psychology, Public Policy, and Law, 9*(3/4), 334-360.

Chamberlain, P. & Reid, J. B. (1998). Comparison of two community alternatives to incarceration for chronic juvenile offenders. *Journal of Consulting and Clinical Psychology, 66*(4), 624-633.

Dishion, T. J., McCord, J., & Poulin, F. (1999). When interventions harm: Peer groups and problem behavior. *American Psychologist, 54*, 755-764.

Edelson, J. L. (1999). Children's witnessing of adult domestic violence. *Journal of Interpersonal Violence, 14*(8), 839-70.

Festinger, L. (1957). *A theory of cognitive dissonance.* Stanford, CA: Stanford University Press.

Ford, M. E. & Linney, J. A. (1995). Comparative analysis of juvenile sexual offenders, violent nonsexual offenders, and status offenders. *Journal of Interpersonal Violence, 10*, 56-70.

Frey, D. (1986). Recent research on selective exposure to information. In L. Berkowitz (Ed.), *Advances in experimental social psychology,* Vol. 19, (pp. 41-80). New York: Academic Press.

Gretton, H. M., McBride, M., Hare, R. D., O'Shaughnessy, R., & Kumka, G. (2001). Psychopathy and recidivism in adolescent sexual offenders. *Criminal Justice and Behavior, 28*, 427-449.

Haney, C. & Zimbardo, P. (1998). The past and future of U.S. prison policy: Twenty-five years after the Stanford Prison Experiment. *American Psychologist, 53*, 709-727.

Hecker, T. & Steinberg, L. (2002). Psychological evaluation at juvenile court disposition. *Professional Psychology: Research and Practice, 33*(3), 300-306.

Heilbrun, K., DeMatteo, D., & Marczyk, G. (2004). Pragmatic psychology, forensic mental health assessment, and the case of Thomas Johnson: Applying principles to promote quality. *Psychology, Public Policy, and Law, 10*(1/2), 31-70.

Jonas, E., Schulz-Hardt, S., Frey, D., & Thelen, N. (2001). Confirmation bias in sequential information search after preliminary decisions: An expansion of dissonance theoretical research on selective exposure to information. *Journal of Personality and Social Psychology, 80*(4), 557-571.

Otto, R. K. & Heilbrun, K. (2002). The practice of forensic psychology: A look toward the future in light of the past. *American Psychologist, 57*, 5-18.

Poulin, F., Dishion, T. J., & Burraston, B. (2001). Three-year iatrogenic effects associated with aggregating high-risk adolescents in cognitive behavioral preventative interventions. *Applied Developmental Science, 5*, 214-224.

Rice, M. E. & Harris, G. T. (1997). Cross-validation and extension of the Violence Risk Appraisal guide for child molesters and rapists. *Law and Human Behavior, 21*, 231-241.

Rosenthal, R. (2002). Covert communication in classrooms, clinics, courtrooms, and cubicles. *American Psychologist*, 839-848.

Shortt, J. W., Capaldi, D. M., Dishion, T. J., Bank, L., & Owen, L. D. (2003). The role of adolescent friends, romantic partners, and siblings in the emergence of the adult antisocial lifestyle. *Journal of Family Psychology, 17*(4), 521-533.

Trivits, L. C. & Repucci, N. D. (2002). Application of Megan's Law to juveniles. *American Psychologist, 57*, 690-704.

Ward, T. & Stewart, C. A. (2003). The treatment of sexual offenders: Risk management and good lives. *Professional Psychology: Research and Practice, 34*(4), 353-360.

Winick, B. J. (1998). Sexual offender law in the 1990s: A therapeutic jurisprudence analysis. *Psychology, Public Policy, and Law, 4*(1/2), 505-570.

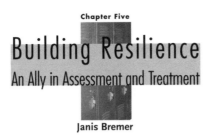

Chapter Five

Building Resilience
An Ally in Assessment and Treatment

Janis Bremer

Resilience, a construct defined in the child development literature of the 1970s, refers to the ability of a child to maintain positive growth and socially appropriate behavior in the face of adverse circumstances. "By resilience we mean the phenomenon of people functioning well in spite of adverse experiences, of relative resistance to risk factors or of overcoming stress experiences" (Rutter et al., 1998). The ability to withstand neglect, abuse, learning disabilities, family tragedies, marginalized neighborhoods, or others of the many risks or threats that cross our paths throughout childhood is not seriously considered in the treatment of juveniles who cause sexual harm to others.

Yet resiliency, the knowledge and skills to bounce back from harm to self, is a characteristic that prevents antisocial or criminal behavior. Turning away from the negative and choosing the positive and accepting compromise in the recognition of others are internalizations of a pro-social orientation that provides real community safety. This chapter discusses conceptual and practical aspects of resilience. Case examples illustrate the importance of considering resilience in both assessment and treatment. The chapter concludes with discussion of the *Protective Factors Scale* (Bremer, 2001), which is included in appendix B.

It is clear now, 30 years later, that resilience is a complex phenomenon. "Resilience functions as a multi-determined and ever-changing product of interacting forces within an individual's family, social groups, community, society, and world" (Waller, 2001). The individual, family, and community can link together in a growth-enhancing cycle. When a single component of a child's world is detrimental to development, another component may provide the structure and safety to maintain pro-social development. The general delinquency field has directed attention to the notion of resiliency in looking at both prevention and intervention. Resilience is a concept that goes hand in hand with risk, for without present risk, or adverse circumstances, there cannot be a resilient action or reaction. Resilience in child development is more often referred to as a mediator when risk factors for developmental difficulties are present and the child develops with normative personal and interpersonal functioning. Risks may be within the individual (genetic predisposition), in the family (domestic violence), and/or in the community (high crime). Resilience allows the child to "walk through" adversity and continue a positive, responsible life course.

In the current postmodern discourse (Ungar, 2004), antisocial behavior is reframed as resilient action. The antisocial behavior is seen as a way for the child or adolescent to continue to feel personal strength, thus continuing growth and development in the face of adversity. Although this approach provides a positive counterplot for an individual youth, it redefines the term "resilience" as an internal motivation. In its original conceptualization by Rutter (1979), resilience involves far more than internal motivation, as can be seen from the definition. The movement into antisocial behavior, including sexual harm to others, is the weak response to risk, not the resilient response. These antisocial behaviors, particularly those which create the havoc caused by sexually harming behavior, are a response based on a lack of resiliency. The underlying reasons for sexually harming behaviors may include a drive for internal conflict resolution. For example, Tom, at age 12, feels confused by his memories of sexual molestation at age 7 by his older male cousin. By reiterating what was done to him, he attempts to make sense of the experience. However, resilience is an outcome-based process, just as risk is an outcome-based process. Neither resilience nor risk is just the process itself. Tom's inability to use socially appropriate means of making sense of his own victimization by going to a trusted adult is the outcome of a lack of social resilience. The risk Tom posed as a victim of child sexual abuse by a male is a defined risk after he himself sexually harms another.

Resilience in recovery is a multidimensional structure that finds and builds strengths in areas of weakness or risk, as well as redirecting attention to strengths. How can we bring resiliency into play when a weak, or antisocial, response such as sexually harmful behavior has occurred? Joe, age 14 years, out of peer insecurity, hormonal surges related to puberty, and a macho community style, decides he needs to explore sexuality by engaging the little sister whom he baby-sits in sexual touch. Joe sexually abuses his much younger, vulnerable sister. Joe lacks the personal strength to resist due to uncontrollable random arousal related to puberty (hormonal surging). He lacks a peer social network that might provide social information and responses that lead to same-age sexual exploration. He is embedded in his home community and has no perspective on other male norms. Working with Joe, educating him about his developing sexuality and sexual responsivity, identifying skills he can bring to a peer group, and providing access to a more balanced notion of "maleness" all can provide him with strengths to use when he is overwhelmed by his emerging sexuality.

Resiliency is a factor in recovery from life difficulties that create problem behaviors for a given individual. Although there is notably less research in this area, a recognized relationship exists between resilience and recovery from adversity such as violent homes and other high-risk situations. Adults' efforts to control or take charge of a problem child are typically only successful for a limited time period (Kagan, 2004). Two paths bring us to the study of resiliency within the issue of youth's engaging in harming sexual behaviors, as in Joe's example. One is that the risks (outside of characteristics of the offense behavior itself) are essentially the same as those leading to other forms of antisocial behavior. Therefore the protective factors that create resilience for antisocial behavior in general will impact many youth who engage in sexually harming behaviors. It may be the complex interaction of risks, combined with the developmental period of puberty, that result in a poor sexual behavior choice. The other pathway is that therapy essentially intervenes by strengthening a positive core identity, by building resilience at the individual level. This is not a traditional approach in the field of treating sexually harmful behavior. Many of the programs developed to treat this population focus on the risks alone and ways to manage them directly. Resiliency is not a direct management response; it is a complex dynamic that shifts Joe's focus from managing risks to utilizing strengths.

The building blocks of the resiliency construct are known as protective factors. Protective factors are the result of concrete events in a youth's life that provide resiliency. The literature on resiliency is a collection of studies on the protective factors that prevent antisocial behavior in at-risk populations. These are referred to as factors or protective processes (Rutter, 1979). Protective factors are qualities or conditions that might mitigate a juvenile's exposure to conditions that put him or her at risk for delinquency. The big deal about protective factors is that these are elements of personality, family function, or community environment that mediate the negative impact of adverse circumstances without conscious awareness in many instances. This is the shift from managing oneself to simply responding from a different orientation.

The fact that protective factors exist at many levels (individual, family, community, society) defines the necessary structure for recovery from adversity. The fact that this is a multitiered system requires attention. The simplistic view of individual child or adolescent "therapy" outside of a systems perspective will not necessarily foster the growth of resilience. Taking a systems approach is far more effective. Even within the original literature on treating sexually abusing youth (National Task Force, 1988) recognition of the relevance of a support network or "treatment team" is explicitly defined. Bringing the construct of resiliency into play provides the basis and a clear understanding of the relevance of multisystems engagement with each of our youth. Conversely, a focus on only the individual can be seen as possible but more difficult when a systems lens is in place. Simply put, when you work with only one of the four levels of influence, 75% of the forces impinging on these youth may be working against them.

Therapy, in whatever form it takes, traditionally works through individual motivation. The postmodern approach taken by Ungar (2004) and proponents of narrative therapy (White, 1995) take a unique stance by considering the antisocial behavior of troubled youth as a sign of their resilience. This is a valid approach when the individual—and not the system—is the client. It allows for definition of the person separately from the problem. There is a group of youth for whom this may be the only workable approach, due to the entrenched antisocial environment (family, community) within which they must live. Their antisocial behavior is framed as the only way they can maintain a sense of well-being. It is seen as a latent sign of health. There is full recognition that this manner of maintaining a sense of self-efficacy is wrong and that harm to others, regardless of the need, is unacceptable. The therapeutic shift that occurs is one of finding "parallel responses" that are social rather than antisocial.

Many youth who do not live under these dire circumstances engage in sexually harming behavior. Their family dynamics provide resilience and lend themselves to social change. They reside in mainstream communities. These youth did not show resilience to stresses entering their lives at different points, and a systems approach to treatment provides a stronger and more holistic buffer to any future risks.

One of the overriding concerns regarding sexual harm to others is whether it is a developmentally persistent behavior. Of particular concern is the question of early onset and persistence. Whether the behavior is first noticed in childhood (prepubertal) or adolescence (pubescent), the first question is, "Will this child become an adult sex offender?" Take John, who is brought to a counselor because, at age 8, he is teaching younger children in his elementary school sexual touch games. Or Tom, at age 13, who is found showing his two young siblings how to masturbate each other. How does a risk process operate over time, and how do we understand intervention to introduce protection against continuing such behavior? Although the research is only beginning to emerge, it does not support a single developmental pathway from child to adolescent to adult sex offending (Burton, 2000; Chaffin, Letourneau, & Silovsky, 2002). Persistence then is not a given and may, in fact, occur only infrequently. We know clinically that persistence occurs at times when there is no intervention. Studies of adult abusers indicate that a majority of these men began their offending behaviors as adolescents (Abel, Mittelman, & Becker, 1985; Longo & Groth, 1983). This data provided the impetus for the development of sex-offense-specific programs for children and youth. Longitudinal studies that investigate the presence of protective mechanisms would help us better understand the dance between adversity and resiliency.

It is clear from the literature on antisocial behavior that risk and protective factors interact over time in a complex and variable way. Links between risks and protective factors vary along the life course in a way that encourages us to move youth out of the risk arena and into a more positive, protective life experience. A well-respected but little-used proposal for effective intervention in our field is Alan Jenkins' *Invitations to Responsibility* (1990). His entire approach is based on a positive growth developmental model. Current research on attachment and the impact of trauma points to the use of positive adult and peer relationship development as an essential component of treatment (Creeden & Howland, 2000). The work currently being done that links attachment style to sexually abusive behavior is specifically about developing a protective factor regarding risk to harm others. The resolution of trauma is specifically aimed at enabling youth to make use of the protective factors in their environment and to shift their way of functioning so that this becomes an internal protection.

What forms do protective factors take, and what are key protective factors to consider within these forms? Protective factors may be either static or dynamic. Static factors are unchangeable. If they are present, then they can be used to build strength. If identified static protective factors are not present, compensatory dynamic protective mechanisms can be put in place to mediate the risk created by the absence of a particular static protective mechanism. A simple example is Mike. If Mike is hyperactive, then he does not have the protective mechanism of using executive functioning (cognitive problem solving) to plan behavior. A way to compensate for the lack of that particular protection is the use of effective medication. Medication that allows for the concentration and focus to use executive functioning, and thus plan behavior, mediates hyperactivity. Developmental assets that act as protective factors may be static or dynamic.

An example of one static protective factor is high intelligence in childhood (Fergusson & Lynskey, 1996). Genetic strength is another static protective factor (Rutter et al., 1998). Temperament is also a static protective factor, but can also be a risk factor (Werner & Smith, 1992).

The early attachment relations literature (Ainsworth, 1970; Bowlby, 1975) directs our attention to the development of a secure attachment with a primary caregiver during infancy as another protective factor. This impacts at the individual and familial levels of influence. A secure attachment provides the underlying ability to self-regulate (Karr-Morse & Wiley, 1997). A sociable demeanor, faith in oneself, self-confidence, and the ability to self-regulate are all individual factors associated with resilience. A close relationship with a caring parent, one who provides consistency with warmth, or caring adults who provide consistent parenting, as well as ties to an extended family, socioeconomic resources, involvement in pro-social organizations, and effective schools are environmental supports (Resnick, Ireland, & Borowsky, 2004). In a review of the literature, Luthar, Cicchetti, and Becker (2000) found four critical factors for promoting resilience. These are positive connections to caring and competent adults, development of cognitive and self-regulation abilities, positive beliefs about oneself, and motivation to act effectively. The close alignment of these two clusters of factors is easy to see.

Factors at the familial level include family discipline practices and communication style. At the community level, neighborhood cohesiveness and community organization help create resilience. At the environmental or cultural level, factors such as poverty and media exposure influence developmental direction (National Youth Violence Prevention Resource Center, 2001). Studies indicate that it is not typically a single factor or situation that causes a youth to engage in delinquent behavior. Multiple factors contribute to and shape behaviors over the course of youth development.

Traditional intervention with delinquency is oriented to building strengths from a deficit perspective. Needs assessments are primarily conducted in the juvenile justice system as a way of revealing which types of services might benefit a youth. Additionally, they can identify the seriousness of these needs. Needs assessments try to identify needs in all areas of life. What needs assessments do not do is identify current strengths or assets. The "one down" position of needs assessment creates resistance and defiance. Defining a youth's life by what's wrong rather than what's right impedes motivation for positive change.

Incorporating present protective factors in treatment reduces the resistance to the need for change. The literature on delinquency prevention and treatment shows, without doubt, that punishment is not an effective deterrent for future antisocial behavior. Placing the focus on weakness rather than strength, what is wrong rather than what is right, taking power and control rather than teaching assertiveness are all ways to perpetuate a sense of helplessness, a "bad me" identity and the lack of social belonging that promotes pro-social behavior. The general delinquency or antisocial literature is rife with examples of protective factors and their role in buffeting the adverse effects present in a youth's life (cf. Gilgun, 2005). A review of the international literature (National Institute for Mental Health, 2000) has identified a small number of instruments relevant to this task, though none have taken on the ambitious task of integrating the multiple perspectives of a global community of researchers. These instruments include the *Resiliency Scale* (Jew, Green, & Kroger, 1999), the *Clinical Assessment Package for Assessing Client Risks and Strengths* (Gilgun, 1999), the *Behavioral and Emotional Rating Scales* (Epstein & Sharma, 1998), the *Adolescent Resiliency Attitudes Scale* (Biscoe & Harris, 1994), the *Individual Protective Factor Index* (Springer & Phillips, 1997), the *Healthy Kids Resilience Scale* (Constantine, Bernard & Diaz, 1999), the *Adolescent Resilience Scale* (Oshio, Nakaya, Kaneko, & Nagamine, 2002), the *Adolescent Social Self-Efficacy Scale* (Connolly, 1989), and the *Protective Factors Scale* (Bremer, 2001). These instruments cover an array of domains that can be loosely gathered under five attribute subheadings: individual, interpersonal, family, community, and social/cultural. The *Protective Factors Scale* (Bremer, 2001) was specifically designed for youth with sexual behavior concerns.

Perhaps due to the emotionally laden arena of sexual abuse, the use and development of protective factors has not been a focal point in our field. One must ask whether this is due to concerns about appearances of ignoring accountability and responsibility or whether it simply feels like rewarding offense behavior. Using a strength-based approach to treatment does not mean a sexual offense is excused or explained away. This does not mean a sexual offense is taken lightly or that a young person does not have to take responsibility for harm done. It does mean that the approach to resolving sexual harming behavior is focusing on acceptance of the person (not the behavior), providing help to develop a sense of self-efficacy, growth of a positive identity, and promoting a feeling of inclusiveness.

The understanding of protective factors in developing resilience to adversity has a long-standing history in the field of developmental psychology. Yet even within the most recent publications on the treatment of juveniles who sexually harm others (Rich, 2003) only 3 of over 400 pages address the role of protective factors. Risk factors and the concept of risk take up almost 40 pages, or 10% of the book. Risk assessment and reduction is clearly a critical component of treatment to end sexual harm to others. Again, however, does this focus actually serve to promote safety through inclusiveness and promotion of a positive identity?

Using protective factors in evaluation, treatment planning, and the assessment of treatment outcome starts with existing assets and promotes positive growth. At the evaluation or intake phase, assessing protective factors as well as risk provides a systematic means of determining how open a setting the youth is able to tolerate while still maintaining decent behavior. This placement on the continuum of care relates to the need for physical containment, frequency of adult supervision, and frequency for therapeutic contact. Mike, a 16-year-old with a variety of caretakers, early physical abuse, and a history of truancy needs structure and daily therapeutic intervention as his life experience of adversity and lack of care left him with neither personal resources nor the knowledge of how to use community resources. Joe, on the other hand, shows the ability to respond to the care of his parents and recognizes his intellectual ability and physical prowess in sports. His sexually harming behavior is bounded by positive attributes in his life. Joe is able to attend seriously to his behavioral difficulties while living in an open community and attending therapy twice a week. When a youth stands in a position of personal strength, knowledge of his skills, and social recognition, he will have a greater ability to face down his wrong behavior. The caveat is that sometimes those supports must be external until sufficient personal strength develops.

The *Protective Factors Scale* (PFS; Bremer, 2001), incorporates a strengths-building approach to assessment and treatment, and is simply a different lens that may prove more useful in the long run than a negative or deficit-based lens. The PFS emerged from the *Intervention Strategy Factors* (ISF; Bremer, 1993). This original formulation was a collection of all the factors considered necessary for effective intervention in this population during the 1980s. The ISF included 6 areas: sexuality, offense-related, social, personal self-control, emotional, and psychological. There were a total of 35 different factors across the 6 areas. These 35 factors could be used to determine both an effective level of intervention (open community to locked correctional facility) and a treatment plan in cases where intervention would be necessary. This original formulation was based on the best clinical practices of the day and focused more on deficits and the professional as the knowledge base. In working with the ISF, it became apparent that a simpler, strength-based focus would augment sex-offense-specific programming. Researching the resiliency literature, in combination with identifying possible risk factors for juvenile reoffending, led to the development of the current PFS. This measure of 10 factors within 3 arenas (personal development, sexuality, and environmental support) covers key areas to develop resilience. A protective factors or resiliency measure can also be used in conjunction with a risk-assessment tool to create a balanced approach to treatment.

Current risk-assessment tools are used to roughly determine the threat a youth poses to the community. These are attempts at considering possible continued harm to the victim(s) or others. The *Estimated Risk Assessment for Sexual Offense Recidivism* (Worling & Curwen, 2000) is an empirically guided tool in wide use. The *Juvenile Sexual Offense Assessment Protocol–II* (Prentky & Righthand, 2003) is a revision of the JSOAP, modeled after adult actuarial risk assessment tools. The JSORRAT–II (Epperson et al., 2005) is in development. A lack of valid and reliable research defining risk factors means the tools developed thus far are based on a combination of adult sex-offense-specific research, emerging research on adolescents, best practice in the field, and theoretically guided assumptions. Given the developmental fluidity of adolescence, predictive validity for risk assessment may be difficult to achieve. Thus the use of these tools to determine where to build strengths rather than as a basis for generalized legal consequences and restrictions is more appropriate.

Accessing the positive factors that promote resiliency opens the door to engaging youth in treatment. Assessing risk factors defines possible areas of weakness. Identifying protective factors that have not been present informs areas in which to build strengths. Developing strengths can be directly related to areas of weakness to reduce risk. In the future, these strengths become protective factors, developing resilience to adversity or stressors, thus reducing the identified risks for continuing with sexually harming behaviors.

Identifying the presence and absence of protective factors within a psychosexual evaluation provides a salient summary that moves logically into treatment planning. Lacking peer social skills, control of sexual arousal, and balanced male models in his community, Joe does have areas of strength to give him hope in moving forward. He attends school regularly and gets above-average grades. His problem-solving ability and organizational skills can be brought to use in order to develop better peer social relationships. His problem-solving personal strength also lends itself to understanding how to gain a sense of mastery over the overwhelming arousal that comes with uneven hormonal surges. Identifying his strengths and weaknesses at evaluation leads to including cognitive behavioral techniques such as "head-heart-penis" balancing before he acts. This is a technique whereby a youth is taught to sense whether one of these three aspects of self is leading rather than a balance between them. Joe has family support and a stable family experience. These strengths allow family therapy to be employed in a variety of ways. His parents are available to supervise safety plans and maintain safe relations between the siblings. They can learn to offer emotional support when Joe feels hurt by peer rejection. His father can be helped to understand the impact of his own and his neighborhood's "macho" attitudes and the impact on his son's developing sexual identity. As Joe builds a stronger sense of personal identity, he gains the strength and resilience to face the stresses that led to his molesting his young sister.

Using a summary of strengths in the evaluation of 16-year-old Mike clearly shows that residential placement is needed to stabilize him. This level of external structure is necessary as he must build strengths before he can address his sexually harming behavior in a serious, meaningful way. Mike's sociability with peers makes the residential peer group a natural place to start building strengths. He is a talented musician—a skill that lends itself to expressing and reimagining feelings. These examples show how accounting for strengths and protective factors can produce better individualized treatment plans and more effective treatment.

There is always a place of strength to build from with any youth. Finding this strength entails defining the external structure that maintains personal and community safety during the process. If we want to avoid treatment that only considers immediate outcomes, then we need to lay the groundwork for internalized change that comes with the development of a positive self-identity. Developing resiliency through building factors known to prevent wrong responses to adversity or life stressors creates the ultimate safety net for our clients, their families, and communities. Resilience in our youth is the ultimate safety net and our most effective treatment ally.

References

Abel, G., Mittelman, M. S., & Becker, J. (1985). Sexual offenders: Results of assessment and recommendations for treatment. In H. H. Ben-Aron, S. I. Hucker, & C. D. Webster (Eds.), *Clinical criminology: The assessment and treatment of criminal behavior* (pp. 191-205). Toronto, Ontario, Canada: Clarke Institute of Psychiatry, University of Toronto.

Ainsworth, M. (1970). Attachment, exploration and separation: Illustrated by the behavior of one-year-olds in a strange situation. *Child Development, 41,* 49-67.

Ainsworth, M., Blehar, M., Waters, E., & Wall, S. (1978). *Patterns of attachment.* Mahwah, NJ: Lawrence Erlbaum Associates.

Biscoe, B. & Harris, B. (1994). *Adolescent Resiliency Attitudes Scale Manual.* Oklahoma City, OK: Eagle Ridge Institute, Inc.

Blaske, D. M., Borduin, C. M., Henggeler, S. W., & Mann, B. J. (1989). Individual, family, and peer characteristics of adolescent sex offenders and assaultive offenders. *Developmental Psychology, 25 (5),* 846-855.

Bowlby, J. (1975). *Attachment and loss, Volume II: Separation anxiety and anger.* Middlesex, England: Penguin Books.

Bremer, J. F. (1993, February). The treatment of children and adolescents with aberrant sexual behaviors. *Bailliere's Clinical Paediatrics International Practice and Research 1 (1),* 269-283.

Bremer, J. F. (1998). Challenges in the assessment and treatment of sexually abusive youth. *The Irish Journal of Psychology 19 (1),* 82-92.

Bremer, J. F. (2001, May). *The Protective Factors Scale: Assessing youth with sexual concerns.* Plenary address at the 16th annual conference of the National Adolescent Perpetration Network, Kansas City, MO.

Burton, D. (2000). Were adolescent sexual offenders children with sexual behavior problems? *Sexual Abuse: A Journal of Research and Treatment 12 (1),* 37-48.

Burton, D. & Schatz, R. (2003, July). *Meta-analysis of the abuse rates of adolescent sexual abusers.* Paper presented at the 8th International Family Violence Conference, Portsmouth, NH.

Carr, M. B. & Vandiver, T. A. (2001, Fall). *Risk and protective factors among youth offenders. Adolescence.* Available from www.findarticles.com/p/articles/mi_m2248/is_143_36/ai_82535314.

Chaffin, M., Letourneau, E., & Silovsky, J. (2002). Adults, adolescents and children who abuse children: A developmental perspective. In J. E. B. Myers, L. Berliner, J. Briere, C. T. Hendrix, C. Jenny, & T. E. Reid (Eds.), *APSAC Handbook on Child Maltreatment, 2nd ed.* (pp. 205-232). Thousand Oaks, CA: Sage.

Connolly, J. (1989). Social self-efficacy in adolescence: Relations with self-concept, social adjustment and mental health. *Canadian Journal of Behavioural Science, 21,* 258-269.

Constantine, N., Bernard, B., & Diaz, M. (1999, June). *Measuring protective factors and resilience traits in youth: The Healthy Kids Resilience Assessment.* Paper presented at 7th Annual Meeting of the Society for Prevention Research, New Orleans, LA.

Creeden, K. & Howland, J. (2000). *Integrating trauma and attachment theory into the treatment of juvenile sexual behavior problems.* Presented at the annual conference of the Association for the Treatment of Sexual Abusers, San Diego, CA.

Epperson, D. L., Ralston, C. A., Fowers, D., & DeWitt, J. (2005, April). *Development of the Juvenile Sexual Offense Recidivism Risk Assessment Tool (J-SORRAT).* Presented at the Conference of the Minnesota Association for the Treatment of Sexual Abusers, Minneapolis, MN.

Epstein, M. H. & Sharma, J. (1998). *Behavioral and emotional rating scale: A strength based approach to assessment.* Austin, TX: PRO-ED.

Fergusson, D. M. & Lynskey, M. T. (1996). Adolescent resiliency to family adversity. *Journal of Child Psychology and Psychiatry, 37,* 281-292.

Gilgun, J. F. (1999). CASPARS: New tools for assessing client risks and strengths. *Families in Society 80,* 450-460.

Jenkins, A. (1990). *Invitations to Responsibility: The therapeutic engagement of men who are violent and abusive.* Adelaide, Australia: Dulwich Centre Publications.

Jessor, R. (1993). Successful adolescent development among youth in high-risk settings. *American Psychologist, 48 (2),* 117-126.

Jew, C. L., Green, K. E., & Kroger, J. (1999). Development and validation of a measure of resiliency. *Measurement and Evaluation in Counseling and Development, 32, (2),* 75-90.

Kagan, R. (2004). *Rebuilding attachments with traumatized children.* Binghamton, NY: Haworth Press.

Karr-Morse, R. & Wiley, M. (1997). *Ghosts from the Nursery.* New York: The Atlantic Monthly Press.

Longo, R. & Groth, N. (1983). Juvenile sexual offenses in the histories of adult rapists and child molesters. *International Journal of Offender Therapy and Comparative Criminology, 27,* 155 -157.

Luthar, S. S., Cicchetti, D., & Becker, B. (2000). The construct of resilience: A critical evaluation and guidelines for future work. *Child Development, 71,* 543-562.

Matshego, J. (2001, May - July). *Best practices in the international and community-based treatment of juvenile offenders.* Presented at the United Nations Asia and Far East Institute for Prevention of Crime and Treatment of Offenders (UNAFEI), Tokyo, Japan.

National Institute of Mental Health (2000). *Child and adolescent violence research at the NIMH.* Article available from www.nimh.nih.gov/publicat/violenceresfact.cfm.

National Task Force (1988). Preliminary Report from the National Task Force on Juvenile Sexual Offending 1988. *Juvenile and Family Court Journal, 39 (2).*

National Youth Violence Prevention Resource Center (2001). *Youth Violence Research Fact Sheet.* Rockville, MD: Author. Available from www.safeyouth.org.

Oshio, A., Nakaya, M., Kaneko, H., & Nagamine, S. (2002). Development and validation of an adolescent resilience scale. *Japanese Journal of Counseling Science, 35 (1),* 57-65.

Prentky, R. & Righthand, S. (2003). *Juvenile Sex Offender Assessment Protocol–II (JSOAP–II).* Available from Center for Sex Offender Management at www.csom.org.

Resnick, M., Ireland, M., & Borowsky, I. (2004). Youth violence perpetration: What protects? What predicts? Findings from the National Longitudinal Study of Adolescent Health. *Journal of Adolescent Health 35*, 424e1-424e10.

Rich, P. (2003). *Understanding, assessing and rehabilitating juvenile sex offenders.* Hoboken, NJ: John Wiley and Sons.

Rutter, M. (1979). Protective factors in children's responses to stress and disadvantage. In M. W. Kent & J. E. Rolf (Eds.), *Primary prevention of psychopathology, Vol 3: Social competence in children* (pp. 49-74). Hanover, NH: University Press of New England.

Rutter, M. (1990). Psychosocial resilience and protective mechanisms. In J. Rolf, A. Masten, D. Cicchetti, K. Nuechterlein & S. Weintraub (Eds.), *Risk and protective factors in the development of psychopathology* (pp. 181-214). New York: Cambridge University Press.

Rutter, M., Giller, H., & Hagell, A. (1998). *Antisocial behavior by young people.* Cambridge, UK: Cambridge University Press.

Springer, J. F., & Phillips, J. L. (1997). *Individual Protective Factors Index (IPFI): A measure of adolescent resilience.* Folsom, CA: EMT Associates, Inc.

Ungar, M. (2004). *Nurturing hidden resilience in troubled youth.* Toronto, Ontario, Canada: University of Toronto Press.

Waller, M. A. (2001). Resilience in ecosystemic context: Evolution of a concept. *American Journal of Orthopsychiatry, 71 (3)*, 290-297.

Werner, E. E. (1989). High-risk children in young adulthood: A longitudinal study from birth to 32 years. *American Journal of Orthopsychiatry, 59 (1)*, 72-81.

Werner, E. E. & Smith, R. S. (1992) *Overcoming the odds: High risk children from birth to adulthood.* Ithaca, NY: Cornell University Press.

White, J. L., Moffitt, T. E., & Silva, P. A. (1989). A prospective replication of the protective effects of IQ in subjects at high risk for juvenile delinquency. *Journal of Consulting and Clinical Psychology, 57*, 719-724.

White, M. (1995). *Re-authoring lives: Interviews and essays.* Adelaide, Australia: Dulwich Centre Publications.

Worling, J. R. & Curwen, T. (2000). *Estimate of Risk of Adolescent Sexual Offense Recidivism (ERASOR).* Toronto, Ontario, Canada: Safe-T Program, Thistletown Regional Centre for Children and Adolescents, Ontario Ministry of Community and Social Services.

Chapter Six

Assessing Juveniles' Risk Within the Civil Commitment Context

Dennis Doren[1]

The fact that there is even a book chapter on this topic will likely come as a surprise to many people. Despite the various publicized controversies concerning sex offender civil commitment laws (e.g., Janus & Meehl, 1997), little attention has been given to the fact that some states are statutorily allowed to commit juvenile sex offenders who have never been waived into adult court. In fact, one state only commits juvenile versus adult offenders.

Currently 17 states have sex offender civil commitment laws: Arizona, California, Florida, Illinois, Iowa, Kansas, Massachusetts, Minnesota, Missouri, New Jersey, North Dakota, Pennsylvania, South Carolina, Texas, Virginia, Washington, and Wisconsin. The relevant commitment laws are sometimes referred to as "sexual predator" laws, though this phrase is neither exclusive to these commitment laws nor inclusive of all sex offender post-incarceration commitment laws. Hence, the generic description of "sex offender civil commitment law" is considered more appropriate and will be used here. Pennsylvania's law, enacted since February 2004, pertains solely to the commitment of people adjudicated for sex crimes as juveniles. A review of the relevant statutes beyond Pennsylvania's finds that about a third of the other laws allow for the commitment of adjudicated delinquents who committed specific sexual offenses (Doren, 2002). Given this potential, evaluators can and do get called upon to conduct risk assessments of juvenile offenders for potential civil commitments.

Most existing empirical studies and professional writings concerning sex offender recidivism risk assessments involve offenders who committed at least some of their crimes as adults (e.g., Doren, 2002).

---

[1] Dennis M. Doren is the Evaluation Director at the Sand Ridge Secure Treatment Center–Evaluation Unit in Madison, Wisconsin. All opinions expressed in this chapter are those of the author and do not necessarily reflect those of the State of Wisconsin Department of Health and Family Services.

Although some descriptions of risk factors specific to juvenile offenders can be found (e.g., Worling & Langstrom, 2003), the vast majority of empirical work concerning sex offender risk assessment involves adult offenders (e.g., Hanson & Bussiére, 1998; Hanson & Morton-Bourgon, 2004). Still, clinicians can find themselves being required to assess the recidivism risk of juvenile offenders. This chapter is designed to address the issue of conducting such assessments with juvenile offenders within the context of sex offender civil commitment evaluations. The assumption throughout this chapter will be that the offenders are male, in keeping with the great preponderance of male versus female juvenile sexual offenders that we assess for potential civil commitment.

Risk Assessment Methodologies

As Hanson (1998) pointed out, there are various methodologies for conducting a sex offender recidivism risk assessment, ranging through (a) various types of traditional clinical judgments to (b) empirically guided clinical judgment and (c) pure and clinically adjusted actuarial procedures. For a general discussion of those different procedures, the reader is referred to that article.

The first question to be addressed here is whether one procedure or another is currently most appropriate for assessing juvenile offenders. Within the adult sex offender risk assessment process, the use of actuarial instruments (within a clinically adjusted process) clearly represents the favored methodology (Doren, 2002). Demonstrations of the greater relative accuracy of actuarial instruments compared to more traditional clinical procedures continue to be found (e.g., Hanson & Morton-Bourgon, 2004). Therefore, the first issue is whether or not current actuarial methodology is the best procedure for assessing juvenile sex offenders within the civil commitment realm.

Actuarial Procedures with Juvenile Offenders

Currently no actuarial risk assessment instrument is specifically designed for evaluating the sexual recidivism risk of juvenile offenders. This is not to say actuarial risk assessment instrumentation does not exist for use with juveniles, but simply that none have become available that specifically measure the type of risk that is relevant to civil commitment statutes. Other actuarial risk tools for use specifically with juvenile offenders do exist (e.g., *Youth Level of Service/Case Management Inventory*; Hoge & Andrews, 2002). This means that any attempt to use actuarial instruments in the civil commitment assessment for a juvenile sexual offender necessarily involves "adult" based instruments. Of course, this situation can, and likely will change, in time. For instance, Douglas Epperson and his colleagues have conducted preliminary work to develop an instrument specific to juvenile sexual offenders for assessing their sexual recidivism risk (*Juvenile Sexual Offense Recidivism Risk Assessment Tool–II, JSORRAT–II*; Epperson, Ralston, Fowers, & DeWitt, 2005).

With adult offenders, the commonly used actuarial instruments in conducting sex offender civil commitment risk assessments include the *Static-99* (Hanson & Thornton, 2000), the *Rapid Risk Assessment of Sexual Offense Recidivism* (RRASOR; Hanson, 1997), and the *Minnesota Sex Offender Screening Tool–Revised* (MnSOST–R; Epperson et al., 1999). The fact that the samples used to develop these instruments did not include juvenile offenders (except, at most, some waived into adult court) is not the crucial issue for their application to juveniles. If there were supportive empirical tests of the accuracy of these tools with juvenile offenders, then the application of these instruments to such offenders would be straightforward. Unfortunately, such research tests are minimal, typically involve very small sample sizes (e.g., Poole et al., 2000), and are not always supportive to the application of these instruments to adolescent offenders (Morton & Bourgon, 2003).

Given this current situation, the use of the above-listed instruments to assess a juvenile offender involves certain potentially problematic assumptions. Even putting aside theoretical concerns about developmental stage differences between juvenile offenders (or even within subgroups of juvenile offenders) and adult offenders, there are two significant assumptions involving the application of adult instruments to juveniles: (a) typical sexual recidivism rates for juveniles and adults are sufficiently similar and (b) specific risk factors found useful in assessing adult offenders are sufficiently applicable to juveniles. Each of these assumptions, however, may not be fully accurate.

A growing body of empirical findings indicates that the sexual recidivism rate for juvenile sexual offenders tends to be lower than found with adults. For instance, Caldwell (2002) reviewed 13 studies of juvenile sexual offender's sexual recidivism (rearrest) rates and reported a range from about 2% to 13% over a follow-up period ranging from 1 to 9 years (mean weighted follow-up = just over 4.25 years). In contrast,

Hanson & Bussiére (1998) found a mean sexual recidivism rate of 13.4% over a 4- to 5-year follow-up with adult offenders; a rate at the top end compared to the range for juvenile samples.

To be comprehensive in this discussion, it should be pointed out that within sex offender civil commitment statutes the risk commitment criterion is regularly interpreted as representing the time period of the person's "remaining lifetime." Since juveniles can be thought of as having longer expected life spans than adults, one could argue that the longer time period means higher risk than adults would show. This argument presumes various things, however, that have not been shown to be true. For instance, juvenile sexual offenders have relatively high nonsexual criminality rates (Caldwell, 2002), such that it can be expected that many will become incarcerated as adults for nonsexual crimes. No studies to date show the degree to which these people return to sexual offending, or whether their reoffense rates become more similar to adult non-sex offenders. The longer lifetime argument presumes some disproportionate return to sexual offending, a presumption not made herein.

The effect of lower recidivism base rates on the "adult" actuarials probably depends on how great the difference in typical rates tends to be. Doren (2004) found that the risk percentages associated with different scores on the Static-99 and RRASOR tended to remain stable despite changes in samples' underlying base rates within a range from the developmental mean recidivism rate +/-6%. In other words, for the Static-99, the risk percentages determined from the development of the instrument tended to show stability within an underlying recidivism range of 18% +/-6% (i.e., between 12% and 24% within 5 years). For the RRASOR, the comparable stability range (surrounding a mean of 15%) was 9% to 21%. Beyond those ranges for underlying recidivism base rates, the risk percentages tended to shift to increasing degrees.

The lower end of the "stability" ranges overlap the highest recidivism rates for juvenile sexual offenders documented by Caldwell (2002), including when the difference in follow-up time periods is taken into consideration. This means that for some juvenile samples, the issue of having a different underlying base rate (compared to typical adult rates) as a concern for applying the adult actuarial instruments is not significant. On average it can be expected that the risk percentages associated with the adult instruments will overestimate the sexual recidivism rates for juvenile offenders assessed with those instruments.

Even that conclusion has another caveat attached to it, stemming from the concern about the application of adult-based risk factors to juveniles. The current sexual recidivism risk actuarial instruments were developed based on research findings with adult offenders. The risk factors included in those instruments came from such research. Unless research shows that these same factors apply to juvenile offenders with reasonable effectiveness, the instruments could be inaccurate if used with juveniles, even when base rate differences are found minimal.

So, do juvenile sexual offenders show the same risk factors? The answer appears to be sometimes yes and sometimes no, depending on the specific risk factor. For example, Worling and Langstrom (2003) found support for some actuarial items but not for others. Specifically, as compared to the items on the MnSOST–R, RRASOR, and Static-99, support was found with adolescent offenders for the meaningfulness of

   a. prior criminal sanctions for sexual assault(s) (on all three instruments),

   b. stranger victim (on the MnSOST-R and Static-99), and

   c. incomplete offense-specific treatment (on the MnSOST-R).

A weak degree of empirical support was found for

   a. male victim (on the RRASOR and Static-99),

   b. use of force/threat of force (on the MnSOST-R), and

   c. victims of a variety of ages (on the MnSOST-R).

A lack of empirical support was found for a history of nonsexual crimes, which is included on the Static-99. Additionally, the reader should be aware that all three instruments have one "age" item that, if applied to people younger than 18, is inclusive of all juvenile offenders without discrimination.

Overall, if some factors on the current instruments matter and some do not matter, this constellation suggests that the adult actuarials may not be as accurate for juvenile offenders as they are for adult offenders. The inclusion of risk factors that are of little use in assessing juveniles' recidivism likelihood amounts to "noise" in the system, which interferes with the music the instruments otherwise play.

Summary and Conclusions Concerning Using Current Actuarials with Juveniles

This chapter described three issues relative to the application of current actuarial instruments to juveniles within the context of sexual offender civil commitment evaluations. These included (a) the lack of sufficient empirical demonstration of the accuracy in this application, (b) the effect of lower typical recidivism base rates, and (c) the potential inclusion of factors that apply to adults but not to juveniles. When put together, the conclusion is drawn that there is reason for unease in using these instruments to assess a juvenile offender's sexual recidivism risk.

To be clear, this conclusion does not say that such instruments should never be used to assess a juvenile offender. The issue of a difference in underlying base rate may be addressed either in specific samples of juveniles (where a higher rate is known, for instance) or by selecting a subgroup of juveniles where the higher rate can reasonably be assumed not to be significantly different from the adults' rate. In this latter category, juveniles who last offended at age 17, for instance, may fit the bill, as there is little reason to presume that offenders who are 17-year-olds are so different from 18-year-old offenders. People whose most recent sexual offense was at 16 may not be so different either. The younger the juvenile at the time of the most recent sexual offense, however, the more a significant concern should be raised.

The same argument can be made concerning the applicability of the risk factors in the current instruments. The meaning of having a male victim may be very different for a 12-year-old sexual offender than for a 17-year-old, as the latter situation may be correlated with pedophilia while the former circumstance often is not (cf., Caldwell, 2002).

Until more research is conducted specifically testing the applicability of the current "adult" actuarial instruments to different groups of juveniles, the use of such instruments in assessing juveniles is by extrapolation from the findings with adult offenders. It appears that such extrapolation to older juveniles is reasonable, and to younger juveniles is not. Even with older juveniles, however, the potential issues may still necessitate viewing high scores on an instrument as simply suggestive of high risk, but not as clearly indicative of it as such scores are with adult offenders.

Empirically Guided Clinical Judgment

If actuarial procedures are not always available for assessing a juvenile offender within the civil commitment context, then the next methodology for us to consider is the use of structured clinical judgment, or what has also been termed the empirically guided clinical approach. The concept behind this method is that an empirically supported structure to clinical judgment maintains an empirical basis for final conclusions while still allowing clinicians to weigh each risk (and protective) factor according to what seems appropriate to the case.

Studies concerning the relevant adult-tested instruments show reasonable results, though not necessarily as accurate as the actuarials do (cf., Hanson & Morton-Bourgon, 2004). As is similar (though even more extreme) compared to what we found in reviewing the current actuarials, the typical structured list instruments for use with adult offenders have quite regularly not been tested with juvenile sexual offender samples (including instruments such as the *Sexual Violence Risk–20* [SVR–20; Boer, Hart, Kropp, & Webster, 1997] and *Risk for Sexual Violence Protocol* [RSVP; Hart, Kropp, & Laws, 2004; Kropp, 2000].) Unlike what was found with actuarial instruments, however, some structured lists have been specifically designed for use with juvenile offenders in assessing their sexual recidivism likelihood.

As stated in earlier chapters, the main instruments that are currently available in that regard are the ERASOR and ERASOR–II (Worling & Curwen, 2000 & 2001 respectively) and the JSOAP (Prentky & Righthand, 2001) and JSOAP–II (Prentky & Righthand, 2002, 2003). These lists of risk considerations both involve about 26 items (versus the far smaller number of items on the aforementioned actuarial instruments), so the clinician has a much broader scope of characteristics to consider in any application of these instruments. Concomitantly, the items often are easier for jurors and judges to understand as compared to actuarial items, as the items on these lists often seem more in keeping with "common sense."

There are disadvantages to the application of these instruments in the civil commitment realm. The main issue is trying to figure out how to assess whether the individual juvenile offender shows a risk higher or lower than the statutory threshold for commitment. For example, an evaluator may rightly conclude that an offender's risk is "high," but the question still remains whether or not that risk is high enough to meet a statutory threshold such as "more likely than not" (the specified threshold in Wisconsin, for instance, where commitments of juvenile offenders is statutorily permitted). To reach that commitment threshold, the individual would need to stand out as particularly higher in risk than the underlying juvenile sexual offender base rate would indicate on average. How many, and which risk factors represent such a degree of risk?

This may seem like a particularly hard task given the paucity of research in this regard. It may not be as difficult as it seems, however. Unstructured clinical judgment can apparently serve to make predictions (versus risk assessment) of who will versus who will not reoffend to a degree beyond chance, as found in the meta-analysis by Hanson & Morton-Bourgon (2004). Conducting risk assessments compared to a specific threshold (i.e., making determinations of risk above versus below a specific risk threshold) allows for less exactness (while still being accurate) than making predictions does. (For instance, instead of assessing a 0% chance of recidivating, that being what a prediction of non-recidivism means, the risk assessment conclusion of below threshold is accurate when the offender's risk falls anywhere from 0% up to just under the commitment threshold, such as just under 50%.) Hence, it seems quite plausible that conducting risk assessments relative to a statutory threshold is a statistically easier task than making predictions. If unstructured clinical judgment can be accurate to a degree beyond chance when involved with the more difficult task (predictions), then it seems very likely that the use of structured clinical judgment (e.g., using the ERASOR or JSOAP) to conduct risk assessments in the civil commitment realm is also accurate at least equal to, and probably greater than, unguided clinical predictions.

Each instrument also presents its own problems. The ERASOR (or ERASOR–II) has only minimally been empirically tested for its predictive accuracy relative to sexual reoffending, where the support for predictive validity was mixed (Morton & Bourgon, 2003). Additionally, the instrument has also been tested only minimally for its inter-rater reliability (Worling, 2004) and concurrent validity (Bourgon, 2002). This alone would seem to raise significant concerns about using the instrument for assessing risk within the civil commitment realm. Interestingly, a similar situation existed with the SVR–20 a few years back, yet in training presentations and court testimony some professionals were promoting its use in conducting civil commitment assessments of adult offenders (citations from the author upon request). It seems that where the field is desperate to find something to avoid unguided clinical judgment (or unwanted actuarial instrumentation), an untested structure appears better than no structure at all.

A second issue in the application of the ERASOR within the civil commitment realm is that numerous items refer to the person's history specifically within the past 6 months. Most juvenile offenders being considered for possible civil commitments have been incarcerated for longer than 6 consecutive months; often years. This makes the application of these ERASOR items problematic, as the juveniles typically did not have the same opportunity to do the specified behaviors as juveniles who were not incarcerated for that same time period.

The JSOAP and JSOAP–II also bring their own issue. Simply put, while these instruments have gone through more empirical testing than the ERASOR (e.g., Prentky et al., 2000; Righthand et al., 2005), the manual still describes the JSOAP–II as "an experimental scale" (Prentky & Righthand, 2003). Using an instrument for a forensic evaluation when the developers use such a label can be a problematic "sell" during testimony. On the other hand, the two developers offer a current perspective that may serve to clarify what they meant. When asked, Robert Prentky stated, "I always use the JSOAP when evaluating juveniles, including young adults who have been targeted for civil commitment solely because of juvenile offenses.... From a strictly empirical standpoint, JSOAP appears to be a sound scale, with ample evidence of its reliability and validity" (personal communication, May 10, 2005). Sue Righthand pointed out that "empirically guided assessments are better than unstructured opinions, and (using the instrument) would be preferable to winging it so to speak, relying solely on clinical experience and judgment" (personal communication, May 9, 2005). Dr. Prentky's comments also included, "Sue and I tend to be exceptionally cautious, because of the flagrant abuse among psychologists, not because of the science."

Summary and Conclusions Concerning Empirically Guided Clinical Judgment

Again, "adult" instruments were found, but none that had been tested for accuracy specifically using juvenile offenders. Unlike what was found concerning the lack of actuarials specific to the assessment of juveniles, however, some instruments for use within the empirically guided approach specific to juveniles were found. While having some strengths to recommend them, their degree of supportive empirical testing was rather to quite minimal. Additionally, each of the two instruments brought its own issues to the civil commitment evaluation task.

With that last set of caveats said, there still seems to be reason to presume that the use of either of these instruments may serve to increase risk assessment accuracy compared to unguided clinical judgment. That view would indicate that one or both of these instruments should be used despite their shortcomings, if the methodological option for an evaluator is unguided clinical judgment. The problem of knowing when a statutory risk threshold has been surpassed would still remain. On the other hand, this issue exists when using unguided clinical judgment, so the use of either of these structured lists would not make things any worse in that regard, and potentially better.

Conducting the Civil Commitment Risk Assessment

As the above discussion suggests, there is no obvious and straightforward answer to the question about the best way to conduct a civil commitment risk assessment with a juvenile offender. Some specific issues first need to be addressed to determine which methodology or combination of methodologies is appropriate.

Issue of Age at Last Sexual Offense

Probably the first issue to be determined is the age at which the offender was known to commit his last relevant sexual offense. A common scenario for referred offenders discharging from a juvenile correctional or treatment facility is that the person has already reached the age of majority (at least 18, sometimes as old as 20 before being released). Some evaluators might therefore view these people as adults and assess their risk accordingly using the RRASOR, Static-99, and/or MnSOST-R. This can be improper, however, as the real statistical issue is the degree to which it was possible these people could have been in any (developmental or cross-validation) sample upon which that instrument has been tested. While people being released at age 18 and older were in such samples for all of these actuarial instruments, these subjects were quite regularly also people who offended as adults, not solely as juveniles. Someone who is released from incarceration at age 19 (from a juvenile facility) who last offended at age 13 comes from a very different base rate sample than has been used with the current actuarials.

USING ACTUARIAL INSTRUMENTS. If the juvenile last offended at age 16 or 17, an argument can be made that the best assessment device is one or more of the current "adult" actuarials. As explicated above, there is reason to believe that these people do not differ enough in the relevant ways from other people in the samples used to test the instruments. Using a current actuarial with a person younger than that at the time of his last sexual offense is probably pushing that argument.

If actuarials are used, then the second issue becomes how to interpret the derived scores. Again, the younger the offender being assessed, the more the evaluator needs to be concerned about the effect of relatively lower underlying base rates for reoffending and the concomitant lowering of the risk percentages associated with the actuarial scores.

There is a meaningful way to compensate for those lower rates, to a point anyway. With typical adult offenders, the risk percentages are taken as they are (with the understanding of surrounding confidence intervals due to sampling error). If one has reason to presume a relatively lowered underlying recidivism base rate, such as is the case with application to juveniles, then taking the existing risk percentages as they are would seem improper. On the other hand, there is still reason to presume that the rank ordering of the scale scores still represents ranking ordering of risk (for older adolescents, where the issue of potentially different risk factors is not also prominent). If an older juvenile scores highly on an actuarial instrument, the adult-associated risk percentage may be inflated for this person, but the rank ordering would indicate he still represents a higher risk than most juvenile sexual offenders. This finding can be considered as a "hurdle jumped" in assessing the degree of risk needed for someone to meet criteria for commitment, though not necessarily as indicating that threshold has been met.[1] Other signs of high risk would still be needed to draw the conclusion that the person represents a sufficiently high enough risk for the statutory criterion to be met.

Even so, the actuarial process can be used in this way to serve as the starting and anchoring point for a risk assessment of an older juve-

---

[1] Thanks to Patricia Coffey, personal communication over years, for the metaphor.

nile offender. Of course, a low-risk finding from the actuarials would strongly indicate that the offender does not meet the risk criterion for commitment, at least without some rare and strong indicator of risk.

USING EMPIRICALLY GUIDED CLINICAL JUDGMENT. If the subject last offended in his teens, including through age 17, then evaluators have the option of using the empirically guided clinical approach. There does not automatically seem to be an obvious choice between using the ERASOR–II or the JSOAP–II, such that it is not uncommon to see both being employed in the same assessment. Since the item content from these two instruments overlap in important ways, it is expected that the two different instruments' results are quite similar.

As mentioned above, the two main issues in using these instruments are (a) scoring the ERASOR items that include the phrase "during the past 6 months," and (b) deciding whether the scales indicate above-threshold risk, while presuming that these subjects have lower-than-commitment levels of risk due to juveniles' relatively low recidivism base rates. In practice, the scoring issue on the ERASOR is not serious. Because the instrument is simply to guide clinical judgment, evaluators can use clinical judgment concerning how to use these items in the individual case.

The more problematic second issue represents the essential point for a sex offender civil commitment risk assessment overall: whether the offender shows lower- or higher-than-threshold sexual recidivism risk— the civil commitment risk question. The fact is that even the use of actuarial instruments with adult offenders involves this same issue, especially in states where the statutory threshold is statistically ambiguous (e.g., using the undefined term "likely"), so the fact that using the guided lists involves this issue is not peculiar to that methodology.

Given these understandings, the most common and reasonable approach to conducting a civil commitment risk assessment for a subject whose last sexual offense was somewhere between ages 13 and 15 is the use of the ERASOR–II and/or JSOAP–II. Using these instruments with people who last offended at age 16 or 17 is just as reasonable, probably along with the adult actuarials.

Issue of Other Clinical Factors

No matter how old the juvenile offender was at his last sexual offense or the time of assessment, and no matter which methodology the evaluator used, at some point clinical judgment comes into play. It is, of course, best if that clinical judgment is at least based on an empirical foundation, and simply represents the application of general research results to the specific case.

For example, the adult literature shows a consistent finding that a high degree of psychopathy coupled with sexual deviance is associated with particularly high sexual recidivism rates (Harris et al., 2003; Hildebrand, deRuiter, & deVogel, 2004; Rice & Harris, 1997). This combination has never been tested with adolescents; however, Gretton et al., (2001) looked at the issue for general violence and criminality recidivism with adolescents. It would seem reasonable to apply this adult-based knowledge clinically in assessing an adolescent to whom it is applicable. This presumes that a reasonable measure of sexual deviance can be obtained for the adolescent subject. Caldwell (2002) reviews findings that suggest this is potentially very difficult. Measurement of the degree of psychopathy should be done with the Psychopathy Checklist—either the Revised (Hare, 1991, 2004) or the Youth Version (Forth et al., 2004) depending on the age of the subject at the time of the offense.

Indicated above during the discussion of the potential application of adult actuarials to older juvenile offenders was that evaluators would likely still need to look for non-actuarial signs of high risk beyond even high scores on the instruments. This process is a clinical one, by definition, as it represents going beyond existing instrumentation. The main thing evaluators typically look for beyond the actuarial characteristics is a repetitive pattern of sexual misbehaviors and offending despite intervening consequences—not necessarily of a criminal justice system nature.

For instance, evaluators of juveniles often see circumstances in which the family handled the matter internally when the subject was caught the first time, and the subject was punished in some way by the family but nothing more. For people we later determine to higher risk, there is a repetition of the sexual offending, sometimes even with escalation in either seriousness (i.e., harm to victim, and/or use of weapon) or frequency or both. The legal system may get involved, but due to circumstances of the case no adjudication may result; only a temporary movement from the home or school may occur. If the person then repeats his offending, this type of repetitive pattern is something that evaluators will view as having relevance from a clinical perspective, as indicative of a drive and preference for sexual offending as opposed to general "acting out" or general antisociality.

Use of clinical judgment of this type should be described in evaluation reports as specifically that. By definition, we have less certainty about our unguided clinical judgment compared to what research has been able to tell us. While it is overtly stated here that some degree of clinical judgment is currently necessary in assessing juvenile offenders' risk, we should also be honest with the readers of our reports that certain information is more clearly accurate than other information.

This brings us to the circumstance where we have virtually nothing to guide us from the empirical world: when the offender's last sexual offense occurred before he was 13. Any application of even our existing empirically guided lists still represents an extrapolation of their research basis to this type of offender. The good news is that very few such people are referred for commitment, by the very nature of the fact that they typically would have already gone about 6 or more years without incident and often with some intervening treatment. The bad news is that if an evaluator has such a case, the only methodological option is unguided clinical judgment. To reiterate from above, unguided clinical judgment can still be better than chance, but we also have to admit it represents our least accurate methodology for assessing recidivism risk.

Issue of Confidence in Our Opinion

The bottom line to any risk assessment is the evaluator's opinion about whether or not the subject represents a sexual recidivism risk beyond the statutory threshold for commitment. There are two facets to such an opinion: the general level of risk assessed (relative to the statutory threshold) and the degree to which the evaluator feels confident that a determination of risk relative to the legal threshold can be made under the circumstances. How an evaluator draws a conclusion depends on both factors.

As described above, it is currently more difficult to determine when an offender's risk is above the statutory risk threshold when that offender is a juvenile versus an adult. The juvenile sexual recidivism base rate is lower, the available assessment instrumentation is not as exact (being empirically guided versus actuarial), and we know less about which characteristics truly represent risk factors for this type of reoffending. The relatively lower base rate for juveniles suggests that it is more likely an evaluator should conclude a juvenile offender does not meet the risk commitment threshold than it is for adult offenders. The latter two characteristics speak to a greater degree of ambiguity compared to analogous adult risk assessments.

An increased degree of ambiguity relates directly to the issue evaluators face every time they conduct a risk assessment: the degree to which the evaluator has confidence in forming a bottom-line opinion. In part, there is the issue of "a reasonable degree of professional certainty," a phrase that may be defined differently across evaluators (a subject beyond the scope of this chapter). Then, there is simply the issue of feeling confident enough in the information available to come to an opinion.

It seems reasonable to believe that some potential evaluators would simply conclude that the type of information available is not "good enough" to make these judgments. Of course, "good enough" is a value judgment and not a scientific standard. Even for those evaluators who feel the information is at least at times sufficient, acknowledgment of the degree unguided clinical judgment plays in the assessment would seem prudent.

Conclusion

Civil commitment risk assessments involving people who last offended sexually as a juvenile are more problematic than are the same assessments with adult offenders. The lesser degree of empirical foundation brings a greater need for unguided clinical judgment. While this does not necessarily mean a lesser degree of accuracy, it can easily lead to a lesser degree of confidence in drawing a bottom-line opinion.

The apparent fact that juvenile sexual offenders, on average, show lower sexual recidivism rates (over a follow-up period up to a decade) than do adult offenders also means that it is reasonable to expect a smaller proportion of juvenile offenders will meet commitment criteria. This is increasingly true the younger the offender is at the time of his most recent sexual offense.

In combination, these factors would appear to make it rather rare for a younger offender to be found to meet criteria for commitment, at least if the statutory risk threshold is at all high. This situation could change when better risk assessment instrumentation becomes available and if and when subgroups of high-risk juvenile offenders are then differentiated.

For older juvenile offenders, there is the potential to use current actuarial instruments to assist in the assessment. This would seem to facilitate the evaluation greatly, both to rule in and rule out potential commitments. On the other extreme, the proper risk assessment for at least most younger juvenile offenders would appear to result in an opinion of "does not meet" or "I cannot tell" to a sufficient degree of professional certainty. Exceptions would be based on clinical considerations unique to the case.

References

Boer, D. P., Hart, S. D., Kropp, P. R., & Webster, C. D. (1997). *Manual for the sexual violence risk–20.* Burnaby, Canada: The Mental Health, Law, and Policy Institute, Simon Fraser University.

Bourgon, G. (2002, Oct). *"The ERASOR": Evaluating its psychometric properties.* Presented at the 21st Annual Conference of the Association for the Treatment of Sexual Abusers, Montreal, Quebec, Canada.

Caldwell, M. F. (2002). What we do not know about juvenile sexual reoffense risk. *Child Maltreatment, 7*(4), 291-302.

Doren, D. M. (2002). *Evaluating sex offenders: A manual for civil commitments and beyond.* Thousand Oaks, CA: Sage Publications.

Doren, D. M. (2004). Stability of the interpretative risk percentages for the RRASOR and Static-99. *Sexual Abuse: A Journal of Research and Treatment, 16*(1), 25-36.

Epperson, D. L., Ralston, C. A., Fowers, D., & DeWitt, J. (2005, April). *Development of the Juvenile Sexual Offense Recidivism Risk Assessment Tool (J-SORRAT).* Presented at the Conference of the Minnesota Association for the Treatment of Sexual Abusers, Minneapolis, MN.

Epperson, D. L., Kaul, J. D., Huot, S. J., Hesselton, D., Alexander, W., & Goldman, R. (1999). *Minnesota Sex Offender Screening Tool–Revised (MnSOST–R): Development, performance, and recommended risk level cut scores.* Available from www.psychology.iastate.edu/faculty/epperson/mnsost_download.htm.

Forth, A. E., Kosson, D., & Hare, R. D. (2004). *The Hare Psychopathy Checklist: Youth Version.* Toronto, Canada: Multi-Health Systems.

Gretton, H. M., McBride, M., Hare, R. D., O'Shaughnessy, R., & Kumka, G. (2001). Psychopathy and recidivism in adolescent sex offenders. *Criminal Justice and Behavior, 28,* 427-449.

Hanson, R. K. (1997). *The development of a brief actuarial risk scale for sexual offense recidivism.* Department of the Solicitor General of Canada, Ottawa, Ontario. Available from www.psepc.gc.ca/publications/corrections/199704_e.pdf.

Hanson, R. K. (1998). What do we know about sex offender risk assessment? *Psychology, Public Policy, and Law, 4*(1/2), 50-72.

Hanson, R. K. & Bussiére, M. T. (1998). Predicting relapse: A meta-analysis of sexual offender recidivism studies. *Journal of Consulting and Clinical Psychology, 66*(2), 348-362.

Hanson, R. K. & Morton-Bourgon, K. E. (2004). *Predictors of sexual recidivism: An updated meta-analysis.* Available from www.psepc.gc.ca/publications/corrections/pdf/200402_e.pdf.

Hanson, R. K. & Thornton, D. (2000). Improving risk assessments for sex offenders: A comparison of three actuarial scales. *Law and Human Behavior, 24*(1), 119-136.

Hare, R. D. (1991). *Manual for The Hare Psychopathy Checklist–Revised.* Toronto, Ontario, Canada: Multi-Health Systems.

Hare, R. D. (2004) *Manual for The Hare Psychopathy Checklist–Revised, 2nd ed.* Toronto, Ontario, Canada: Multi-Health Systems.

Harris, G. T., Rice, M. E., Quinsey, V. L., Lalumiére, M. L., Boer, D., & Lang, C. (2003). A multisite comparison of actuarial risk instruments for sex offenders. *Psychological Assessment, 15*(3), 413-425.

Hart, S. D., Kropp, P. R., & Laws, R. L. (2004). *The Risk for Sexual Violence Protocol (RSVP).* Burnaby, British Columbia, Canada: Mental Health, Law, and Policy Institute, Simon Fraser University. Available from the Mental Health, Law and Policy Institute via e-mail (mhlpi@sfu.ca), URL (www.sfu.ca/psyc/groups/mhlpi), or telephone (604-291-5868). Also available from Richard Laws at the Pacific Psychological Assessment Corporation (www.pacific-psych.com).

Hildebrand, M., de Ruiter, C., & de Vogel, V. (2004). Psychopathy and sexual deviance in treated rapists: Association with sexual and nonsexual recidivism. *Sexual Abuse: A Journal of Research and Treatment, 16*(1), 1-24.

Hoge, R. D. & Andrews, D. A. (2002). *Youth Level of Service/Case Management Inventory: User's Manual.* Toronto, Ontario, Canada: Multi-Health Systems.

Janus, E. S. & Meehl, P. E. (1997). Assessing the legal standard for predictions of dangerousness in sex offender commitment proceedings. *Psychology, Public Policy, and Law, 3*(1), 33-64.

Kropp, P. R. (2000, Nov.). *The Risk for Sexual Violence Protocol (RSVP).* Presented at the 19th Annual Conference of the Association for the Treatment of Sexual Abusers, San Diego, CA.

Morton, K. E. & Bourgon, G. (2003). *Validation of a measure designed to predict sexual recidivism among adolescent sexual offenders.* Presented at the Conference of the Canadian Psychological Association, Hamilton, Ontario, Canada.

Poole, D., Liedecke, D., & Marbibi, M. (2000). *Risk assessment and recidivism in juvenile sexual offenders: A validation study of the Static 99.* Austin, TX: Texas Youth Commission.

Prentky, R. A., Harris, B., Frizzell, K., & Righthand, S. (2000). An actuarial procedure for assessing risk with juvenile sex offenders. *Sexual Abuse: A Journal of Research and Treatment, 12*(2), 71-93.

Prentky, R. A. & Righthand, S. (2001). *Juvenile Sex Offender Assessment Protocol (J-SOAP): Manual.* Bridgewater, MA.

Prentky, R. A. & Righthand, S. (2002). *Juvenile Sex Offender Assessment Protocol–II (J-SOAP-II): Manual.* Bridgewater, MA.

Prentky, R. & Righthand, S. (2003). *Juvenile Sex Offender Assessment Protocol II: Manual.* Washington, DC: Office of Juvenile Justice and Delinquency Prevention.

Rice, M. E. & Harris, G. T. (1997). Cross-validation and extension of the violence risk appraisal guide for child molesters and rapists. *Law and Human Behavior, 21*(2), 231-241.

Righthand, S., Prentky, R. A., Knight, R. A., Carpenter, E., Hecker, J. E., & Nangle, D. (2005). Factor structure and validation of the Juvenile Sex Offender Assessment Protocol (J-SOAP). *Sexual Abuse: A Journal of Research and Treatment, 17*(1), 13-30.

Worling, J. R. (2004). The Estimate of Risk of Adolescent Sexual Offense Recidivism (ERASOR): Preliminary data. *Sexual Abuse: A Journal of Research and Treatment, 16*(3) 235-254.

Worling, J. R. & Curwen, T. (2000). *Estimate of Risk of Adolescent Sexual Offense Recidivism (ERASOR)–Version 1.2.* Unpublished manuscript. Toronto, Ontario, Canada: Ontario Ministry of Community and Social Services.

Worling, J. R. & Curwen, T. (2001). Estimate of Risk of Adolescent Sexual Offense Recidivism (The ERASOR–Version 2.0). In M.C. Calder (Ed.), *Juveniles and children who sexually abuse: Frameworks for assessment* (pp. 372-397). Lyme Regis, U.K.: Russell House Publishing.

Worling, J. R. & Langstrám, N. (2003). Assessment of criminal recidivism risk with adolescents who have offended sexually. *Trauma, Violence, & Abuse, 4*(4), 341-362.

Chapter Seven

Actuarial Risk Assessment With Juveniles Who Offend Sexually:

Development of the Juvenile Sexual Offense Recidivism Risk Assessment Tool–II (JSORRAT–II)

Douglas L. Epperson
Christopher A. Ralston
David Fowers
John DeWitt
Kathleen S. Gore

The general public has demonstrated increasing concern about sexual violence in their communities over the past 15 years. This apprehension has focused more and more on the danger posed by sexual offenders released into the community who subsequently perpetrate additional sexual offenses (repeat offenders). The public's anxiety is reflected in numerous legislative mandates for more effective risk management techniques to reduce the threat to public safety posed by known sexual offenders released to the community. In addition, state and federal governments have enacted registration and community notification statutes for convicted sexual offenders, and 16 states have passed laws that enable the state to commit high-risk sexual offenders to forensic hospitals instead of releasing them into the community at the end of their prison sentences (Doren, 2002; Lieb & Goodkin, 2005).

To understand the role of effective risk management, it is important to first clarify the key concepts of risk, risk management, danger or threat to the community, and risk reduction. In our model, risk is inherent in the individual; it is comprised of those individual characteristics that make an individual more or less likely to commit new sexual offenses in the future. Examples of such characteristics, or risk factors, would include the level of drive to engage in such acts, presence or absence of distorted sexual attitudes, quality of judgment and/or impulse control, and degree of psychopathy. Risk, as the composite of risk factors, can be operationalized as the offender's likelihood of committing additional sexual offenses if released into the community with no external constraints placed on his or her behavior (see the dotted line in Figure 7.A).

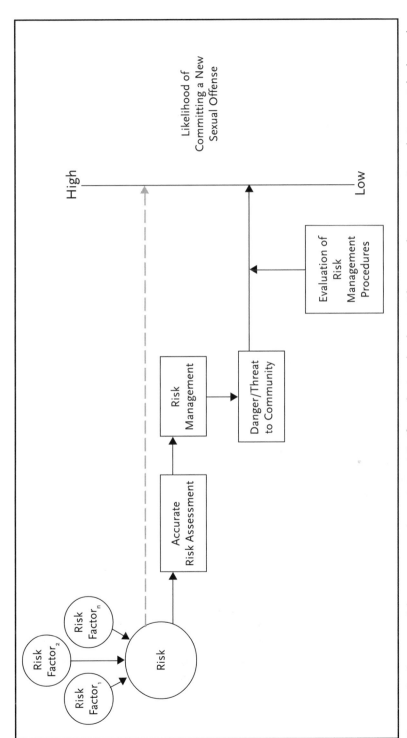

Figure 7.A. Accurate risk assessment is a prerequisite for reducing the danger/threat to the community, relative to risk, through effective risk management (note that the effectiveness of risk management procedures must be evaluated).

It is important to note that environmental factors are not considered to be risk factors under this conceptualization; instead, they are viewed as components of risk management. Risk management in our model includes all efforts external to the individual intended to reduce the danger or threat to the public relative to the level of risk presented by the individual. Examples of risk management include placement in supervised settings, increased individual supervision, and random testing for substance use. Operationally, the danger or threat to the community is the reduced likelihood, relative to risk, of an offender's committing a new sexual offense given the level of risk management implemented. If there is no risk management or it is ineffectively applied, then the danger or threat to the public is equal to the risk of the individual. However, with effective risk management, the threat or danger to the public is reduced (see Figure 7.A).

There are two key implications of this conceptualization for risk assessment and risk management. The first is that the model specifies that risk is inherent in the individual and is unchanged by external constraints in the environment. These external constraints, so long as they remain in effect, reduce the danger or threat to the community by reducing the likelihood that the level of risk will manifest itself; however, risk remains unchanged because the individual remains unchanged. Second, the model emphasizes that although risk management components do not reduce risk, they should be selected based on risk to effectively reduce the public's exposure to danger. For example, it makes little sense to invest in intensive supervision for a very low-risk offender, particularly when resources are limited, which is an almost universal situation for departments of corrections, youth corrections, and public safety. Such a practice would waste precious resources on an individual whose threat to the public is already so low that it cannot be reduced much further. It also may actually increase the risk of that individual through contagion effects by exposing him or her to higher-risk offenders (e.g., Gifford-Smith, Dodge, Dishion, & McCord, 2005). Additionally, such practices can unnecessarily deprive individuals of liberty interests by providing a more restrictive environment than is warranted without commensurate benefit to society.

Alternatively, a very high-risk offender may require a significant investment in risk-management efforts to substantially reduce the danger or threat to the community posed by this individual. To be effective, risk management requires that scarce resources be invested carefully by matching the level of risk management to the level of risk presented by the individual. Accurate assessment of risk, therefore, is absolutely critical for this necessary matching process to occur. The absence of risk assessment produces undifferentiated, "one size fits all," risk-management practices that are often too intense and costly for low-risk offenders and insufficient to effectively reduce the danger to the public posed by high-risk offenders. Inaccurate risk assessment produces mismatched, and therefore largely ineffective, risk-management efforts.

As indicated in Figure 7.A, the empirical evaluation of risk-management procedures, including legislatively mandated ones, is a second type of assessment that is central to effective risk management. Risk-management procedures cannot simply be assumed to reduce danger or threat to the public; instead, we must evaluate them empirically to assess their effectiveness. If specific risk-management components prove ineffective for particular levels of risk, then they should be discontinued and replaced with more promising procedures.

Although risk is inherent in the individual, it is not static, so danger or threat to the public can be reduced through risk reduction as well as through effective risk management. Risk reduction necessarily results through changes in the individual because risk is inherent in the individual. The majority of such changes presumably would occur through treatment, and they might include decreased deviant sex drive, decreased distortions in sexual attitudes, decreased psychopathy, and increased impulse control, among others—often labeled stable dynamic variables (e.g., Hanson & Harris, 2000, 2001). Just as effective risk management requires accurate risk assessment, so does effective treatment. Specifically, accurate risk assessment informs decisions about the necessary length and intensity of treatment, with higher risk offenders presumably requiring a longer-term and more intense treatment experience to effectively lower their risk and divert them toward a non-offending path. Of course, a psychological needs assessment also would be necessary to provide focus to treatment (see Figure 7.B).

In the same way that risk management practices should match the risk levels of individuals, the intensity and duration of treatment should also be matched to risk level. The absence of risk assessment produces "one size fits all" treatments in regard to intensity and duration, and inaccurate risk assessment produces mismatched treatment placements. In an era of restricted resources, this often translates into treatments that are too intense and costly for very low-risk offenders and inadequate for high-risk offenders. This approach to treatment also results in mixing low-risk and high-risk offenders, which may actually

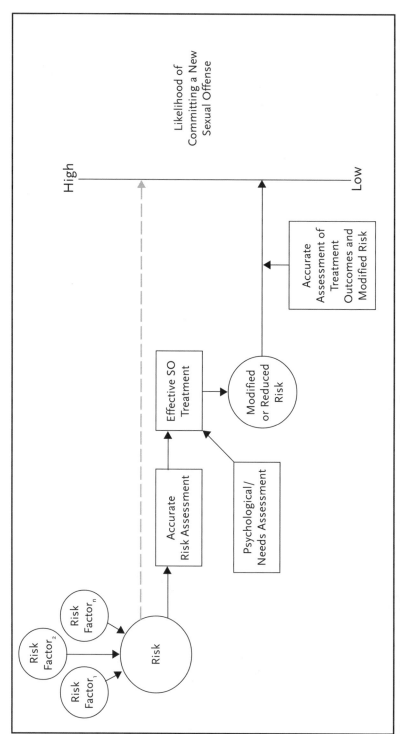

Figure 7.B. Accurate risk assessment is a prerequisite for effective treatment to reduce risk (note that accurate measures of treatment outcomes and resulting reductions in risk would be required to assess the modified level of risk).

increase the risk of initially low-risk offenders through contagion effects (Boxer, Guerra, Huesmann, & Morales, 2004). Such contagion effects may be particularly problematic with juveniles, who are more malleable than adults. Therefore, an important part of treatment may involve segregation of low-risk juveniles from higher-risk juveniles. In fact, for some very low-risk juvenile sexual offenders, detection, segregation from higher-risk offenders, and a basic psycho-educational program may be the only intervention needed. Resources saved with lower-risk offenders could then be invested in longer-term, intensive treatment for higher-risk offenders.

A second level of assessment is also required to reduce risk through treatment, specifically the assessment of treatment outcomes and the resulting modified level of risk. The achievement of treatment outcomes and their resulting impact on risk must be carefully measured. Historically, treatment outcomes have been assessed simply at the very broad level of whether offenders completed or failed to complete treatment (e.g., Hanson & Bussiére, 1998; Hanson & Morton-Bourgon, 2004). As an initial step to advance the assessment of modified risk, we must continue to develop specific treatment goals, evaluate the achievement of each of those goals, and assess the impact of each goal attainment on risk. Some of the most promising work in this area is being conducted by Karl Hanson and Andrew Harris in conjunction with the development of a dynamic risk assessment tool, the *Sex Offender Needs Assessment Rating* (SONAR; Hanson & Harris, 2001)

Risk Assessment with Adult Sexual Offenders

As discussed above, accurate risk assessment plays a central role in both risk management and treatment for sexual offenders. Furthermore, it has been well established over the past several decades that unguided clinical judgment is generally unable to produce reliable and accurate predictions of either general violence (e.g., Monahan, 1981; Bonta, Law, & Hanson, 1998) or sexual violence (e.g., Hanson & Bussiére, 1998; Hanson & Morton-Bourgon, 2004) whereas the general superiority of statistical (actuarial) prediction over clinical prediction is well documented in the pioneering work of Paul Meehl (1954) and subsequent researchers (e.g., Grove & Meehl, 1996; Grove, Zald, Lebow, Snitz, & Nelson, 1995, 2000; Swets, Dawes, & Monahan, 2000). Unfortunately, despite such conclusions, sexual offender risk assessment continued to rely heavily on unguided clinical judgment until the middle to late 1990s. Significant gains in risk assessment with sexual offenders were realized in the 1990s based on extensive primary research and meta-analyses to identify variables that were empirically linked to sexual recidivism and the resulting development of actuarial risk assessment tools for sexual offenders. These developments largely focused on adult, male, sexual offenders because this was the group that committed the largest proportion of known sexual offenses and, therefore, was immediately subjected to the legislation described earlier.

The most commonly used actuarial risk assessment tools for adult sexual offenders include the *Sex Offender Risk Assessment Guide* (SORAG; Quinsey, Rice, & Harris, 1995), the *Rapid Risk Assessment of Sexual Offense Recidivism* (RRASOR; Hanson, 1997), the *Minnesota Sex Offender Screening Tool–Revised* (MnSOST-R; Epperson et al., 1998, 2000), and the *Static-99* (Hanson & Thornton, 1999, 2000). These tools largely built on the earlier success of actuarial methods to predict general recidivism and the successful development of was later named the *Violence Risk Appraisal Guide* (VRAG; Harris et al., 1993) as an actuarial risk assessment tool for general violent recidivism (Quinsey et al.). These empirically validated tools have substantially exceeded the level of accuracy produced by clinical prediction, and none of the tools has consistently emerged as more accurate than the others (Hanson & Morton-Bourgon, 2004; Langton, Barbaree, Harkins, Seto, & Peacock, 2002). Because of their greater and more consistent accuracy, these actuarial risk assessment tools are widely used to inform a variety of release-related decisions, including decisions regarding civil commitment, level of community notification, and level of supervision (Doren, 2002).

Risk Assessment with Juvenile Sexual Offenders

Although adults were the initial focus of most risk assessment and risk management research, accurate risk assessment with juveniles is just as important as with adults. It offers many of the same advantages, including the ability to more efficiently allocate limited resources by matching placement, programming, and treatment intensity with risk, as well as the ability to segregate lower-risk juvenile sexual offenders from higher-risk offenders. Such advantages may be even more important for juveniles relative to adults given the greater likelihood of treatment success when interventions occur at younger ages and given that contagion effects from mixing lower- and higher-risk offenders have been clearly documented with juveniles (e.g., Boxer et al., 2005). Nonetheless, empirically based risk assessment tools have been slow to develop for juveniles.

At the present time, only four such tools have been presented and described in published articles: *Juvenile Sex Offender Assessment Protocol* (JSOAP; Prentky et al., 2000), now in its second version (JSOAP–II; Prentky & Righthand, 2003; Righthand et al., 2005); *Estimate of Risk of Adolescent Sexual Offense Recidivism* (ERASOR; Worling & Curwen, 2001; Worling, 2001, 2004); *Juvenile Risk Assessment Tool* (J–RAT; Rich, 2001a, 2003); and *Risk Assessment Matrix* (RAM; Christodoulides, Richardson, Graham, Kennedy, & Kelly, 2005). In addition, Phil Rich has developed several variants of the J–RAT for specialized populations and/or for reassessing and monitoring risk during treatment (Rich, 2001b).

Each of these tools was developed based on a review of the literature and/or clinical observation, and they include a mixture of static and dynamic risk factors or items. The JSOAP–II contains 28 items, the ERASOR contains 25 items, the J–RAT contains 118 items, and the RAM contains 26 items. These tools were carefully conceptualized and developed by leaders in the field, and each of the tools possesses many strengths. The tools would, however, be best characterized as structured- or guided-clinical assessment tools, rather than actuarial tools, primarily because they provide no empirically derived rules for how to weight and combine risk factors into an overall assessment of risk. Instead, the final risk judgment is largely left to the clinician doing the assessment. In addition, although several of these tools are empirically based, the development samples used were generally small and specific to clinical settings, raising some questions about whether the samples were representative of the broader range of juvenile sexual offenders. Finally, we could locate only one study that validated any of these tools against observed sexual recidivism, and this study was based on a sample of 54 (6 sexual recidivists) and produced somewhat mixed results (Hecker et al., 2002).

Thus, there appeared to be an opportunity to contribute to the literature by developing an actuarial juvenile sexual recidivism risk assessment tool on a large and broadly representative sample. The planned second step of this endeavor is, of course, a validation study with an independent sample. The hope is that such a tool will augment existing tools and bring increased accuracy to risk assessment with juvenile sexual offenders. This is, of course, an empirical question to be answered through future research.

Development of the JSORRAT–II

The slower development of empirically validated risk assessment tools for adolescents is probably due to several factors. One potential reason is the fact that adults commit most sexual offenses. However, based on data for 1991–96 from the National Incident Based Reporting System, Snyder (2000) reported that juveniles committed 23% of all sexual offenses and 40% of sexual offenses against children age 11 or younger. Such substantial numbers point to the need for empirically derived measures of risk for juvenile sexual offenders.

A second possible reason is that, at least initially, legislative mandates such as community notification were targeted at adults, resulting in less urgency to develop risk assessment tools for juveniles. A related possible reason was that some feared that the development of empirically validated risk assessment tools for juveniles would hasten the application of such legislation to adolescents. As a point of fact, we began development of the JSORRAT–II only after it became apparent that many states were already engaging in community notifications for adolescent sexual offenders, in some cases for all juvenile sexual offenders, despite the lack of appropriately developed and validated risk assessment tools.

We believe that broad community notification for juveniles who offend sexually is generally a mistaken strategy because of the many likely negative effects for the juvenile and his or her family that are not offset by comparable benefits to society. Potential negative effects include ostracism, stigmatism, harassment, and withdrawal of social support for both the offender and his or her family. In addition, the offender may experience physical harm or the threat of physical harm as well as the loss of important developmental opportunities, such as employment and organizational membership (e.g., sports teams, clubs). Although no empirical studies of the effects of broad community notification on juvenile sexual offenders have been published, a study by Zivits, Crim, and Farkas (2000) documented the presence of many of these effects with adult sexual offenders.

If there were compelling, offsetting benefits to society, particularly a documented decrease in sexual recidivism associated with community notification, such negative effects arguably might be tolerable. Although community notification statutes are politically popular, no empirical evidence demonstrates that they constitute an effective risk management strategy to reduce juvenile sexual recidivism. Ironically, the discouragement, fear, and/or anger that may be experienced by juvenile sexual offenders subjected to community notification and its associated negative consequences may interfere with treatment designed to reduce risk. In fact, the chances of a reoffense may actually increase under such conditions.

Within this context, community notification is a particularly misguided strategy when it fails to recognize the tremendous heterogeneity among juvenile sexual offenders based on the nature of their crimes (e.g., Knight & Prentky, 1993), their risk for sexual recidivism, and their potential to respond favorably to detection, education, and treatment (e.g., Walker, McGovern, Poey, & Otis, 2004). Consequently, it seemed that an appropriately developed and validated actuarial tool would provide an empirical basis for attempting to limit the scope of community notification in states that notify on adolescent sexual offenders, in addition to providing critical information for placement, programming, treatment, and resource allocations decisions.

Goals of the JSORRAT—II

Given the significant contributions of empirically developed and validated actuarial risk assessment tools for adults, we assumed that the same approaches could be effective in risk assessment with juveniles. We also believed that only shorter-term predictions would be possible given the incomplete level of development in adolescence. Consequently, our goal was to develop a tool that would assess the risk of juvenile sexual recidivism, then subsequently evaluate the ability of that tool to also assess the risk of longer-term sexual recidivism.

Whereas adult risk-assessment tools have probably been used most extensively in conjunction with forensic decisions, such as civil commitment and community notification, the intended application of the JSORRAT—II necessarily differs because of its target population. Our hope is that accurate risk-assessment tools for juveniles will be used to better segregate lower-risk juveniles from higher-risk juveniles, better match treatment length and intensity with risk (noting that psychological and other assessments will be necessary to appropriately focus treatment), and better match placement supervision/security with risk. As noted earlier, accurate risk assessment may also aid in limiting the scope of community notification for adolescents.

To achieve the goal of developing a reliable and accurate actuarial risk-assessment tool for juveniles that could inform the types of decisions just described, the tool needed to have a number of characteristics. First, the tool would have to be broadly applicable to a range of juvenile sexual offenders, including those who have not received treatment. Consequently, we followed the lead of several adult risk-assessment tools and limited potential items to those for which information would be available in typical juvenile court and youth corrections files. Second, we focused on data sources for which we had greater confidence in their reliability and consistency across case files. For example, when looking at past history of sexual offending, we looked at incidents that were officially documented and not simply alleged. Third, in designing data collection instruments, we tried to make data points as behaviorally anchored as possible (e.g., events that either occurred or did not occur, as opposed to assessing mood states or personality characteristics). However, there were some instances in which this was less possible due to the nature of the information required. Finally, we were committed to developing a risk-assessment tool that was as simple and intuitive as possible without losing accuracy.

Sample

The development sample used was exhaustive and included 636 male juveniles adjudicated for a sexual offense in the state of Utah between 1990 and 1992 while under the jurisdiction of the juvenile court, which is generally from age 12 through age 17. Because of some flexibility regarding the ages during which the juvenile court has jurisdiction in Utah, four people in our sample were 11 years old at intake for the index sexual offense and 10 people were 18 years old at intake for the index sexual offense.

Because this was an exhaustive sample of all eligible juveniles for whom we could find records, it included the full spectrum of juveniles who offend sexually, both geographically within the state and in regard to their offense histories and characteristics. The majority of the sample (76.4%) was Caucasian, 7.7% were Hispanic/Latino, 2.2% were African American, 1.6% were Asian American, 1.4% were Native American, 1.1% were multiethnic or other, and 9.6% were unspecified. As noted earlier, ages in our sample ranged from 11 to 18 years old at intake for the index sexual offense, and the average age was 15.18 (sd = 1.57). Approximately one quarter (22.6%) of the sample received a secure placement for their index sexual offense, 8.2% had received some type of sexual offender specific treatment prior to their index offense, and 44.5% received some type of sexual-offender-specific treatment during their involvement with the juvenile justice system for the index sexual offense.

Data Collection Materials and Procedures

CASE FILE PREPARATION AND CONTENT. Juvenile judicial files and youth corrections case files for the 636 adolescents in the sample were located and copied by staff of the Utah Juvenile Court and the Utah Division of Juvenile Justice Services. The files were then redacted and edited to appear as they did when the juvenile exited the juvenile justice system for their 1990–92 index sexual offense. This work was completed by staff from the same two agencies and by volunteers from a statewide organization of caseworkers and treatment providers for juveniles who offend sexually. By editing the files in this manner, we emulated a prospective research method while working with archival files.

After the files were located, copied, redacted, and edited, they were shipped to Iowa State University for review and data extraction. The case files varied somewhat in their content, but all the files contained a record of criminal involvement with the juvenile justice system up to and including the index sexual offense. This record typically included arrest, investigation, court, and youth corrections reports. Among other information, these reports described the juvenile's past sexual offense perpetrations and the index sexual offense, including information about events leading up to sexual offenses, the nature of the offenses, and information about the victim or victims. The majority of files also had caseworker reports and/or psychological evaluations that provided background information for the juvenile and his family regarding educational history, social functioning, substance abuse and mental health issues, and treatment history. Finally, a number of files contained histories of familial involvement with the courts and the Department of Human Services regarding child neglect and child sexual, physical, and emotional abuse.

CASE FILE REVIEW, DATA EXTRACTION, AND DATA ENTRY. Eight research assistants at Iowa State University who had no knowledge of the juveniles or their sexual recidivism outcomes reviewed the case files and extracted data into codebooks—one background codebook for each juvenile. Items recorded in the codebook provided demographic data and information about care-giving structure, family relationships, child abuse history, educational history (academic and behavioral), consenting sexual history, substance abuse history, mental health history, treatment history (substance abuse, mental health, and sexual-offender-specific), nonsexual offense charges and adjudications, and sexual offense charges and adjudications.

In addition to the background codebook, an offense characteristics codebook was completed for each separate victim of sexual offenses perpetrated by the juvenile offender. Consequently, each juvenile could have multiple offense characteristics codebooks. Each offense characteristics codebook provided information about the victim (e.g., gender, age, relationship to the perpetrator), pre-offense behaviors (e.g., stalking, grooming), methods for achieving compliance (e.g., force, threat of force, bribery), offense locations (e.g., school, victim's home, offender's home), specific sexual acts in the offense (e.g., fondling, penetration), role of the juvenile offender in the offense (e.g., sole perpetrator, leader of group, member of group), and post-offense behaviors (e.g., told victim not to tell, threatened harm if victim told, confessed) for each unique victim of a sexual offense.

The research assistants were trained to correctly read the contents of the files and accurately extract data into the codebooks during multiple meetings of one to two hours duration each. Detailed instructions were provided for each individual item in the codebooks during these meetings. Research assistants were then paired and given identical practice cases to do individually. After completing the case, the assistants met with the lead researcher to review the file and discuss any discrepancies in coding. This process was repeated until the research assistants could produce consistent codebooks. The research assistants then coded the case files according to the prescribed protocol. When questions arose, they were directed to the lead researcher for discussion and clarification. The results of those discussions were shared with the entire group in periodic team meetings and through a common log that was kept in the research lab. When all cases had been coded, research assistants entered the data from the codebooks into an electronic spreadsheet. Two separate research assistants entered each codebook, and the records were compared for discrepancies that signaled data entry errors. When discrepancies were encountered, the original codebook was consulted to determine which entry was correct.

SEXUAL RECIDIVISM DATA. Information about sexual recidivism was obtained only after all files had been reviewed. Juvenile sexual recidivism was the outcome of primary interest, and it was defined as a charge for a new sexual offense prior to the age of 18. The Utah Division of Youth Corrections provided this information from a statewide electronic database of juvenile offenders. The base rate in the sample for juvenile sexual recidivism was 13.2% (84 juvenile sexual recidivists in the sample of 636).

Information on adult sexual recidivism, defined as a charge for a new sexual offense after the age of 18, was also obtained through 2003. This information was collected through a check of Utah's state-wide criminal offender data base and the FBI's National Crime Index data base. Offenders in our sample ranged in age from 22 years old to 31 years old at the time the adult recidivism data were collected. A total of 58 offenders sexually recidivated as adults, constituting a 9.1% adult sexual recidivism base rate. Sixteen of the 58 adult sexual recidivists also recidivated as juveniles, and the remaining 42 offenders sexually recidivated for the first time as adults. Anytime recidivism, defined as a new charge for a sexual offense as either a juvenile or young adult prior to 2004, was generated by combining the juvenile and adult recidivism data. The base rate in the sample for anytime sexual recidivism was 19.8% (126 out of 636 recidivated as a juvenile and/or as an adult).

Item Selection Procedures

GENERAL ANALYTIC PROCEDURES. The dependent variable in all analyses was juvenile sexual recidivism, defined as a charge for a new sexual offense subsequent to the index offense while still under the jurisdiction of the juvenile court. All such offenses occurred prior to age 18 in our sample. The analytic procedure followed was designed to identify the set of variables that optimally separated juvenile sexual recidivists from those who did not have any new charges for a juvenile sexual offense. After that set of variables was identified, its ability to predict anytime recidivism, defined as any new charge for a sexual offense regardless of age, was also assessed.

The analytic procedure initially used continuous variables whenever possible and tested for both linear and curvilinear relations between potential predictor variables and juvenile sexual recidivism. The specific steps in item selection analyses are described in more detail

below. To facilitate those analyses, however, variables were first organized hierarchically into families, groups, and subgroups based on
conceptual similarity. For example, one of the variable families was a
history of child abuse. The four groups within this family were sexual
abuse, physical abuse, emotional abuse, and neglect. Within each of
these groups were subgroups of similar variables. Within the sexual
abuse group, for example, one subgroup included the different types
of sexual abuse and another subgroup included several ways of looking at frequency of sexual abuse.

In all, 10 families of variables were evaluated. These families were
history of sexual offending, sexual offense characteristics, sexual offender treatment, child abuse, special education, discipline problems
at school, family instability, mental health diagnoses, mental health
treatment, and nonsexual offending.

Item Selection Analyses

Five steps were involved in item selection. STEP 1 involved identifying all individual subgroup variables that were significantly associated
with juvenile sexual recidivism (p < .05). Categorical variables were
tested with chi-square analyses, and continuous variables were tested
through correlation analyses.

STEP 2 identified the best marker variables within each subgroup.
Subgroups that did not yield a single variable significantly associated
with juvenile sexual recidivism were eliminated from further analyses.
In subgroups that yielded multiple variables significantly associated
with juvenile sexual recidivism, simultaneous and hierarchical logistic
regression analyses were used to select the optimal predictors and
eliminate redundant predictors within those subgroups. Specifically,
all the significant variables within one subgroup were entered into a
simultaneous logistic regression model. If the Wald chi-square statistics were significant for each of the variables, indicating that each was
making a unique contribution to the prediction of juvenile sexual recidivism, all variables were retained and no further analyses were
needed. If not all variables were significant, the next action depended
on the number of variables. If there were only two variables in that
subgroup, then the one variable that was significant was retained and
the other was dropped without additional analyses. In cases where
neither variable yielded a significant Wald chi-square statistic when
entered simultaneously because of suppression effects, the stronger

of the two variables was retained. If there were more than two variables, then hierarchical logistic regression analyses were used to assess variables in different orders to determine the optimal set of predictors. If no real pattern emerged, then the variables were collapsed into a single variable. For example, in the subgroup for type of child sexual abuse, the variables for each type of "hands-on" sexual abuse (e.g., fondling, penetration of anus) were correlated with each other, and the presence of each type of hands-on sexual abuse produced a similar increase in juvenile sexual recidivism of about 20%. In this case, those variables were collapsed into a single new variable reflecting the presence or absence of any hands-on sexual abuse.

In STEP 3, the subgroup variables retained in the previous step were analyzed using similar procedures to identify the best marker variables within each group. In analyzing variables at the group level, we utilized a "drill-down" strategy, in which we started at the most general level, then drilled down to more specific levels to determine whether greater specificity enhanced predictive accuracy. Hierarchical logistic regression was used for these analyses. For example, in the sexual abuse group the most general variable, the presence or absence of any sexual abuse, was entered in the first block, then the presence or absence of hands-on sexual abuse was entered in the second block. The presence of hands-on sexual abuse added significantly to the presence of any sexual abuse in predicting juvenile sexual abuse. However, the reverse was not true, so the variable for any sexual abuse was dropped as a potential item and the variable for hands-on sexual abuse was tentatively retained as we drilled down further to look at the impact of frequency of hands-on sexual abuse. In the next analysis, the presence of hands-on sexual abuse was entered in the first block, and the frequency of hands-on sexual abuse was entered in the second block. Frequency of hands-on sexual abuse added significantly to the simple presence of hands-on sexual abuse in the prediction of juvenile sexual recidivism. Because the simple presence or absence of hands-on sexual abuse became nonsignificant, the only variable to emerge from the sexual abuse group was the frequency of hands-on sexual abuse.

STEP 4 involved evaluating all of the surviving group variables within families to identify the best marker variables within each family. To be retained at the fourth step, group variables not only had to make a unique contribution to the prediction of juvenile sexual recidivism relative to other group variables in the same family, but also relative to the sexual offending history family of variables. Given that the best predictor of future behavior is past behavior and support for the application of this principle to sexual offending has been documented (e.g., Hanson & Bussiére, 1998; Hanson & Morton-Bourgon, 2004; Langstrom, 2002; Rasmussen, 1999), we wanted to ensure that variables retained beyond this step added to the prediction of juvenile sexual recidivism beyond that accounted for by sexual offending history.

Using procedures similar to those described in the previous step, the first part of Step 4 identified group variables that made a unique contribution to the prediction of juvenile sexual recidivism relative to other group variables in the same family. In the second part of Step 4, all significant and independent variables in the sexual offending history family were entered in the first block of several hierarchical logistic regression analyses, and the other group variables retained in the first part of this step were entered one group at a time as the second block in separate analyses. Any group variable that did not add significantly to the sexual offending history family of variables in the prediction of juvenile sexual recidivism was dropped from further analyses.

Some of the stronger variables within each of the 10 families are summarized in Table 7.A. Variables in this table with at least one asterisk made a unique contribution to the prediction of juvenile sexual recidivism relative to other variables in the same family. Variables with two asterisks also predicted juvenile sexual recidivism above and beyond the sexual offending history family or were members of that family.

STEP 5, the final step in item selection, identified the optimal number of families through hierarchical logistic regression. The families were entered in the following order: sexual offending history, sexual offense characteristics, child abuse, sexual offender treatment, special education, school discipline, mental health diagnoses, mental health treatment, family instability, and nonsexual offending history. Each block was required to add significantly to the prediction of juvenile sexual recidivism at the p < .05 level, and each variable within the family was required to be significant at the p < .10 level to be retained. When a variable was retained, it remained in the model regardless of how it performed as additional variables were added to the model.

The results of these analyses are summarized in Table 7.B. As indicated there, 12 variables from seven families plus two nonlinear effects for one of those variables emerged from this process as the optimal set of predictors for juvenile sexual recidivism.

Table 7.A

Selected Variables from the Ten Families and Their Bivariate Relations with Juvenile Sexual Recidivism

Variable	Total N	Sex Recid. N	Sex Recid. %	χ^2	p
Sexual Offending History					
** Number of juvenile sexual offense adjudications				72.56	<.0005
One	452	28	6.2%		
Two	118	31	26.3%		
Three	37	13	35.1%		
Four or more	29	12	41.4%		
** Duration of charged sexual offending history				113.33	<.0005
0 months (only one charge)	416	22	5.3%		
0.01 to 5.99 months	144	25	17.4%		
6.00 to 11.99 months	27	10	37.0%		
12.00 or more months	49	27	55.1%		
** Was any charged sexual offense committed under supervision?				23.38	<.0005
No	505	50	9.9%		
Yes	131	34	26.0%		
** Number of victims in charged sexual offenses				55.54	<.0005
One	442	30	6.8%		
Two	116	28	24.1%		
Three or more	78	26	33.3%		
Number of juvenile sexual offense charges				75.05	<.0005
One	416	22	5.3%		
Two	130	30	23.1%		
Three	43	13	30.2%		
Four or more	47	19	40.4%		
Sexual Offense Characteristics					
** Was any felony-level, charged sexual offense committed in a public place?				24.26	<.0005
No	523	53	10.1%		
Yes	113	31	27.4%		
** Was any charged sexual offense preceded by deception or grooming?				18.55	<.0005
No	506	52	10.3%		
Yes	130	32	24.6%		

Table 7.A (Continued)

Variable	Total N	Sex Recid. N	Sex Recid. %	^{2}	p
** Number of different location categories in which charged sexual offenses occurred				44.65	<.0005
One	549	53	9.7%		
Two	67	23	34.3%		
Three or more	20	8	40.0%		
* Pattern of multiple acts and multiple event contacts				12.92	<.0005
Neither	282	22	7.8%		
One or both	354	62	17.5%		
Number of different relation groups offended against in felony level sex offenses (sibling group, extended family/friends/classmates, stranger/acquaintance)				34.40	<.0005
One	315	28	8.9%		
Two	294	43	14.6%		
Three	27	13	48.1%		
Gender of victims in charged sexual offenses				9.37	<.009
Exclusively female victims	441	57	12.9%		
Exclusively male victims	75	9	12.0%		
Both male and female victims	58	16	27.6%		
Use of force/threat of force in charged sexual offenses				11.06	<.001
No	413	41	9.9%		
Yes	223	43	19.3%		
Did the offender ever perpetrate a charged sexual offense alone or as the leader of a group?				13.85	<.0005
No	185	10	5.4%		
Yes	451	74	16.4%		
MENTAL HEALTH DIAGNOSES					
** Was the offender ever diagnosed with a self-regulatory disorder? (ADD, ADHD, Impulse Control, Conduct, or Oppositional Defiant Disorder)				26.89	<.0005
No	478	44	9.2%		
Yes	158	40	25.3%		
Was the offender ever diagnosed with an affective disorder? (Depression, Anxiety, Bipolar, PTSD)				19.44	<.0005
No	508	52	10.2%		
Yes	128	32	25.0%		

Table 7.A (Continued)

Variable	Total N	Sex Recid. N	Sex Recid. %	χ^2	p
Sexual-Offender-Specific Treatment History					
** Sexual offender treatment program status prior to index offense				114.62	<.0005
Never entered	584	53	9.1%		
Entered and completed all	26	12	46.2%		
Entered and did not complete at least once	26	19	73.1%		
** Offender's level of denial for index offense at discharge				24.15	<.0005
No denial	478	45	9.4%		
Denies, minimizes impact, or claims consensual	158	39	24.7%		
* Sexual Offender Treatment for Index Offense				33.53	<.0005
Never entered	353	33	9.3%		
Entered and completed	174	18	10.3%		
Entered and did not complete	109	33	30.3%		
Prior and index sexual offender treatment failures				84.83	<.0005
No SO treatment failures	516	44	8.5%		
Failed prior or index but not both	105	28	26.7%		
Failed both prior and index	15	12	80.0%		
Abuse History					
** Number of hands-on sexual abuse incidents experienced as the victim (official report)				41.11	<.0005
None	533	52	9.8%		
One to four times	77	20	26.0%		
Five or more times	26	12	46.2%		
** Number of incidents of physical abuse experienced as the victim (official report)				27.94	<.0005
None	537	61	11.4%		
One to four times	84	14	16.7%		
Five or more times	15	9	60.0%		
Special Education History					
** Did the offender receive any special education placements in K-12?				45.26	<.0005
No	454	34	7.5%		
Yes	182	50	27.5%		

Table 7.A (Continued)

Variable	Total N	Sex Recid. N	Sex Recid. %	²	p
DISCIPLINE PROBLEMS IN SCHOOL					
** Number of different educational periods with discipline problems (elementary, middle school, high school)				27.13	<.0005
None or one	481	45	9.4%		
Two	109	25	22.9%		
Three	46	14	30.4%		
NON-SEXUAL OFFENDING HISTORY					
** Number of juvenile adjudications for non-sexual offenses				15.86	<.0005
None or one	333	27	8.1%		
Two or more	303	57	18.8%		
FAMILY INSTABILITY					
** Did the offender experience physical separation from biological or adoptive parents prior to age 16?				42.40	<.0005
No	509	45	8.8%		
Yes	127	39	30.7%		
** Severe difficulty relating to siblings (no sibs=no)				27.70	<.0005
No	468	42	9.0%		
Yes	168	42	25.0%		
Severe difficulty relating to parents				29.19	<.0005
No	536	54	10.1%		
Yes	100	30	30.0%		
MENTAL HEALTH TREATMENT HISTORY					
* Mental health treatment status prior to index offense				17.52	<.0005
None	486	52	10.7%		
Completed all	122	22	18.0%		
Did not complete at least one	28	10	35.7%		

* Variables with one asterisk made a unique contribution to the prediction of juvenile sexual recidivism relative to other variables in the same family.

** Variables with two asterisks made a unique contribution to the prediction of juvenile sexual recidivism relative to other variables in the same family and also contributed uniquely beyond the sex offending history variable family (or were in that family).

Note: Variables without an asterisk did not make a unique contribution to the predictions of sexual recidivism beyond the other variables in the same family.

Table 7.B

Results of Hierarchical Logistic Regression Analyses with the Final Variable Families

Block	Variable	Variable Wald X^2 (df = 1)	p	Block X^2	df	p
Sexual Offending History				108.05	6	.001
	Number of adjudications for juvenile sexual offenses, including index offense – linear effect	6.61	.010			
	Number of victims in charged sexual offenses – linear effect	3.90	.048			
	Number of victims – quadratic effect	3.73	.054			
	Number of victims – cubic effect	3.09	.079			
	Commission of a charged sexual offense while under supervision of the court	5.33	.021			
	Duration of charged sexual offending history	25.81	.001			
Sexual Offense Characteristics				17.69	2	.001
	Commission of a felony-level, charged sexual offense in a public place	8.81	.003			
	Use of deception or grooming in a charged sexual offense	8.07	.004			

Table 7.B (continued)

Block	Variable	Variable Wald X² (df = 1)	p	Block X²	df	p
Child Abuse History				18.52	2	.001
	Number of officially documented, "hands-on," sexual abuse incidents experienced as the victim	8.93	.003			
	Number of officially documented, physical abuse incidents experienced as the victim	4.79	.029			
Sexual Offender Treatment History				24.53	1	.001
	Completion status in prior sexual offender treatments	23.55	.001			
Special Education History				12.26	1	.001
	Any placement in special education	12.32	.001			
School Discipline History				4.39	1	.036
	Number of educational periods with discipline problems (elementary, middle school, high school)	4.46	.035			

Table 7.B (continued)

Block	Variable	Variable Wald X^2 (df = 1)	p	Block X^2	df	p
Non-Sexual Offending History				6.40	1	.011
	Number of adjudications for non-sexual offenses	6.16	.013			

Note: The Block X^2 is the test of the additive contribution of the current block relative to previous blocks in the prediction of juvenile sexual recidivism. The Wald X^2 statistic is the test of the unique contribution to the prediction of juvenile sexual recidivism for each variable relative to other variables in the same block and those in previous blocks.

Accuracy of the Regression Model with the Development Sample

Assessing the accuracy of the logistic regression model with the development sample does not constitute a validation of the model because the model was "tailor made" for the sample on which it was developed. Therefore, any model or risk-assessment tool must be validated with an independent sample. However, before investing the major resources necessary for an independent validation, it should be confirmed that the model or risk-assessment tool performs well with the development sample. To accomplish this, the ability of the logistic regression model to correctly classify juvenile sexual recidivists and non-recidivists in the development sample was assessed in two ways, both using the predicted probability of juvenile sexual recidivism generated by the regression model for each juvenile sexual offender (JSO) in the sample.

PREDICTED OUTCOMES BY OBSERVED OUTCOMES CLASSIFICATION TABLE. The first method of evaluating the accuracy of the regression model involved the use of a traditional 2 x 2 classification table for a probability cut score of .50. Each JSO with a probability score of .50 .and higher was predicted as positive (to be a sexual recidivist) and each JSO with a probability score below .50 was predicted as negative (to not be a sexual recidivist). The cross-tabulation of predicted outcomes with the observed outcomes is presented in Figure 7.C.

There are a number of different ways to assess the accuracy of the predicted outcomes in the classification table in Figure 7.C. From a risk-assessment perspective, positive predictive power and negative predictive power are two of the most important indices of accuracy. Positive predictive power is the conditional probability of juvenile sexual recidivism occurring given a positive prediction of recidivism. In other words, positive predictive power is equal to the proportion of all individuals predicted to sexually recidivate who actually do sexually recidivate. This is also often referred to as the rate of true positive predictions. As indicated in Figure 7.C, the positive predictive power of the full regression model was .73, meaning that 73% of individuals predicted to reoffend (probability scores of .50 or higher) did sexually recidivate as juveniles (40 out of 55 instances). In contrast to true positive predictions, false positive predictions occur when individuals are predicted to be positive but, in fact, do not sexually recidivate. Therefore, the rate of false positive predictions is equal to 1 minus the true positive rate (1 - .73 = .27), so 27% of the positive predictions in Figure 7.C were false positive predictions (15 out of 55).

Observed Outcome	Predicted Outcome		Row Totals
	Non-Recidivist (Low Risk)	Recidivist (High Risk)	
Non-Recidivist	537	15	552
Recidivist	44	40	84
Column Totals	581	55	636

Measures of Predictive Accuracy

Positive Predictive Power = .73
[40 / 55]

Negative Predictive Power = .92
[537 / 581]

Sensitivity = .48
[40 / 84]

Specificity = .97
[537 / 552]

Overall Accuracy = .91
[(537+40) / 636]

Figure 7.C. Classification table of predicted juvenile sexual recidivism cross tabulated with observed juvenile sexual recidivism and various measures of predictive accuracy for the logistic regression model using a probability cut score of .50.

Categorical Scoring for the Final Twelve JSORRAT–II Variables

Negative predictive power is similar to positive predictive power but focuses on negative predictions (predictions that juvenile sexual recidivism will not occur). Negative predictive power is the conditional probability of juvenile sexual recidivism not occurring given a negative prediction. Of the 581 individuals with negative predictions, 537 actually did not sexually recidivate as juveniles. This yielded a negative predictive power of .92, meaning that 92% of the negative classifications were true negative predictions. Conversely, the rate of false negative predictions was .08 (1 - .92), which reflects that 8% of the negative predictions (44 out of 581) were incorrect because the individual did, in fact, sexually recidivate.

The reason that positive predictive power and negative predictive power are two of the most important measures of accuracy for risk assessment is because these conditional probabilities represent the situation we find ourselves in when conducting risk assessments. At that time, we are trying to assess the risk of a future, unknown outcome based on a score or risk level from validated risk assessment tool. In this situation, it is critical to know the rate of juvenile sexual recidivism for comparable groups of individuals with the same score or risk level on that tool.

Two other important measures of accuracy are sensitivity and specificity. Whereas positive predictive power and negative predictive power are conditional probabilities given a predicted outcome (either positive or negative), sensitivity and specificity are conditional probabilities given an observed outcome (either positive or negative). Sensitivity is the proportion of all individuals who sexually recidivate as juveniles and who were correctly classified or predicted to be positive (recidivists). This proportion is also often referred to as "the hit rate." The sensitivity of the full regression model in the development sample was .48, indicating that 48% of all juvenile sexual recidivists in the sample were correctly predicted as positive using a probability cut score of .50. One minus sensitivity yields the miss rate for sexual recidivists, which is .52 in this example.

Specificity is the proportion of all individuals who do not sexually recidivate as juveniles and who were correctly classified or predicted to be negative (non-recidivists). The specificity of the full regression model in the development sample was .97, indicating that 97% of all juvenile non-recidivists in the sample were correctly predicted as negative using a probability cut score of .50. The proportion of juvenile non-recidivists incorrectly predicted as positive, or to be recidivists, is generally referred to as the false-alarm rate. This is calculated as 1 minus specificity, so the false-alarm rate for the data in Figure 7.C is .03, meaning that 3% of all non-recidivists were falsely predicted to be positive (15 out of 552).

The sensitivity of a validated risk assessment tool is important complementary information to the tool's positive predictive power. To illustrate, consider the hypothetical case of a risk-assessment tool validated for your population using a specified cut score with a positive predictive power of .80 and a sensitivity of .15. With such a tool, there would be a high degree of confidence in positive predictions, or high-risk classifications, given the 80% sexual recidivism rate for high-risk individuals in the normative samples. However, because only 15% of recidivists would be expected to score in the high-risk range, 85% of recidivists would be expected to score in the low-risk range using the specified cut score. Consequently, while false positive predictions would be relatively rare, false negative predictions would be more common.

Some might mistakenly assume that using a cut score on a validated tool that produces such a pattern of positive predictive power and sensitivity would not be valuable. In fact, such a tool could be very useful in informing decisions and actions for which the costs of false positive predictions are clearly higher than the costs of false negative predictions. An example within the context of juvenile sexual offenders would be selection of juveniles for placement in long-term, residential treatment in a high-security facility. Placement of a low-risk juvenile in such a setting through a false positive prediction is very costly at the individual level because of the loss of liberty through the unnecessary placement in a highly restrictive setting. It is also very costly to society because of the much higher expenses required to maintain juveniles in long-term, high-security, residential treatment programs.

Some might argue that the cost of false negative predictions is even higher in such decisions. This argument is based on the assumption that the cost associated with not placing a high-risk juvenile in a high-security facility as a result of a false negative prediction is further victimization. This is not necessarily the case, however, because the alternative to being placed in such facility is generally not to simply release the adolescent. Instead, juveniles considered for, but not placed in, a long-term, high-security facility generally still receive a significant level of treatment and supervision rather than just being returned to the community with no treatment or supervision.

A similar example with adult sexual offenders is the civil commitment of those who have served their prison sentences. The costs of false positive predictions are clearly very high, both to the individual and to society. An individual who is unnecessarily committed suffers an obvious loss of liberty, perhaps for the rest of his or her life. At the societal level, such actions are also very costly, both financially and socially. The financial costs of civil commitment are enormous, generally approaching or exceeding $100,000 per year for each person committed, in addition to the significant legal fees associated with each case (Lieb & Goodkin, 2005; Winick & La Fond, 2003). From a social perspective, civil commitment statutes are viewed by some as a threat to constitutionally guaranteed freedoms. Largely because of these costs, most states with civil commitment statutes commit only a small proportion of sexual offenders, generally 10% or less (Lieb, 2005), so sensitivity is not a major issue. Again, the cost of false negative predictions is not necessarily further victimization because high-risk offenders who are not civilly committed are typically subjected to a range of risk management procedures that increase the likelihood of detection in pre-offense behaviors and intervention prior to further victimization.

In an analogous manner, the specificity of a validated risk assessment tool provides important complementary information to the tool's negative predictive power. For example, a given cut score on a validated risk assessment tool may yield a negative predictive power of .99, which is excellent. However, if the specificity of this cut score is only .10, enthusiasm is dampened by the realization that 90% of all non-recidivists would be falsely classified as high risk. Although such a profile of accuracy would not be useful in informing a wide range of decisions, it would be potentially useful in making decisions about low-frequency actions for which the costs associated with false negative predictions are enormous and the costs associated with false positive predictions are relatively small. Determining who to release to the community with minimal supervision would be an example of such a decision.

Overall accuracy is a fifth type of accuracy that can be calculated from the 2 x 2 classification table in Figure 7.C. This is calculated as the sum of the true positive and true negative classifications divided by the total number of cases, so the overall accuracy is .91 for the data in Figure 7.C. The overall accuracy of a specific cut score is often not helpful, however, because identical levels of overall accuracy can result from very different patterns of positive predictive power, negative predictive power, sensitivity, and specificity. As described earlier, differences in these patterns are important.

Implicit in the discussion of the accuracy of specific cut points on validated actuarial risk assessment tools are two important values of actuarial risk assessment. The first value is that good estimates of all of the various measures of accuracy can be obtained for any given cut score on a well-developed and validated actuarial risk-assessment tool, something that is difficult or even impossible with other approaches to risk assessment. The second value is that different cut scores can be selected on a validated risk assessment tool for different decisions. As noted earlier, different cut scores on the same risk-assessment tool generate different patterns or profiles of accuracy. Positive predictive power and specificity increase as higher cut scores are selected, but sensitivity and negative predictive power decreases. The reverse pattern is observed when lower cut scores are selected. This characteristic enables users to select the cut score that generates the most appropriate accuracy profile given the relative costs of false positive and false negative predictions associated with the contemplated decision or action. Although the developer must provide complete information regarding accuracy profiles for various cut scores and provide guidance in the potential use of cut scores, the selection of specific cut scores for particular decisions or actions is ultimately made by users (e.g., program administrators, probation administrators, courts, etc.).

AREA UNDER THE ROC CURVE. Because of the possibility and desirability of using different cut scores for different decisions, the accuracy of risk-assessment tools must be assessed across all possible cut scores rather than for just one cut score. The best measure of the overall accuracy of a risk-assessment tool is the area under the receiver operator characteristics (ROC) curve, as discussed in detail by Quinsey et al. (1998), Swets (1996), and Swets et al. (2000). The ROC curve is generated by plotting sensitivity (hit rate) on the Y-axis against 1 minus specificity (false-alarm rate) on the X-axis for all possible cut scores on the risk-assessment tool being evaluated. If done by hand, one would generate a 2 x 2 classification table for each possible cut score, calculate the sensitivity and 1 minus specificity for each of the tables, then plot these values on a graph. The area under the resulting curve reflects the overall accuracy of the risk-assessment tool. This value can range from 0 to 1.0, with a value of .50 being equal to a chance-level of accuracy. Values significantly greater than .50 reflect a significant improvement over chance, and a value of 1.0 reflects perfect predictive accuracy.

Fortunately, several statistical software packages can generate ROC curves and calculate the area under the curves, such as the *Statistical Package for the Social Sciences* (SPSS) versions 10 and higher. The ROC curve for the probability cut scores generated by the full logistic regression model is presented in Figure 7.D. The area under the ROC curve was .91, with a 95% confidence interval of .87 to .94. Because the confidence interval does not include .50, the performance of the full regression model exceeded chance level. In fact, this level of accuracy would generally be considered to be very strong, but it is important to emphasize, again, that this was achieved with the development sample. Application of the full logistic regression model to an independent sample would be expected to produce a smaller area under the ROC curve.

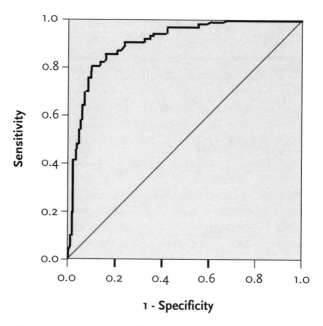

Figure 7.D. ROC curve for the full regression model (area under the curve = .91).

Simplification of the Model

The full logistic regression model clearly performed well with the development sample, but regression models with individual beta weights for each linear and nonlinear effect are complex and difficult for many to understand or implement. Consequently, we wanted to explore a simpler, more robust, categorical scoring system to assess the trade-off between simplicity and information loss. The simple, categorical scoring method used for each of the final 12 variables was applied in the following manner. A score of zero was assigned to the level of each variable associated with the lowest rate of juvenile sexual recidivism, and the score was increased by one for each level of the same variable associated with a meaningful increase in the rate of sexual recidivism. The distribution of variables was truncated at the upper end when the distribution became too thin to create additional categories of adequate size. With one exception, all levels of the final 12 variables included at least 25 offenders. Listed below is the categorical scoring for one variable, number of juvenile sexual offense adjudications, as an example.

Number Juvenile Sexual Offense Adjudications	N	Juvenile Sexual Recidivism Rate	Categorical Score
One	452	6.2%	0
Two	118	26.3%	1
Three	37	35.1%	2
Four or more	29	41.4%	3

When variable levels did not produce meaningfully different rates of juvenile sexual recidivism, those levels were collapsed in the new categorical system. The frequency of officially documented hands-on sexual abuse provides such an example. One, two, three, or four instances of hands-on sexual abuse were each associated with approximately a 25% rate of juvenile sexual recidivism, so these four levels were collapsed into one level, as illustrated below. The scoring of all 12 variables is presented in Table 7.C.

Number of "Hands-On" Sexual Abuse Incidents	N	Juvenile Sexual Recidivism Rate	Categorical Score
None	533	9.8%	0
One to four	77	26.0%	1
Five or more	26	46.2%	2

PERFORMANCE OF THE SIMPLIFIED MODEL. The performance of the simplified model was assessed by using the total score from the 12, categorically scored variables as the predictor in an ROC analysis. The area under the ROC curve for the simplified model was .89 (95% CI of .85 to .92). This value is not significantly different from that of the full regression model, so very little loss of information was associated with the simplified model. Consequently, the simplified model

Table 7.C

Variable	N	Juvenile Sexual Recidivism Rate	Categorical Score
Number of juvenile sexual offense adjudications			
One	452	6.2%	0
Two	118	26.3%	1
Three	37	35.1%	2
Four or more	29	41.4%	3
Number of victims in charged sexual offenses			
One	442	6.8%	0
Two	116	24.1%	1
Three or more	78	33.3%	2
Length of charged sexual offending			
0 Months (only one charge)	416	5.3%	0
0.01 to 5.99 months	144	17.4%	1
6.00 to 11.99 months	27	37.0%	2
12.00 or more months	49	55.1%	3
Was any charged sexual offense committed while under supervision?			
No	505	9.9%	0
Yes	131	26.0%	1
Was any felony-level, charged, sex offense committed in a public place?			
No	523	10.1%	0
Yes	113	27.4%	1
Was any charged sexual offense preceded by deception or grooming?			
No	506	10.3%	0
Yes	130	24.6%	1
Sexual offender treatment program status prior to index offense			
Never entered	584	9.1%	0
Entered and completed all	26	46.2%	1
Entered and did not complete at least once	26	73.1%	2
Number of "hands-on" sexual abuse incidents experienced as the victim (official report)			
None	533	9.8%	0
One to four times	77	26.0%	1
Five or more times	26	46.2%	2

Table 7.C (continued)

Variable	N	Juvenile Sexual Recidivism Rate	Categorical Score
Number of physical abuse incidents experienced as the victim			
None	537	11.4%	0
One to four times	84	16.7%	1
Five or more times	15	60.0%	2
Did the offender receive any special education placement in K-12?			
No	454	7.5%	0
Yes	182	27.5%	1
Number of different educational periods with discipline problems (elementary, middle school, high school)			
None or one	481	9.4%	0
Two	109	22.9%	1
Three	46	30.4%	2
Number of juvenile non-sexual offense adjudications			
None or one	333	8.1%	0
Two or more	303	18.8%	1

was used in all subsequent analyses, and it was named the *Juvenile Sexual Offense Recidivism Risk Assessment Tool–II* (JSORRAT–II).

JSORRAT–II Scores and Associated Juvenile Sexual Recidivism Rates in the Development Sample

The range of possible scores on the JSORRAT–II is 0 to 21, and the range of actual scores in the development sample was 0 to 15. The observed rates of juvenile sexual recidivism associated with each score in the development sample are presented by the heavier of the two lines in Figure 7.E. The lighter line reflects the "smoothed" relation between JSORRAT–II scores and juvenile sexual recidivism. The "smoothed" curve was generated by regressing JSORRAT–II total scores onto juvenile sexual recidivism with logistic regression, then plotting the predicted probabilities for each JSORRAT–II score.

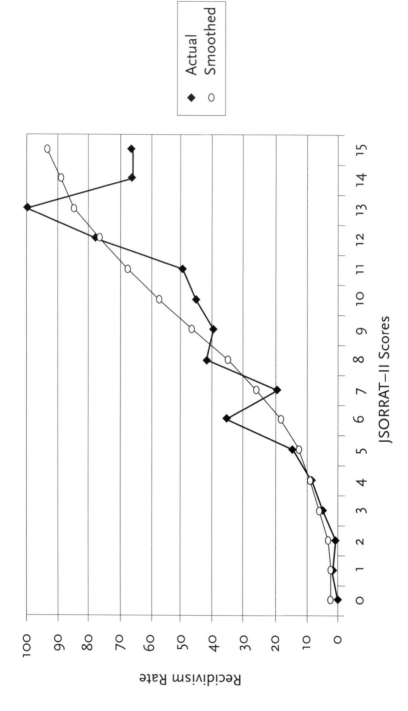

Figure 7.E. JSORRAT–II Scores and Associated Juvenile Sexual Recidivism Rates

Establishment of formal risk levels requires validation of the JSORRAT–II. However, to explore the possible usefulness of the JSORRAT–II, potential risk levels were created based on visual inspection of the actual rates of juvenile sexual recidivism associated with JSORRAT–II scores. These potential risk levels and the associated scores, selection ratios (proportion of offenders classified within each level), and juvenile sexual recidivism rates are presented in Table 7.D. Also presented in Table 7.D are the 95% confidence intervals for the rates of juvenile sexual recidivism associated with each potential risk level.

The spread of juvenile sexual recidivism rates associated with the potential risk levels in Table 7.D is substantial, ranging from 1.0% to 81.8%, and the confidence intervals are largely non-overlapping. Perhaps the most important element of Table 7.D is the combination of the selection ratios (proportion of sample scoring within range) and juvenile sexual recidivism rates associated with each potential risk category. The JSORRAT–II was able to identify 48.0% of the development sample with an extraordinarily low juvenile sexual recidivism rate of 1.0%, and another 21.5% of the development sample with a juvenile sexual recidivism rate of only 6.6%. Collectively, these two groups comprised 69.5% of the development sample and had an overall juvenile sexual recidivism rate of only 2.7%.

There were a number of adolescents in our sample who were relatively old at the time of the index sexual offense. Because some adolescents were at or approaching 18 years of age at the time of their index sexual offense, they may have artificially reduced the juvenile sexual recidivism rates presented in Table 7.D. Selection ratios and juvenile sexual recidivism rates were recalculated separately for adolescents under the age of 17 at their index sexual offense, and again for adolescents under the age of 16 at their index sexual offense, to explore this possibility. Inspection of Table 7.E indicates that very similar patterns were evident in all three groups: the full sample, the under-age-17 sample, and the under-age-16 sample. In addition, the areas under the ROC curve were nearly identical for all three groups (full sample = .89, 17 years old and younger sample = .88, 16 years old and younger sample = .88).

This pattern illustrates the potential value of the JSORRAT–II in making placement, treatment, and programming decisions, which are essentially resource allocation decisions. The 65% to 70% of the development sample who scored 4 or less on the JSORRAT–II may not require intervention beyond detection, segregation from higher-

Table 7.D

Potential Risk Categories for Juvenile Sexual Recidivism Based on
Results from the Development Sample (N = 636).

Potential Risk Level	Score Range	Number Scoring in Range (Selection Ratio)	Number Juvenile Sexual Recidivists	Percent Juvenile Sexual Recidivism	95% Confidence Interval for Recidivism Rates
Low	0 - 2	305 (48.0%)	3	1.0%	0.2% - 3.1%
Moderately Low	3 - 4	137 (21.5%)	9	6.6%	3.2% - 12.5%
Moderate	5 - 7	107 (16.8%)	26	24.3%	16.7% - 33.7%
Moderately High	8 - 11	65 (10.2%)	28	43.1%	31.1% - 55.9%
High	12 +	22 (3.5%)	18	81.8%	59.0% - 94.0%

risk juvenile offenders, and a relatively brief psycho-educational program. The resources saved with this group could be allocated to the
other approximately 30% of the sample with a more significant risk of
continuing a pattern of juvenile sexual offending. This pattern must,
of course, be validated before establishing risk levels or making con-
clusive judgments, but the emergence of this pattern in the development sample is encouraging and illustrative of the potential value of
the JSORRAT–II in making resource allocation decisions.

Performance of the JSORRAT–II in Predicting Anytime Recidivism

The JSORRAT–II was developed to assess the risk of juvenile sexual
recidivism, but we also subsequently evaluated its ability to predict
sexual recidivism as either a juvenile or a young adult, which we labeled "anytime sexual recidivism." To conduct this evaluation, we
determined sexual recidivism statuses through 2003 for the members
of our sample. At the time of this determination, the youngest member of our sample was 22 years old and the oldest member of our
sample was 31 years old. Juvenile sexual recidivism data through age
18 was already available, and information on sexual recidivism after
age 18 was obtained through checks with the Utah statewide criminal
record database, Utah prison records, and the FBI's National Crime

Table 7.E

Selections Ratios and Juvenile Sexual Recidivism Rates by Potential Risk Level for the Full Development Sample, for Offenders Under Age 17 at the Index Sexual Offense (N = 524), and for Offenders Under Age 16 at the Index Sexual Offense (N = 433).

Potential Risk Level	Score Range	Selection Ratio			Juvenile Sexual Recidivism Rate		
		Full Sample	Under Age 17 at Index Sex Offense	Under Age 16 at Index Sex Offense	Full Sample[a]	Under Age 17 at Index Sex Offense[b]	Under Age 16 at Index Sex Offense[c]
Low	0 - 2	48.0%	45.2%	43.6%	1.0%	1.3%	1.6%
Moderately Low	3 - 4	21.5%	21.9%	22.4%	6.6%	7.8%	7.2%
Moderate	5 - 7	16.8%	17.6%	18.9%	24.3%	25.0%	28.0%
Moderately High	8 - 11	10.2%	11.2%	10.6%	43.1%	47.5%	47.8%
High	12 +	3.5%	4.0%	4.4%	81.8%	85.7%	89.5%

[a] Juvenile sexual recidivism base rate = 13.2%. Area under the ROC curve = .89.

[b] Juvenile sexual recidivism base rate = 15.5%. Area under the ROC curve = .88.

[c] Juvenile sexual recidivism base rate = 16.6%. Area under the ROC curve = .88.

Index database. As was the case for juvenile sexual recidivism, our criterion for sexual recidivism was a charge for a new sexual offense. A total of 126 offenders sexually recidivated prior to 2004. Sixty-eight offenders recidivated only as juveniles, 16 offenders recidivated both as juveniles and as adults, and 42 offenders recidivated only as adults.

ROC analysis of the prediction of anytime sexual recidivism using total scores from the JSORRAT–II yielded an area under the curve of .79, with a 95% confidence interval of .74 to .84. Although the level of predictive accuracy reflected is quite reasonable and well above chance levels, the area under the ROC curve of .79 is significantly lower than that obtained for juvenile sexual recidivism (.89 with a 95% CI of .85 to .92). This difference suggested that the JSORRAT–II was less predictive of sexual recidivism during young adulthood than during adolescence, so a separate ROC analysis was conducted using sexual recidivism during adulthood as the outcome variable. This analysis produced an area under the curve of .64, with a 95% CI of .55 to .73. Although this level of accuracy still exceeds chance levels, it is substantially lower than the level of accuracy achieved with juvenile sexual recidivism.

Consideration and exploration of this substantial decline in accuracy generated several potential explanations. Two of these are related to the age of offenders at the time of their index sexual offense. Exploration of the data indicated that offenders who sexually recidivated only as adults were considerably older at the time of their index sexual offense (16.13 years) than were those who sexually recidivated only as juveniles (14.44 years), those who sexually recidivated both as juveniles and as adults (14.03 years), and those who did not sexually recidivate (15.33 years). One possibility raised by this observation is that offenders who entered the system at an older age simply did not have enough documented history on which to make predictions. A second possibility, which is not mutually exclusive with the previous one, is that juvenile sexual offenses committed after age 16, when much maturation has occurred, are more reflective and predictive of adult sexual offending than juvenile sexual offenses committed at an earlier age. In other words, this would be an additional risk factor for adult sexual recidivism.

Additional ROC analyses were performed to explore the impact of age at index offense on the accuracy of the JSORRAT–II in predicting anytime and adult sexual recidivism. The first set of analyses was performed only on those offenders who were under the age of 17 at the time of their index sexual offense (N = 524). These analyses generated areas under the ROC curve of .84 for anytime sexual recidivism (95% CI .80 to .89) and .73 for adult sexual recidivism (95% CI .65 to .82). The second set of analyses was performed only on those offenders who were under the age of 16 at the time of their index sexual offense (N = 433). These analyses generated very similar areas under the ROC curve: .84 for anytime sexual recidivism (95% CI .79 to .88) and .72 for adult sexual recidivism (95% CI .63 to .81). The improvement in validity indices with the exclusion of older offenders lends credibility to these two possible explanations.

Rates of adult sexual recidivism associated with each of the five potential risk categories constructed in conjunction with juvenile sexual recidivism are presented in Table 7.F for the full sample, the under age 17 at index sexual offense sample, and the under age 16 at index sexual offense sample. The adult sexual recidivism base rates and the adult sexual recidivism rates associated with each potential risk category were very similar for the under age 17 and under age 16 samples. The adult sexual recidivism base rates for both samples were approximately half the juvenile sexual recidivism base rates for each of the same two samples. This had little impact on the adult sexual recidivism rates associated with the low and moderately low categories for these two samples, which were very comparable to the parallel rates of juvenile sexual recidivism for the same two samples. In contrast, the rates of adult sexual recidivism associated with the top three categories were substantially lower than comparable rates of juvenile sexual recidivism for these two samples. Specifically, adult sexual recidivism rates were approximately only one third of the comparable juvenile sexual recidivism rates. Consequently, whereas the spread of juvenile sexual recidivism rates ranged from about 1% to about 85% across the five categories, the spread of adult sexual recidivism rates only ranged from about 3% to about 30%. In addition, the highest rate of adult sexual recidivism is comparable to that for the moderate level of juvenile sexual recidivism.

Two other possible explanations for the lower accuracy in predicting adult sexual recidivism remain viable. The first of these is that a substantially different set of variables is needed to predict eventual adult sexual recidivism with greater accuracy for offenders who are still juveniles. Alternatively, it simply may not be possible to achieve greater accuracy in predictions of adult sexual offending behavior based on adolescent behavior because of the complexity and magnitude of developmental changes occurring during adolescence.

Table 7.F

Adult Sexual Recidivism Rates by Potential Risk Level for the Full Development Sample, for Offenders Under Age 17 at the Index Sexual Offense (N = 524), and for Offenders Under Age 16 at the Index Sexual Offense (N = 433).

Potential Risk Level	Score Range	Adult Sexual Recidivism Rate		
		Full Sample[a]	Under Age 17 at Index Sex Offense[b]	Under Age 16 at Index Sex Offense[c]
Low	0 – 2	5.9%	3.0%	3.2%
Moderately Low	3 – 4	6.6%	6.1%	7.2%
Moderate	5 – 7	9.3%	7.6%	8.5%
Moderately High	8 – 11	23.1%	20.3%	17.4%
High	12 +	27.3%	28.6%	33.3%

[a]Adult base rate = 9.1%. Area under the ROC curve = .64.

[b]Adult base rate = 7.4%. Area under the ROC curve = .73.

[c]Adult base rate = 7.9%. Area under the ROC curve = .72.

Factor Structure of the Twelve JSORRAT–II Items

Although the items of the JSORRAT–II emerged through an empirical selections process, it is still helpful to try to understand the underlying constructs that these items might reflect. An exploratory principle-components analysis of the 12 items was conducted to examine potential underlying structure. Examination of the scree plot in Figure 7.F suggested a four-factor solution, and the rotated factor structure, using a varimax rotation, is presented in Table 7.G.

The first factor is defined by number of sexual offense adjudications, length of sexual offending history, and number of sexual offense victims. All three variables clearly tap the persistence of sexual offending behavior, and these variables may be behavioral proxies for the magnitude/persistence of the drive to engage in sexual offending behaviors.

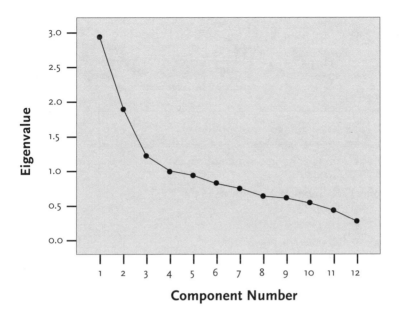

Figure 7.F. Scree plot for the exploratory components analysis of the 12 JSORRAT–II items

The second factor is defined by number of adjudications for non-sexual offenses, number of educational periods (elementary school, middle school, high school) with discipline problems, commission of a sexual offense while under supervision, and placement in special education. The items defining Factor 2 strongly suggest an antisocial orientation with problems conforming to rules and relating appropriately with authorities. The one loading that might raise questions is that of placement in special education. It is important to remember, however, that this variable included behaviorally disordered placements. In addition, many children with other special education placements may also have problems with rule violations.

The third factor is defined by number of physical abuse incidents, number of sexual abuse incidents, and, to a lesser degree, prior sexual offending treatment status. The items on this factor suggest a traumatic history of child sexual and physical abuse. The fact that prior sexual

Table 7.G

Rotated Four-Factor Structure for the JSORRAT–II Items

JSORRAT–II Item	Factor			
	1	2	3	4
1. Number of adjudications for sexual offenses	**.882**	.035	.044	.036
2. Number of victims in charged sexual offenses	**.793**	.012	.067	.213
3. Length of sexual offending history based on charged sexual offenses	**.858**	.105	.098	.041
4. Commission of a charged sexual offense while under supervision	.273	**.686**	-.087	-.119
5. Commission of a charged felony-level sexual offense in a public place	.176	-.019	.003	**.797**
6. Use of deception or grooming in a charged sexual offense	.032	.060	.081	**.610**
7. Prior sexual offender treatment status	.376	.005	**.473**	.059
8. Number of officially documented "hands-on" sexual abuse incidents	.106	.033	**.754**	.123
9. Number of officially documented physical abuse incidents	-.055	.214	**.777**	-.030
10. Placement in special education	.071	**.590**	.243	.290
11. Number of educational periods with discipline problems	-.058	**.705**	.217	.103
12. Number of adjudications for non-sexual offenses	-.043	**.762**	.007	-.058

Note: Extraction method was principal components. Varimax rotation with Kaiser normalization was used.

offender treatment history also loads on this factor, and also somewhat on the first factor, indicates that adolescents with a significant history of child abuse or sexual offending were more likely to have been referred to prior sexual offending treatment. It also suggests that they were more likely not to have done well in treatment. One hypothesized possibility for this association may reside in the interplay between prior violations of trust, particularly from those in a position of authority, and participation in treatment that requires high degrees of trust.

The fourth factor is defined by commission of a sexual offense in a public place and the use of deception or grooming in a sexual offense. The interpretation of this factor is less evident, but one possibility is that this factor is the "flip side" of the first factor. Although some adolescents are charged for sexual offenses as the result of exploratory sexual behavior, such exploratory offending behavior usually ceases following detection and sanctions. Factor 1 does not seem to tap that type of behavior. Rather, the items of Factor 1 reflect more persistent engagement in sexual offending behavior, suggestive of a greater drive to engage in such behaviors. However, a number of people have similar urges but do not act on them because of internal controls (good judgment and strong impulse control). Consequently, the "flip side" of drive to engage in sexual offending behaviors is the lack of judgment and impulse control to not act on such urges. Offending in public clearly exposes the individual to greater risk of detection; therefore, it may reflect impaired judgment and impulse control, as well as greater drive to engage in such acts. Although the case is less obvious for deception and grooming, the item loading on this component may also reflect a tendency to target victims outside the immediate family, requiring additional planning and exposing the juvenile to a greater risk of detection. Again, this may be reflective of impaired judgment and impulse control as well as a greater drive to engage in sexual offending behaviors.

Summary and Conclusions

The primary purpose of the research program described in this chapter was to develop an actuarial risk assessment tool for juvenile sexual recidivism that was relatively brief, based primarily on behaviorally anchored information that was routinely available for most juvenile sexual offenders, and relatively simple and intuitive to use. The resulting tool, the JSORRAT–II, appears to have met those goals. Consisting of 12 items and designed to be scored through a file review, the JSORRAT–II is relatively brief and easy to use. All informa-tion required to score the JSORRAT–II should be contained in typical juvenile court and youth corrections files. Because nearly all of the items are behaviorally anchored, scoring of the JSORRAT–II requires little interpretation by the evaluator. Consequently, the JSORRAT–II can be scored easily and objectively with a modest amount of train-ing. Finally, the categorical scoring and the use of simple total scores make the JSORRAT–II uncomplicated and intuitive to use.

An additional benefit of the JSORRAT–II is the factor structure that emerged, which was relatively interpretable and meaningful. The first two factors, high/persistent drive to engage in sexual offending be-havior and an antisocial orientation, were consistent with the first two factors on the JSOAP (Prentky et al., 2000) and with research on adult sexual recidivism (e.g., Hanson & Morton-Bourgon, 2004). The third factor, history of child abuse, is more controversial. On the one hand, a greater history of child abuse, particularly child sexual abuse, clearly distinguished juvenile sexual offenders from juvenile non-sexual offenders in a meta-analysis by Seto and Lalumiére (2004), but the research regarding the relation of child abuse to sexual recidivism has been more mixed. Treatment failure, which also loaded on this factor, has been linked to sexual recidivism for both juveniles and adults (e.g., Hanson & Morton-Bourgon, 2004; Worling & Langstrom, 2002). Although items on the fourth factor, which are suggestive of impaired judgment and/or impulse control, have not emerged in research on juvenile sexual recidivism, they have emerged in research on adult sexual recidivism (e.g., Epperson et al., 1998).

The ultimate, required characteristic of a risk assessment tool is pre-dictive accuracy. The JSORRAT–II performed very well with the devel-opment sample, as reflected by its area under the ROC curve of .89 (95% CI of .85 to .92) for juvenile sexual recidivism. In addition, the JSORRAT–II yielded a wide dispersion of juvenile sexual recidivism rates associated with JSORRAT–II scores categories, ranging from 1% to 82% with largely non-overlapping confidence intervals. More spe-cifically, the JSORRAT–II identified nearly half of the sample with an extraordinarily low 1% rate of juvenile sexual recidivism. At the other end of the spectrum, the JSORRAT–II identified approximately 15% of the sample with very significant rates of juvenile sexual recidivism (43% to 82%). If this general pattern holds up on validation, the JSORRAT–II has the potential to greatly inform a range of resource allocations decisions regarding placement, programming, and treat-ment. In other words, valuable resources once invested across all juveniles, including those in the lowest-risk categories, could be diverted to those juveniles requiring the most intense placements and treatments. In addition, the pattern described above demonstrates the potential of the JSORRAT–II to identify low-risk adolescents that should be segregated from higher-risk adolescents.

One potential limitation of our study was the inclusion of older adolescents (age 17 to 18 at the time of the index sexual offense) in our sample because they would have been at risk for juvenile sexual recidivism for only a very short time. However, the potential impact of their inclusion was assessed by redoing all analyses of juvenile sexual recidivism using only those people in our sample who were under age 17 at the time of the index sexual offense, and then redoing the analyses again for those people in our sample who were under age 16 at the time of their index sexual offense. Although these restrictions slightly elevated the juvenile sexual recidivism base rate from 13.2% to about 16%, the resulting areas under the ROC curve and the rates of juvenile sexual recidivism associated with JSORRAT–II score categories were extremely similar to those for the full sample. Consequently, the inclusion of older adolescent in the sample does not appear to have significantly altered the results related to juvenile sexual recidivism.

The predictive accuracy of the JSORRAT–II with adult sexual recidivism in the development sample was considerably lower than that for juvenile sexual recidivism. The area under the ROC curve for adult sexual recidivism with the full sample was only .64, and that value increased to .72 when offenders who were over age 16 at the time of their index offense were excluded from analyses, reflecting a moderate level of predictive accuracy. This lower level of accuracy with adult sexual recidivism is not surprising, given that the JSORRAT–II was developed on and optimized for juvenile sexual recidivism.

These results do, however, seriously call into question the possibility of making lifelong predictions based on risk assessments of juveniles. Not only were the areas under the ROC curve much lower for adult sexual recidivism than for juvenile sexual recidivism, so were the adult sexual recidivism base rates and the recidivism rates associated with the five score categories (see Table 7.F). As indicated in Table 7.F, rates of adult sexual recidivism do not exceed single digits until a score of 8 or higher. More specifically, approximately 86% of the development sample scored below 8 on the JSORRAT–II, meaning that the rate of adult sexual recidivism for this large group was at or below the base rate of 9%. The remaining approximately 14% of the sample sexually recidivated as adults at about a 24% rate.

Admittedly, the offenders in our sample have only been followed into young adulthood, on average until age 27. However, based on the adult sexual recidivism rates in our sample and the degree of accuracy achieved in predicting adult sexual recidivism, it would be extraordinarily difficult to justify the imposition long-term sanctions or sanctions with long-term negative consequences to the juvenile. This would be particularly true when there are no empirically documented, major benefits to society from those sanctions. Prescott (2004) and Worling (2003) have argued that juvenile sexual offender risk assessments should have an expiration date. Our data suggest that, with rare exceptions, this date should be no later than age 18 unless more accurate predictive tools become available for juvenile sexual offenders.

The planned second step of the research program is to validate the JSORRAT–II with an independent sample that is large and representative of the broad spectrum of juveniles who offend sexually, both within Utah and other states. Conclusions about the performance of the JSORRAT–II must remain tentative until it has been successfully validated. Given the sampling methods used and the strong indices of predictive accuracy for juvenile sexual recidivism achieved in the development sample, we would expect that a validation in Utah with a similar sample would be successful, though with some shrinkage in the indices of predictive validity. However, this remains an unproven assumption until the validation study is completed.

The probability of successful validation studies with samples from other states is more difficult to estimate for a variety of reasons. As Caldwell (2002) and Miner (2002) noted, past studies intended to identify risk factors for juvenile sexual recidivism produced inconsistent results. Presumably, at least some of this past inconsistency in findings is due to the studies' being conducted in different locales and with different populations. This observation certainly would question the likelihood of our research's identified risk factors being successfully replicated with a sample from a different state. However, many of those past studies were based on relatively small samples of convenience, often from treatment centers, which introduced considerable potential bias and error. Consequently, the failure of risk factors to replicate across studies may be due more to small and biased samples rather than to systematic differences in juvenile sexual offenders, broadly speaking, across states. Because our sample was large (N = 636) and sampled the full range of sexual offending, we are hopeful that our findings might prove to be more robust.

In addition, several of the variables on the JSORRAT–II have been found to be associated with sexual recidivism in at least one other study. These include total number of adjudications for sexual offenses (Langstrom, 2002; Schram, Milloy, & Rowe, 1991), number of sexual offense victims (Langstrom, 2002; Rasmussen, 1999; Worling, 2002), sexual offender treatment status (Worling & Curwen, 2000), child sexual abuse (Rasmussen, 1999; Rubinstein, Yeager, Goodstein, & Lewis, 1993), and number of adjudications for nonsexual offenses (Knight & Prentky, 1993; Prentky & Knight, 1993). Several other variables on the JSORRAT–II have been associated with juvenile sexual offending in general or included on other risk assessment tools. These include special education placement or learning problems (Kahn & Chambers, 1991) and school behavior problems (Knight & Prentky; Prentky et al., 2000; Schram et al., 1991).

Although there are some reasons to be optimistic about the successful replication of results in different states, as summarized above, there are also some reasons for pessimism. Our sample was large and representative of the full range of sexual offending, but it also was drawn entirely within the state of Utah. As a result, juveniles of color comprised only 14.0% of our sample (ethnicity was unspecified for another 9.6% of the sample), so the sample was predominantly Caucasian. Although we did not collect data on religious background, the demographics of Utah strongly suggest that the majority of our sample came from Mormon (Church of Jesus Christ of Latter Day Saints) families, another way in which Utah is systematically different from many other states. In our opinion, the greatest potential threat to the generalizability of our findings is the likely jurisdictional differences across states in the way that juvenile sexual offenses are charged, adjudicated, and disposed. Jurisdictional differences across counties in Utah are fully represented within our sample, so that is not the issue; rather, differences across states are the potential issue. We are encouraged by the fact that adult actuarial risk assessment tools have proven to be fairly robust in this respect. However, it is our impression that jurisdictional differences across states are much greater for juvenile sexual offenders than for adult sexual offenders. Ultimately, of course, the generalizability of our findings to other settings is an empirical question, one that we hope to answer through planned validations studies that have been initiated.

Some may view the absence of dynamic variables as a limitation of the JSORRAT–II. Indeed, it is a limitation in the sense that it limits the use of the JSORRAT–II to initial risk assessments used to inform level of programming, treatment, and placement/supervision, and it precludes the JSORRAT–II from being used as a measure of treatment outcome or modified risk. However, within the context of the risk-assessment model introduced at the beginning of this chapter, this would be construed as an intended purpose rather than as a limitation. The power of empirically identified, static variables to provide relatively long-term estimates of risk with adult sexual offenders is well documented (e.g., Hanson & Morton-Bourgon), and there is reason to believe that they can do the same for adolescents, though the term may be shorter. The use of validated measures of risk to inform programming, treatment, and placement/supervisions decisions permits better utilization of resources by matching the duration and intensity of interventions and placements with needs assessments providing focus, and prevents contagion effects by segregating lower-risk juveniles from higher-risk juveniles. Interventions must target specific goals, and research must link the achievement of those goals to risk reduction, eventually quantifying risk reduction, or modified risk. Ultimately, research on treatment outcomes and risk reduction may produce a single instrument that can be used for both initial and modified risk assessment with juveniles. Until that time, the best tools available for initial risk assessment should be used to inform treatment, and resources should be devoted to developing more refined measures of treatment outcomes and their relationship to risk.

In conclusion, the JSORRAT–II is a promising juvenile sexual recidivism risk assessment tool that performed very well in the development sample. However, it has not yet been validated with an independent sample. Until it has been successfully validated, the JSORRAT–II should be used only for research and to experimentally and tentatively inform treatment and programming decisions; it should not be used to inform forensic decisions. A copy of the JSORRAT–II scoring guidelines and a score recording sheet are attached as an appendix to this chapter to facilitate research on the JSORRAT–II and to permit its appropriate experimental use in clinical settings.

References

Bonta, J., Law, M., & Hanson, K. (1998). The prediction of criminal and violent recidivism among mentally disordered offenders: A meta-analysis. *Psychological Bulletin, 123,* 123-142.

Boxer, P., Guerra, N. G., Huesmann, L. R., & Morales, J. (2005). Proximal peer-level effects of a small-group selected prevention on aggression in elementary school children: An investigation of the peer contagion hypothesis. *Journal of Abnormal Child Psychology, 33,* 325-338.

Caldwell, M. F. (2002). What we do know about juvenile sexual reoffense risk. *Child Maltreatment: Journal of the American Professional Society on the Abuse of Children, 7,* 291-302.

Christodoulides, T. E., Richardson, G., Graham, F., Kennedy, P. J., & Kelly, T. P. (2005). Risk assessment with adolescent sex offenders. *Journal of Sexual Aggression, 11,* 37-48.

Doren, D. M. (2002). *Evaluating sex offenders: A manual for civil commitments and beyond.* Thousand Oaks, CA: Sage Publications, Inc.

Epperson, D. L., Kaul, J. D., & Hesselton, D. (1998, October). *Final report of the development of the Minnesota Sex Offender Screening Tool–Revised (MnSOST-R).* Presentation at the 17th Annual Research and Treatment Conference of the Association for the Treatment of Sexual Abusers, Vancouver, British Columbia, Canada.

Epperson, D. L., Kaul, J. D., Huot, S. J., Hesselton, D., Alexander, W. & Goldman, R. (2000, November). *Cross-validation of the Minnesota Sex Offender Screening Tool-Revised.* Paper presented at the 19th annual conference of the Association for the Treatment of Sexual Abusers, San Diego, CA.

Grove, W. M. & Meehl, P. E. (1996). Comparative efficiency of informal (subjective, impressionistic) and formal (mechanical, algorithmic) prediction procedures: The clinical-statistical controversy. *Psychology, Public Policy, & Law, 2,* 293-323.

Grove, W. M., Zald, D. H., Lebow, B. S., Snitz, B. E., & Nelson, C. (2000). Clinical versus mechanical prediction: A meta-analysis. *Psychological Assessment, 12,* 19-30.

Hanson, R. K. (1997). *The development of a brief actuarial risk scale for sexual offense recidivism.* (User Report 97-04). Ottawa, Canada: Department of the Solicitor General of Canada.

Hanson, R. K., & Bussiére, M. T. (1998). Predicting relapse: A meta-analysis of sexual offender recidivism studies. *Journal of Consulting & Clinical Psychology, 66,* 348-362.

Hanson, R. K. & Harris, A. J. R. (2000). Where should we intervene? Dynamic predictors of sexual assault recidivism. *Criminal Justice & Behavior, 27,* 6-35.

Hanson, R. K. & Harris, A. J. R. (2001). A structured approach to evaluating change among sexual offenders. *Sexual Abuse: Journal of Research & Treatment, 13,* 105-122.

Hanson, R. K. & Morton-Bourgon, K. (2004). *Predictors of sexual recidivism: An updated meta-analysis.* Corrections User Report No. 2004-02: Public Safety and Emergency Preparedness Canada.

Hanson, R. K. & Thornton, D. (1999). *Static 99: Improving Actuarial Risk Assessments for Sex Offenders.* Ottawa: Department of the Solicitor General of Canada.

Hanson, R. K. & Thornton, D. (2000). Improving risk assessments for sex offenders: A comparison of three actuarial scales. *Law & Human Behavior, 24,* 119-136.

Harris, G. T., Rice, M. E., & Quinsey, V. L. (1993). Violent recidivism of mentally disordered offenders: The development of a statistical prediction instrument. *Criminal Justice & Behavior, 20,* 315-335.

Hecker, J., Scoular, J., Righthand, S., & Nangle, D. (2002, October). *Predictive validity of the J-SOAP over 10-plus years: Implications for risk assessment.* Paper presented at the 21st Annual Meeting of the Association for Treatment of Sexual Abusers, Montreal, Quebec, Canada.

Kahn, T. J. & Chambers, H. J. (1991). Assessing reoffense risk with juvenile sexual offenders. *Child Welfare, 70,* 333-345.

Knight, R. A. & Prentky, R. A. (1993). Exploring characteristics for classifying juvenile sex offenders. In H. E. Barbaree & W. L. Marshall (Eds.), *Juvenile sex offender* (pp. 45-83). New York: Guilford Press.

Langton, C. M., Barbaree, H. E., Harkins, L., Seto, M. C., & Peacock, E. J. (2002). *Evaluating the predictive validity of seven risk assessment instruments for sex offenders.* Paper presented at the 21st annual conference of the Association for the Treatment of Sexual Abusers, Montreal, Canada.

Langstrom, N. (2002). Long-term follow-up of criminal recidivism in young sex offenders: Temporal patterns and risk factors. *Psychology, Crime & Law: Special Swedish Studies on Psychology, Crime and Law, 8,* 41-58.

Lieb, R. & Goodkin, K. (2005). *Involuntary commitment of sexually violent predators: Comparing state laws.* Washington State Institute for Public Policy (Document No. 05-03-1101).

Meehl, P. E. (1954). *Clinical vs. statistical prediction: A theoretical analysis and a review of the evidence.* Minneapolis, MN, US: University of Minnesota Press.

Miner, M. H. (2002). Factors associated with recidivism in juveniles: An analysis of serious juvenile sex offenders. *Journal of Research in Crime & Delinquency, 39,* 421-436.

Monahan, J. (1981). The clinical prediction of violent behavior. *Crime & Delinquency Issues: A Monograph Series, ADM 81-921,* 134.

Prentky, R. A. & Knight, R. A. (1993). Age of onset of sexual assault: Criminal and life history correlates. In G. C. Hall, R. Hirschman, J. R. Graham, & M. S. Zaragoza (Eds.), *Sexual aggression: Issues in etiology, assessment, and treatment* (pp. 43-62). Washington, DC: Taylor & Francis

Prentky, R., Harris, B., Frizell, K., & Righthand, S. (2000). An actuarial procedure for assessing risk with juvenile sex offenders. *Sexual Abuse: Journal of Research & Treatment, 12,* 71-93.

Prentky, R. A. & Righthand, S. (2003). *Juvenile sex offender assessment protocol: Manual.* Bridgewater, MA: Justice Resource Institute.

Prescott, D. (2004, May). *The current state of adolescent risk assessment and need assessment.* Seminar presented at the 19th annual conference of the National Adolescent Perpetration Network, Portland, OR.

Quinsey, V. L., Rice, M. E., & Harris, G. T. (1995). Actuarial prediction of sexual recidivism. *Journal of Interpersonal Violence, 10,* 85-105.

Quinsey, V. L., Harris, G. T., Rice, M. E., & Cormier, C. A. (1998). *Violent offenders: Appraising and managing risk.* Washington, DC: American Psychological Association.

Rasmussen, L. A. (1999). Factors related to recidivism among juvenile sexual offenders. *Sexual Abuse: Journal of Research & Treatment, 11,* 69-86.

Rich, P. (2001a). *J-RAT: Juvenile (Clinical) Risk Assessment Tool Assessment of Risk for Sexual Re-Offending (J-RAT: V.2).* Retrieved May 31, 2005 from www.stetsonschool.org/Clinical_Materials/Assessment_Tools/assessment_tools.html.

Rich, P. (2001b). *IM-RAT: Interim Modified Risk Assessment Tool for Sexual Re-Offending Response to Treatment (IM-RAT: V2).* Retrieved May 31, 2005 from www.stetsonschool.org/Clinical_Materials/Assessment_Tools/assessment_tools.html.

Rich, P. (2003). *Understanding, assessing, and rehabilitating juvenile sexual offenders.* Hoboken, NJ: John Wiley & Sones.

Righthand, S., Prentky, R., Knight, R., Carpenter, E., Hecker, J. E., & Nangle, D. (2005). Factor structure and validation of the juvenile sex offender assessment protocol (J-SOAP). *Sexual Abuse: Journal of Research & Treatment, 17,* 13-30.

Rubinstein, M., Yeager, C. A., Goodstein, C., & Lewis, D. O. (1993). Sexually assaultive male juveniles: A follow-up. *American Journal of Psychiatry, 150,* 262-265.

Schram, D. D., Milloy, C. D., & Rowe, W. E. (1991, September). *Juvenile sex offenders: A follow-up study of reoffense behavior.* Olympia, WA: Washington State Institute for Public Policy.

Seto, M., & Lalumiére, M. (2004, October). *The uniqueness of juvenile sex offenders: A meta-analysis.* Paper presented at the 23rd Annual Conference of the Association for the Treatment of Sexual Abusers, Albuquerque, NM.

Snyder, H. N. (2000). *Sexual Assault of Young Children as Reported to Law Enforcement: Victim, Incident, and Offender Characteristics.* A NIBRS Statistical Report (No. NCJ182990). U.S.; Pennsylvania: Bureau of Justice Statistics Clearinghouse.

Swets, J. A. (1996). *Signal detection theory and ROC analysis in psychology and diagnostics: Collected papers.* Hillsdale, NJ, England: Lawrence Erlbaum Associates, Inc.

Swets, J. A., Dawes, R. M., & Monahan, J. (2000). Psychological science can improve diagnostic decisions. *Psychological Science in the Public Interest, 1,* 1-26.

Walker, D. F., McGovern, S. K., Poey, E. L., & Otis, K. E. (2004). Treatment effectiveness for male adolescent sexual offenders: A meta-analysis and review. *Journal of Child Sexual Abuse: Special Identifying and Treating Youth Who Sexually Offend: Current Approaches, Techniques, and Research, 13,* 281-293.

Winick, B. J. & La Fond, J. Q. (2003). *Protecting society from sexually dangerous offenders: Law, justice, and therapy.* Washington, DC, U.S.: American Psychological Association.

Worling, J. R. (2002). Assessing risk of sexual assault recidivism with adolescent sexual offenders. In M. C. Calder (Ed.), *Young people who sexual abuse: Building the evidence base for your practice* (pp. 365-375). Lyme Regis, U.K.: Russell House Publishing.

Worling, J. R. (2003, October). *Introduction to adolescent sexual abuser assessment, treatment, and supervision.* Seminar presented at the 22nd annual conference of the Association for the Treatment of Sexual Abusers, St. Louis, MO.

Worling, J. R. (2004). The estimate of risk of adolescent sexual offense recidivism (ERASOR): Preliminary psychometric data. *Sexual Abuse: Journal of Research & Treatment, 16,* 235-254.

Worling, J. R. & Curwen, T. (2000). Adolescent sexual offender recidivism: Success of specialized treatment and implications for risk prediction. *Child Abuse & Neglect, 24,* 965-982.

Worling, J. R., & Langstrom, N. (2002). Assessment of criminal recidivism risk with adolescents who have offended sexually. *Trauma, Violence, and Abuse, 4,* 341-362.

Zevitz, R. G., Crim, D., & Farkas, M. A. (2000). Sex offender community notification: Managing high risk criminals or exacting further vengeance? *Behavioral Sciences and the Law, 18,* 375-391

Chapter Eight

Putting It All Together
Anchor Points and Communication

David Prescott

This chapter provides ideas for the practical application of the concepts presented throughout the book. It begins with a discussion of how to walk into an assessment situation (whether a formal evaluation or incident review) and begin to understand its key elements. By keeping in mind some simple routines (e.g., consider historical variables first) and framework (e.g., the dynamic risk domains), professionals are better poised to keep themselves grounded.

Anchor Points

The following points offer a rough order of events. Depending on the circumstances, this order may vary. For example, a brief review of an incident may not allow for a comprehensive file review prior to an interview. However, some aspects of this sequence can be very helpful to professionals seeking to stay focused and avoid the pitfall of considering too much information:

> REVIEW THE FILE. As noted earlier, professionals who assume they know a case well enough to forego a file review are probably making a mistake. Skipping a file review should be considered a diagnostic indicator for the professional. File reviews emphasize important historical information and can serve as a reminder that what the professional sees is not necessarily what they really have.

> SEPARATE RISK, NEED, RESPONSIVITY, AND READINESS. Files and clinical interviews can produce large amounts of information. It is useful for the professional to consider whether various aspects are more related to the risk, need, or responsivity principles (described in chapter two). Professionals will also wish to consider readiness to engage in strategies for reducing risk and providing assistance to victims. In this way, the professional can partition off information that seems important but is not empirically associated

with risk for further consideration in treatment and risk management plans.

Professionals should begin by looking for historical markers such as persistence (despite detection? detection and sanction? detection, sanction, and treatment?) and prior treatment experience (completed? If not, why not?). This facilitates the consideration of risk prior to the formation of opinions about the individual, which may prejudice the less diligent practitioner (Williams, 1975). For this reason, wherever possible, professionals should consider risk before making assessments of need, responsivity, and readiness.

INTERVIEW WITH OPEN-ENDED QUESTIONS. Research suggests that this is much more difficult than it might seem (Sternberg, Lamb, Esplin, Orbach, & Hershkowitz, 2002). Further, young people, even older adolescents, can be far more suggestible and susceptible to interviewer cues and bias than adults realize. Adults can unknowingly provide information about what they want and expect to youth who edit their answers accordingly.

The trend among professionals working with sexually abusive youth has been to narrow interviews to simple facts, to "break down denial," and to chase after various details rather than to listen to the youth's story. While all mental health professionals will want to have skills for gently moving people back on track in clinical interviews, it is easy to forget that many narratives contain useful information about a young person's attitudes, relationships, and worldview.

Even denial itself can contain useful information. The attendant objections can be pro-social and indicative of the values that the youth would like to live by. For example, the statement "I would never do that ... my mom would kill me" suggests a very different orientation from "I would never do that, and you're an idiot for thinking I would."

INTERVIEW WITHOUT IMMEDIATE DEMAND FOR FULL DISCLOSURE. Obtaining a truthful account is obviously important. However, interviewer enthusiasm for a short-term disclosure can create long-term problems. For example, youths attempting to disclose before they are entirely ready are subject to introducing distortions and even lies that become all the more difficult to retract later in treatment. Further, in some circumstances, asking too much of a youth in an interview can leave him susceptible to deterioration or harmful behavior (including self-injury) or the belief that adult professionals are intrusive or can't be trusted. In many instances, taking disclosure slowly can build a level of tension that will motivate the youth to provide a better disclosure.

Although sexual aggression is cause for great concern, this does not mean that professionals cannot express compassion as well. Professionals should honor the individual while deploring the behavior. While it can be tempting to begin an interview by saying "We're here to talk about what you did," it may be more productive to say "People are very concerned about this incident. Before we discuss it, how are you doing? Is everything okay?" It is possible to be very compassionate and very direct at the same time.

LOOK PAST DENIAL, MINIMIZATION, REMORSE, AND EMPATHY. It is all too easy for professionals to apply meaning to these elements, while there is too little evidence of their predictive value. Additionally, these aspects can change dramatically over brief periods of time and from one interviewer to the next. In some cases, the youth may simply not like the professional. In the case of empathy, individuals may be very empathic in general, but not for their specific victims (Hanson, 2003). As noted earlier, these aspects can inform assessments of readiness and responsivity, but professionals should avoid the temptation to adjust a risk assessment based on them.

LOOK PAST REFERRAL OFFENSE. There is no question that referral (also known as "index") offenses are extremely important in treatment planning and general consideration. After all, at least on one occasion, the young person has been willing to engage in this behavior. However, because of the evidence that referral offenses are not predictive, professionals should partition them out of decisions based on risk. Predictive validity does not come out of having multiple offenses; it comes out of having persisted despite detection and interventions. Professionals should be highly cautious in considering situations where a youth acknowledges large numbers of victims prior to being detected for the first time. Sexual abusers very often have undetected victims, but some youth are more willing to disclose this than others. In the adult literature, having multiple victims has not proven to be predictive. While having multiple victims may indicate indiscriminate behavior or a dynamic factor such as sexual preoccupation, professionals should be cautious in interpreting this element.

CONSIDER THE DYNAMIC FACTORS IN CHAPTER THREE. After considering risk, need, and responsivity, the five domains can serve as useful bins for information, and as a framework for considering that information. These domains also lend themselves to report structure, where the professional can describe them one at a time.

CONSIDER DEVELOPMENTAL/CONTEXTUAL FACTORS. Research has not yet devised a way to look directly at an individual's long-term willingness to engage in harmful behavior. As one professional noted, "You can't just peel back someone's skull and look inside." However, one can first look at historical variables to form a core assessment, then look at dynamic variables to refine that assessment and consider the elements that might contribute to a reoffense process, and then consider the youth's development and context to refine the assessment further still. Developmental and contextual factors can be either aggravating or mitigating, and can inform treatment and management strategies.

CONSIDER ASSETS/PROTECTIVE FACTORS. Many of these will show up among the developmental and contextual factors, but paying special attention to them in their own right will be essential in understanding and treating the youth.

CONSIDER BASE RATES. As one gathers information, it is worthwhile to explicitly ground one's assessment within the base rates of interest.

Report Writing

If risk assessment isn't already risky enough, discussion about communicating findings is truly dangerous. Writing can be a highly sensitive and emotionally charged topic, with divergent opinions spanning from comma usage to the proper placement of a report's summary. The following discussion provides recommendations for professionals looking for new ideas for report writing, but is by no means the final word on style or content. A sample assessment is included as an appendix, which may be useful as a template for structuring a report.

To paraphrase the words of Mark Twain, "It may well be that all professionals want to have written good reports, but almost none want to write them." It is easy to forget that practicing writing can help organize thoughts and promote speaking skills. As in all things, practice makes perfect. The form and content of an assessment report will depend on the referral question, the youth, and his situation.

By the time many assessors start producing reports, they have long forgotten the rules of writing they learned in high school. Some may never have learned them at all. In order to have influence in whatever setting a report appears, it is highly advisable for professionals to review some basic rules of writing. The following are basic guidelines:

AVOID THE PASSIVE VOICE. Sexual abuse produces complicated language. It is easy to emphasize what happened to someone rather than saying what someone did. Whether signaling the emotional distress of the writer or reflecting the language of victim impact statements, professionals working with sexual abuse lean too heavily on the passive voice. For example, many authors sympathizing with the victim will say, "She was fondled by him over her clothes on five occasions." However, the same sentence is more accurately stated "He fondled her over her clothes on five occasions." Although it may seem a small difference, this also places the responsibility for the action back onto the actor.

THE STRENGTH OF LANGUAGE IS IN NOUNS AND VERBS, NOT ADJECTIVES. Reports should be about facts, actions, and the people involved. Professionals risk sacrificing language when they are at a loss for describing these elements. In those moments when professionals have to search for the right language, it becomes easy to depend on adjectives to make the case. For example, the sentence "Mr. X has engaged in explosive outbursts and has been disruptive in five out of the seven most recent group sessions" is far more descriptive than "Mr. X is resistant in group." Adjectives can also say more about the attitude of the author than the subject, as in "Mr. X's treatment progress has been poor."

THE FIRST WORDS IN A SENTENCE ARE OFTEN THE MOST IMPORTANT. Readers are referred to the works of Chomsky (2002), Rudacille (1994), and Sapir (1988) for further discussion of the reasons for this. In some cases, this can mandate the use of the passive voice. "Mr. X was convicted of..." is far more common than "The court convicted Mr. X..." Mr. X is the most important part of that sentence, because it is about his conviction.

Listening to the order of words in a clinical interview (including where a subject starts his/her story) or observing their sequence in a written sentence yields significant information about the person using them. This may be one reason that professionals quickly resort to the passive voice—in many cases because they are identifying with the victim. As a result, sentences turn into "the victim was molested by Mr. X" rather than "Mr. X molested the victim." Professionals should keep the order of words in mind when interviewing and writing. Although not specific to report writing, consider the following story, overheard at a breakfast diner:

> *I woke up on the floor again, at 4:30 this morning. We all had been out drinking, and when they all went to bed they didn't even move me. I got up and said "whatever" and went out to clean my truck. Then at 6:00 a.m. some other friends come over to see if I want to go fishing. So we went for a while. Then when I get home my girlfriend calls me an asshole. Whatever.... She's been really sick, and I invited her to come along anyway, but she didn't want to. I gotta work the whole rest of the week.*

This man's story begins with waking up on the floor, apparently without much concern. It is noteworthy that his girlfriend, her illness, and their relationship are not mentioned until the end. His use of the word "whatever" appears both dismissive of what would cause others great concern and reflective of a passive orientation to his own life. At least in this paragraph, he does not express an understanding of how his girlfriend came to call him a rude name. Clearly, one cannot make inferences based on one paragraph, but it does illustrate how the details of language can speak volumes. It also illustrates how useful quotes can be within the body of a report.

AVOID WORDS ENDING IN "LY." Again, careful organization of the facts and words makes relying on descriptive but unfocused language unnecessary. "Mr. X is moving slowly in treatment" provides less information and more opinion than "Mr. X has yet to complete the introductory blocks of the treatment program."

ALWAYS REVIEW A PRINTED COPY OF A REPORT PRIOR TO SIGN-ING AND DISTRIBUTING IT. This prevents embarrassing errors and ensures a better text. No matter how great the author, everyone's work improves after a thorough review and edit. This is even more important when working off a preestablished template or taking shortcuts, such as "cutting and pasting" from other reports where other individuals' names may appear. Although these practices lack wisdom and are potentially dangerous, they are common among practitioners, as evidenced by their mistakes.

Have a supervisor or colleague review your report in accordance with confidentiality requirements. For the same reasons noted above, an objective review can help to identify areas of consideration that the writer may have missed. The text of reports can be crucial to those impacted by sexual abuse. Authors and poets often establish methods for sharing work to improve their use of language, and yet this is rarely the case amongst sexual abuse professionals.

Review your report from the vantage point of diverse victims and attorneys. It can be easy to forget the importance of restoration to victims in the rush to discuss the abuser.

Word-processing spell checkers are helpful, but beware of incorrect replacement "suggestions." Many egregious, though often humorous, errors result from professionals' failure to pay attention to this tool. In one case, "Mr. X sexually assaulted her" became "Mr. X sexily assaulted her." Corruption of unusual names is also common, as when a colleague named Analdo became "Anal do."

The following recommendations are more specific to reports on sexually abusive youth:

CONSIDER THE REPORT AS A VEHICLE FOR LEADING THE READER TO OBVIOUS CONCLUSIONS. It is easy to forget the audience when juggling the elements to be included in a report. It can be helpful to construct a chronologically oriented report so that the reader comes to the same conclusions as the author before reading them. The summary and recommendations sections are not the place to add new information.

IN SOME CASES, A SUMMARY OF FINDINGS MAY BE USEFUL AT THE OUTSET. For example, "This report details a number of reasons why social services may wish to consider residential treatment" may allow readers to focus on the details rather than simply turning to the last page for a summary statement.

AVOID JARGON (e.g., "issue," "dynamic," "cycle") AND OVERUSE OF ABBREVIATIONS AND ACRONYMS ("CSA", "SAY"). It is easy for human beings to lose sight of the importance of a topic when authors resort to abbreviations. This essentially asks the reader to do two things at once—decipher information and understand the individual. Resorting to jargon and abbreviations can focus too much attention on the author, who is best left in the background except when absolutely necessary. Coming to terms with sexual abuse is challenging, even in a report. The use of vague jargon and acronyms overshadows the topic's importance. Sexual abuse is about harm. "CSA" is about initials, although it can be useful for research purposes. Further, clinical jargon is rarely helpful. Everyone knows that sexually abusive youth have "issues." The report is at its best when it presents the issues rather than refers to them. "Mr. X struggles with the recent loss of his father and with his mother's relocation" is much clearer than when the author states the obvious: "The loss of his father and his mother's relocation are issues that Mr. X has to deal with."

PROVIDE AN EXPLICIT RECOUNTING OF REFERRAL QUESTION. As mentioned in chapter one, referral sources are not always clear on what they're asking. After all, sexual abuse is complicated and emotionally charged. Stating the explicit purpose of the report (e.g., "for placement and treatment decisions") prevents harmful repercussions in high-stakes situations. "Mr. X was referred for a sexual abuse assessment" does not contribute to an understanding of the individual or the process of the assessment.

PROFESSIONALS SHOULD ASSIGN A TIME LIMITATION TO THEIR REPORTS. While nothing can completely prevent the misuse of a report, this can be an important step.

CONTENT SHOULD BE SPECIFIC. "Mr. X has a number of victims" is less helpful than a specific telling of what is known and not known. Piecing together an understanding of an individual is complicated; this is why there are specialists. Professionals should be clear in the actions and chronology of an individual to prevent further confusion. Human beings often tell their stories in the order of subjective importance (e.g., "I woke up on the floor. I'd been out drinking."). Authors should present facts chronologically and use quotes to illustrate the individual's subjective experience.

PROVIDE A NARRATIVE THAT NOT ONLY DESCRIBES THE YOUTH'S HISTORY, BUT ALSO DESCRIBES ELEMENTS OF HIS LIFE THAT CONTRIBUTE TO A BETTER UNDERSTANDING OF THE INDIVIDUAL. Sometimes asking and reporting personal aspects of a young person's life can improve a reader's understanding. Possible areas to explore include what the young person thinks about when he can't sleep and what it's like to wait at the bus stop. Understanding the youth's struggles can deepen the reader's appreciation of his development and worldview.

PRESENT AS MANY FACTS, AND AS LITTLE OPINION, AS POSSIBLE. A good report leads its audience to incontrovertible conclusions.

AVOID VAGUE LANGUAGE (e.g., "fondled," when "squeezed and twisted" would be more accurate) AND STILTED LANGUAGE ("his treatment progress has been abysmal" versus "he has not made gains in treatment, as evidenced by..."). Individuals' histories become more distorted with each recounting. If the victim reported squeezing and twisting, using the word "fondling" may be the first step toward collusion and lead future treatment providers in the wrong direction.

AVOID PEJORATIVE TERMS (e.g., "predator," "psychopath") WHOSE MEANINGS ARE NOT SPECIFIC. At a time when the rest of the world uses vague but frightening language to describe youth (consider the book title *Savage Spawn*), professionals can more effectively prevent harm and assist victims by using accurate and precise language. It can be more helpful to describe the individual psychopathic traits (Forth et al., 2003) than to simply state that the youth has "psychopathic traits." The latter is imprecise and leaves any reasonable reader with more questions than answers.

EMPHASIZE SIMPLE LANGUAGE OVER VAGUE OR LEGALISTIC TERMS. "He forced her to engage in vaginal intercourse" leaves less room for error than "he raped her." Many professionals use strong language to make their point when the details could make the point more effectively. "Rape" is an emotionally charged word that has been defined differently across legal jurisdictions. It can also betray the strong emotions of the examiner. While it is appropriate to be very clear about what happened, many words sacrifice clarity for emphasis. Likewise, describing someone as "antisocial" is not as helpful as describing their antisocial acts.

BE ON GUARD AGAINST EDITORIALIZING. "Issue-specific treatment will help Tommy reduce his risk for harmful sexual behaviors" is preferable to "Tommy is dangerous without treatment."

Some Examples

Here are examples of writers gone astray while describing sexual harm. The first is adapted from a newspaper account:

In May 2003, it was announced that Mr. K, 51, had been criminally charged by the County District Attorney with a violation of Wis. Stat. 948.02(2) and 939.50(3)(c) which establishes criminal punishment for sexual contact with a child under the age of 16.

The passive voice and legal language obscure the crime. The sentence highlights the fact that the law "establishes criminal punishment" rather than the fact that Mr. K may well have committed a crime. This might have been said more simply:

The County District Attorney has alleged that Mr. K, aged 51, had sex with a person under the age of 16.

In sentence structure, it may be best to simply start at the beginning:

"When he was done hitting her, he..." can be replaced by "He then..." where it is already obvious that "he hit her."

A useful axiom might be to use key language at the start if you can, and at the end if you cannot.

Additionally, it is important to note that little words have meaning, too. "He threatened her life and had intercourse with her" implies a relationship, whereas "He threatened her life and forced her to engage in intercourse" does not. "Mr. X sexually assaulted a little girl" risks editorializing, while "Mr. X sexually assaulted a 4-year-old girl" does not, and is more accurate. "She began to shake violently. Mr. X told her he would kill her if she didn't stop shaking" is awkward and risks editorializing by mentioning the "shaking" twice. This is better expressed as "Mr. X said he would kill her if she didn't stop shaking." Further, describing it as "masturbating to deviant fantasies of little girls" is unnecessary, and imprecise without a definition of "deviant." Simply stating that "Mr. X describes masturbating to fantasies of his 4-year-old victim" can illustrate the concern with facts.

Finally, *watch for all forms of minimization*:

- "He reports that in the past he would..." versus "He has..."

- "He has deviant arousal patterns" versus "He is aroused by children much younger than himself."

- "His index offense involved the sexual assault of a 6-year-old girl. Records indicate that she was both vaginally and anally penetrated" versus "He forced vaginal and anal intercourse on his most recent victim, a 6-year-old girl."

In closing, the work of Strunck and White (2000) can inspire those getting lost along the way.

DO NOT OVERSTATE:

When you overstate, readers will be instantly on guard, and everything that has preceded your overstatement and everything that follows will be suspect in their minds because they have lost confidence in your judgment or your poise (p. 73).

DO NOT OVERWRITE:

Rich, ornate prose is hard to digest, generally unwholesome, and sometimes nauseating... you must guard against wordiness. The click and flow of a word processor can be seductive. It is always a good idea to reread your writing later and ruthlessly delete the excess (p. 72).

PLACE YOURSELF IN THE BACKGROUND:

To achieve style, begin by affecting none—that is, place yourself in the background. A careful and honest writer does not need to worry about style. Fortunately, the act of composition, or creation, disciplines the mind; writing is one way to go about thinking, and the practice and habit of writing not only drain the mind but supply it, too (p. 70).

BE CLEAR:

When you become hopelessly mired in a sentence, it is best to start fresh; do not try to fight your way through the terrible odds of syntax. Usually what is wrong is that the construction has become too involved at some point; the sentence needs to be broken apart and replaced by two or more shorter sentences (p. 79).

DO NOT INJECT OPINION:

Unless there is a good reason for its being there, do not inject opinion into a piece of writing. We all have opinions about almost everything, and the temptation to toss them in is great.... Opinions scattered indiscriminately about leave the mark of egotism on a work (pp. 79-80).

References

Chomsky, N. (2002). *On nature and language.* Cambridge, UK: Cambridge University Press.

Forth, A. E., Kosson, D. S., & Hare, R. D. (2003). *Psychopathy Checklist: Youth Version.* Toronto, Ontario, Canada: Multi-Health Systems.

Hanson, R. K (2003). Empathy deficits of sexual offenders: A conceptual model. *Journal of Sexual Aggression, 9,* 13-23.

Rudacille, W. C. (1994). *Identifying lies in disguise.* Dubuque, IA: Kendall Hunt Publishing Company.

Sapir, A. (1988). *SCAN–Scientific Content Analysis.* Audiotape of workshop. Phoenix, AZ: Laboratory for Scientific Interrogation, Inc. Available from www.lsiscan.com.

Sternberg, K. E., Lamb, M. E., Esplin, P. W., Orbach, Y., & Hershkowitz (2002). Using a structured interview protocol to improve the quality of investigative interviews (pp.409-436). In M. L. Eisen, J. A. Quas, & G. S. Goodman (Eds.), *Memory and suggestibility in the forensic interview.* Mahwah, NJ: Lawrence Erlbaum Associates.

Strunk, W. & White, E. B. (2000). *The elements of style, 4th ed.* Boston: Allyn and Bacon.

Williams, M. (1975). Aspects of the psychology of imprisonment. In S. McConville (Ed.), *The use of imprisonment: Essays in the changing state of English penal policy* (pp. 32-42). London: Routledge & Kegan Paul Ltd.

Four Reflections in Closing

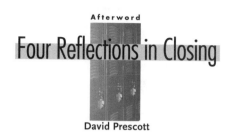

David Prescott

What lessons can we draw from the preceding chapters? Clearly, effective risk assessment involves the solid understanding of risk, youthful development, and the response of young people to risk management and risk reduction. Professionals may want to evaluate these issues in light of the following questions:

Do we want youthful abusers to stop causing harm?

To help assure this, professionals may wish to look beyond assessing basic risk to the assessment of risk, need, responsivity, readiness, and resilience. In these latter areas strengths can be built and changes made. The challenge, of course, is to work from a strength-based perspective and not just talk about it. This can be more challenging than it seems. Human beings have always been on the alert for dangerousness; our survival has depended on it. Across time and cultures, communities have sought to keep themselves safe. While communities want the best for young people in the abstract, this may not always promote their long-term development.

It is not difficult to find examples of adults sacrificing aspects of children's education, development, and even well-being for their own convenience. Professionals may consider that attending only to an individual's dangerousness without accounting for strengths and long-term development may cause us to miss our mark and cause harm. With increasing public anxiety about juvenile sexual abusers comes increasing responsibility to understand the effects of our actions on the young people we assess and treat.

Do we want to increase our accuracy in risk assessment?

Professionals should remain vigilant of our own limitations as observers and human beings. This includes our liabilities, mistaken beliefs, and thinking of ourselves as having all the answers. This likely applies most to those of us who have been in the field the longest. Professionals should understand the scales in use (including their strengths and weaknesses) and reconsider all methods for decision making. Professionals will always want to stick to the fundamentals. Clarifying the referral question and having a transparent process for bringing information together into a formulation and report are especially important.

Do we want our recommendations to be taken seriously?

Professionals should pay close attention to language and its use in all communications (including even our most informal remarks). More than just a fact of human services, writing reports focuses the mind and promotes better practice. Professionals may wish to return to textbooks on grammar and style. Professionals are also encouraged to create recommendations that can both inform and drive the treatment process.

Do we want to punish or rehabilitate?

Individual readers will have to answer this question for themselves. A substantial body of literature shows that punishment does not reduce recidivism (Smith et al., 2002). Research indicates that poorly conceived treatment can create harmful effects (Dishion et al., 1999), but that treatment delivered in a warm, empathic, rewarding, and directive style can produce better outcomes (Marshall et al., 2003). Wherever professionals land on this issue, rehabilitation appears not to work when it's punitive, and punishment is not rehabilitative. Punishment may therefore serve the short-term needs of adults more than the long-term needs of youth. While there is no question that truly high-risk individuals should be kept from harming others, it is not as simple as getting tough on crime. Professionals assessing risk will want to be very clear of their own values and study this area of the literature further in order to make the most effective recommendations.

In the end, effective assessment of abusive youth may begin with a mirror and an accurate assessment of ourselves. As we expand and refine our own perspectives, we can increase our own effectiveness in reducing harm.

References

Dishion, T. J., McCord, J., & Poulin, F. (1999). When interventions harm: Peer groups and problem behavior. *American Psychologist, 54 (9)*, 755-764.

Marshall, W. L., et al. (2003). Process variables in the treatment of sexual offenders: A review of the relevent literature. *Aggression and Violent Behavior, 8*, 205-234.

Smith, P., Goggin, C., & Gendreau, P. (2002). *The effects of prison sentences and intermediate sanctions on recidivism: General effects and individual differences* (User Report 2002-04). Ottawa, Canada: Department of the Solicitor General of Canada. Available from www.psepc-sppcc.gc.ca/publications/corrections/200201_Gendreau_e.pdf

A Sample Report

DAVID PRESCOTT

This report is purely fictional and is intended for educational purposes only. It is typical of cases that professionals have experienced. It is provided as a source of possible ideas for those seeking to change their template or use of language.

BUSYTOWN YOUTH ACADEMY
Busytown, Calisota

Assessment of Ongoing Treatment Needs

STUDENT:	Scooter Firesign
DATE OF BIRTH:	December 12, 1986
SEX:	Male
DATE OF ADMISSION:	April 2, 1999
PROJECTED DATE OF DISCHARGE:	October 2001
PRIMARY CLINICIAN:	Raving Desktop, LCSW
DATE OF REPORT:	March 2, 2001

PURPOSE OF ASSESSMENT

Scooter's DSS caseworker, Mr. Cobra Shrinkwrap, requested an assessment of Scooter's overall risk for problematic behavior to assist the department in case planning and management. An inherent problem in such an assessment is that there is no empirically validated method for determining the risk of young people to engage in criminal activity, particularly those as young as Scooter. However, recent research (cited below) suggests that historical factors as well as interpersonal and contextual factors can both mitigate and contribute to the overall risk of a young person.

Scooter is at an age (14 years) where people change, often dramatically, in a short period of time. For this reason, this assessment should be used only for case planning and treatment purposes and reflects Scooter's functioning only for the next 6 to 12 months.

Background Information

Mr. Cobra Shrinkwrap of the Busytown Department of Child Protective Services (CPS) referred Scooter to the Busytown Youth Academy. Concerns upon admission included a history of physical aggression toward peers, adults, and property, beginning at the age of 2. CPS substantiated allegations of neglect by Scooter's mother when he was between the ages of 2 and 5, and for several years he lived with his maternal grandparents. Scooter has reported a history of sexual abuse by his father since before his admission, and his father was subsequently convicted of First Degree Sexual Assault. Scooter's past teachers described him as impulsive and hyperactive in preplacement documentation. He would frequently run from his classroom, hide, and refuse to return. According to Mr. Shrinkwrap and preplacement documentation, Scooter has reportedly displayed inappropriate sexual behaviors, such as disrobing in front of others and making inappropriate sexual remarks. His mother described his engaging in similar behaviors on a frequent basis, including pulling down his pants, exposing his genitals, and shouting obscenities when angry.

Developmental History

Scooter is the first child born to his mother, Audrey Firesign, and was the result of an uncomplicated, fullterm pregnancy. He reached developmental milestones within normal limits, but had significant problems with ear infections in his early years. CPS substantiated allegations of neglect by Ms. Firesign in 1989 and took custody of Scooter. In 1990, Scooter went to live with his maternal grandmother and grandfather. Although Scooter's father frequently visited, he apparently did not contribute to his care.

By the time Scooter entered kindergarten, he apparently acted out on a regular basis. He reportedly engaged in severe aggression against peers, adults, and property. His grandparents were unable to manage him in their home, despite engaging in a wide range of services.

Scooter was placed at the New Seaport Residential Treatment Center in April of 1994. He remained there until his admission to Busytown Youth Academy roughly 4 years later. In 1995, Scooter alleged that his father had sexual abused him. The Freebird, Calisota District Attorney's office successfully prosecuted Mr. Firesign for First Degree Sexual Assault.

Since Scooter's placement at New Seaport, Ms. Firesign remarried and currently lives with her husband and stepchildren in downtown Freebird, Calisota. By all appearances and reports, her family life is stable. Scooter gets along well with his stepfather, who is an editor for the local newspaper.

CURRENT STATUS

RESIDENTIAL: Scooter resides in South Cottage of the Busytown Youth Academy. This on-campus dormitory for 16 young men provides an intensive level of supervision, structure, and staff interventions. Scooter has a single room with no roommates. Since his admission, he has made slow but substantive progress in managing his behavior.

Scooter is well liked and highly regarded by the staff and his peers. When he is not experiencing a high level of stress, he can be charming and engaging and possess a strong sense of humor. Scooter enjoys playing sports, other outdoor activities, and computer games. Scooter has a strong presentation of wanting to be a good young man. However, when he is upset, angry, or anxious, Scooter can rapidly escalate into assaultive and aggressive behaviors. Since his admission, the frequency of these incidents has decreased, but not the severity. During incidents, Scooter is known to become intimidating, issuing threats against staff and peers. This often includes intent to fabricate allegations of abuse in order to get the staff fired. At other times, Scooter has attempted to bite the staff who try to de-escalate him. To his credit, Scooter has made small gains in his ability to de-escalate himself following incidents.

Elsewhere in the dorm, Scooter has worked to improve his interpersonal relationships through participation in the activities mentioned above. He has made gains in practicing self-care skills by attending to the routines of the dorm and activities of personal hygiene. Scooter has formed positive alliances with the staff who work with him on a regular basis. However, he can be highly suspicious of newer staff, and requires considerable engagement by them in order to prevent problematic behaviors.

EDUCATIONAL: Scooter is educated in a small, self-contained classroom on the main campus of the program. Within this setting he retains a high level of access to his teacher and teacher's assistants. Detailed accounts of his academic progress can be found in his Educational Progress Reports.

Scooter's progress in the classroom has continued to mirror his progress in the residence. His educational day contains frequent scheduled breaks in order to assist him in maintaining his attention and manage strong emotions. Similarly, the classroom activities are punctuated by extensive hands-on educational activities to accommodate his learning style.

CLINICAL: Scooter meets with his clinician on a weekly basis and as necessary to discuss issues outlined in his Treatment Learning Plan. Scooter engages in sessions and frequently asks for additional time with his clinician. Scooter has been able to discuss his aggressive behaviors toward others, but has intense difficulty generalizing insights into his behavior.

FAMILY: Scooter goes home for visits on a regular basis, and for the most part is able to comply with rules and routines. He works with his clinician to develop and maintain an appropriate safety plan. Generally, these visits have been successful, although his mother notes that he can revert to opposition and defiance when his routines become unpredictable, and when he feels he is not getting his way. Under these conditions he quickly becomes upset, angry, or anxious.

CURRENT DIAGNOSIS AND MEDICATIONS

Per a psychiatric evaluation by Dr. Figmund Droid and dated February 31, 2001, Scooter's diagnosis is:

Axis I -   PTSD
            ADHD
            Major Depression, recurrent
            R/o Bipolar Disorder

Axis II -   None

Axis III-   Enuresis

Author's note: Professionals may wish to cite others' diagnoses exactly as they appear in the original [even when appearing to contain inconsistencies] so as not to create additional confusion to those reviewing the original documents.

Scooter is currently prescribed:

List medications, including dosages and times of day taken.

Per a psychological evaluation by Erik Miltonsson, Psy.D., and dated January 1999:

WISC-III:

Verbal IQ-	93
Performance IQ-	73
Full-scale IQ-	82

Dr. Miltonsson notes that the 20-point spread between verbal and performance scores is significant at the .05 level, and that the full-scale score may not adequately represent his overall functioning.

SIGNIFICANT RISK FACTORS

As noted above, no empirically validated method exists for appraising the risk of a young person to engage in harmful behavior. However, recent research suggests that some factors are associated with elevated or attenuated risk.

VIOLENCE: Static factors, or elements fixed in Scooter's history that suggest an elevated level of risk for aggression, include

- Caregiver instability, including neglect, reported abuse, and the deterioration of his birth family.

- Parental alcohol abuse.

- An early onset to persistent behavior problems (from around age 2 to the present).

- A history of aggressive behavior: Scooter's aggression toward others began at a young age, and has persisted for many years. He has been aggressive toward adults and peers within the past several weeks. However, it is important to note that Scooter's aggressive behavior generally involves unarmed fighting (e.g., fists, kicking, spitting, biting) and does not involve weapons beyond occasionally throwing objects at others. Scooter's aggression typically occurs at times when he is experiencing strong emotions and when he is upset and perceives a need to defend himself. His aggression is not highly organized, targeted, planned, or even carefully thought out. Typically, the only purpose for Scooter's aggression is to avoid perceived threats and dangers, and to establish himself as invulnerable in the eyes of others. Scooter's stated thoughts and feelings about violence do not involve specific or sequentially based themes of violence (e.g. "first I'm going to... then I'm going to... after that, I'll..."), but rather appear to serve a self-protective purpose. However, of particular concern is that Scooter can often perceive threat and insult in the otherwise harmless and well-intentioned actions of others.

Dynamic factors, or elements subject to change (and potentially responsive to intervention), include

- Underdeveloped stress management and coping skills: Scooter has difficulty managing strong emotions, even with the provision of a medication regime specifically targeting subjective stress and clinical sessions aimed at developing skills in this area.

Protective factors that can serve to mitigate Scooter's risk for aggression include

- Strong family support for Scooter's placement, treatment, and rejection of aggression.

- Strong attachments and bonds with others, and a desire to improve his interpersonal skills.

- A history of moderate response to treatment targeting aggressive behavior.

- An overall positive attitude to interventions targeting aggressive behavior.

- The absence of a history of nonviolent, nonsexual offending.

- The relative absence of peer delinquency or peer rejection.

- Involvement and interest in pro-social activities such as sports, family activities.

- The relative absence of planned, purposeful, organized violence.

- A generally resilient interpersonal style.

Scooter prefers to engage in activities typical of boys his age, and does not appear to obsessively ruminate on themes of violence. Although he expresses anger and rage at some perceived elements of his personal history, he has no apparent investment in maintaining a violent persona or behavior. He has no history of substance abuse or of interest in weapons.

SEXUAL MISCONDUCT: Although Scooter has a self-reported history of inappropriate sexual behavior directed at others, no specific static factors other than this history indicate an increased level of risk for sexually abusive behavior. He has not been charged or convicted of any sexual offense, and presents with no apparent evidence of deviant preferences or paraphilias, whether related to illegal sexual behavior or not.

Although many of the factors predictive of violence noted above can also be predictive of sexual aggression, Scooter has shown no strong predisposition to sexual behavior during his placement. Although involved in one situation following his admission in which he and another student briefly exposed themselves to each other, Scooter's motivation appeared to be more the excitement of breaking rules than engaging in sexual behavior. Scooter has not been involved in any other reported instances of inappropriate sexual behavior since this time. Although Scooter was apparently detected engaging in problematic behaviors in a previous placement, and persisted despite this detection, the same cannot be said of his recent behavior.

Dynamic factors that suggest an elevated risk for sexual misconduct:

- *Impulsivity.* Scooter's aggressive behavior, as well as his sole instance of sexualized behavior at Busytown Youth Academy, have been primarily impulsive. When agitated, excited, or experiencing strong emotions, Scooter can have serious difficulty weighing the pros and cons of his actions, as well as the effects of his actions on himself and others. At these times, his capacity for reflection and forethought are diminished. While Scooter's aggressive behaviors have been primarily impulsive, it should be noted that Scooter's overall appearance in daily routines can be impulsive as well, suggesting that interventions targeting this factor will be of primary importance in reducing Scooter's risk for a wide range of problem behaviors.

- *Aggressive thinking.* When upset or agitated, Scooter can quickly revert to an active belief that he is a victim of others as well as of circumstances, whether accurate or not. He becomes angry easily and makes statements that justify an aggressive response. He has described a range of permission-giving self-statements, including the belief that others "deserve" his aggression. However, Scooter rarely expresses these same beliefs and attitudes when he is not under stress. Further, when he is not stressed, he expresses disgust both for his actions and the thought patterns that support them.

It should also be noted that Scooter is experiencing puberty. Although this is associated with increased sexual interest and arousal, it is also associated with dynamic and fluid changes of interest and arousal in males (e.g., Hunter & Becker, 1994; Hunter & Goodwin, 1992). For this reason, it is impossible to forecast what level of preoccupation or preference for abusive sexual behavior may or may not emerge in Scooter's future.

Protective factors that can serve to mitigate the risk of sexually abusive behaviors include

- An acceptance of his responsibility for past misconduct with little, if any, minimization.
- An internal motivation for change.
- A beginning ability to understand patterns of appropriate versus inappropriate behavior.
- A relatively stable home environment and family support of treatment.
- A beginning understanding of healthy sexual behavior.
- The presence of community supports (e.g., church).

Despite the above-mentioned factors, Scooter has a history of impulsive and sexualized behaviors. He should be considered at a level of risk to engage in indiscriminate, but not necessarily abusive, sexual behavior if left unsupervised with other children.

GENERAL MISCONDUCT: Scooter has no history of involvement with the legal system. He does not associate with an actively delinquent peer group or friends. He expresses no attitudes supportive of crime or criminality, and displays no overt fascination with topics related to crime. His mother and stepfather are not supportive of crime either overtly or subtly, and are supportive of his placement and treatment. Scooter's family does not live in a high-crime area.

Scooter lacks any historical factors predictive of general misconduct and criminality. However, his impulsivity and susceptibility to peer pressure should caution the supportive adults in his life to provide him with an ongoing level of supervision, education, and pro-social activities to prevent a pattern of illegal behaviors.

Summary and Conclusions

Recent research suggests that an early onset and persistent course of aggressive behavior can be predictive of future aggression. A review of Scooter's past behavior and current circumstances suggests that he is at greater risk for continued physical aggression than for sexual misconduct. However, it is important to note that the majority of Scooter's acting out has occurred within residential settings. While this is not necessarily indicative of functioning in the community, the fact that this aggression has persisted despite numerous interventions is of concern.

During his course of placement at Busytown Youth Academy, Scooter has had relatively successful visitation with his family. However, they have occasionally reported his reversion to defiance. Although Scooter has not been involved in any critical incidents at home to this point, he should be considered at considerable risk for aggressive acting out, particularly when stressed, agitated, upset, or feeling as though no one is listening to him. It is important to note that Scooter's perception of provocation does not necessarily reflect the intentions of others.

Recent research evidence suggests that sexual reoffense after detection and treatment is statistically unusual (Alexander, 1999; Worling & Curwen, 2000). Although any level of risk is undesirable, Scooter has a history of positive response to supervision and interventions. It is anticipated that with the ongoing supervision and intervention of supportive adults, Scooter's risk for sexual behavior problems can be kept reasonably low. However, given Scooter's age and developmental status, he should be considered at risk for indiscriminate (though not necessarily illegal) sexual behavior in the coming years. It is therefore recommended that he continue to be provided with appropriate education around sexuality, as well as interpersonal relationships and boundaries.

Scooter does not have a history of other forms of harmful behavior, and is not considered to be at significant risk for general forms of criminal behavior at this time.

Scooter continues to require a level of care such as residential treatment in order to manage his aggressive behavior. He is persistently aggressive toward others, albeit with the motivations described above. Scooter has been able to make substantive but often very slow progress at Busytown Youth Academy and can be viewed as responsive to interventions. Despite his behavior, he remains well liked by both the staff and his peers. Although his discharge will depend on completion of treatment goals, his current projected discharge date is October, 2001. In the coming months, both before and after his eventual discharge, the adults in Scooter's life should remain vigilant for any signs of escalation in aggressive behavior. This could include (but is not limited to)

- Evidence of planning aggressive events.

- Evidence of increased forethought and purpose to aggression beyond perceived reduction of vulnerability.

- Specifically targeting individuals.

- Evidence of violent fantasies, including sequential ideation of aggressive acts.

- Increased medication noncompliance.

- Increased complaints of mistreatment of others (whether justified or not).

- Deteriorating peer or family relationships.

These "warning signs" could indicate a change in the course and pattern of Scooter's behavior, and should indicate an increased level of risk and imminence of destructive behaviors.

_____   _____
Raving Desktop, LICSW   Date

REFERENCES AND RESOURCES

Authors can provide citations or other resources that may help future professionals here.

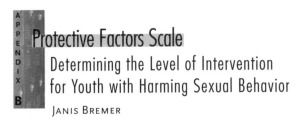

Protective Factors Scale
Determining the Level of Intervention
for Youth with Harming Sexual Behavior

JANIS BREMER

Background

The Protective Factors Scale (PFS) was initially designed as a way to evaluate the adequacy of initial placement orders for treatment (Bremer, 1998). The results of the pilot study indicate that the PFS did predict at what level of placement a youth would successfully complete treatment. It is a placement tool that fits a unique niche. Community safety involves more than just sexual recidivism. A means of determining where to place a youth on the continuum of care (Bengis, 1986) is quite useful. The continuum of care places youth on a range of service from short-term psycho-educational community-based to intensive outpatient treatment, placement in the community, placement out of the community, and correctional secure placement.

Although not mutually exclusive, the hierarchy of sexual offenses, as defined legally, and the meaning of a harmful sexual behavior for the individual are not equivalent. Juvenile court and social services depend on evaluations to guide their decision making. It is our job to explain clearly and cogently to the courts how an individual presents regardless of the petitioned charge. In order to do this in a consistent and valid manner, we must develop empirically driven bases for recommendations. When looking at level-of-placement decisions, a holistic assessment provides both the parameters for community safety and the needed structure to get the youth's attention. The initial PFS had good inter-rater reliability (Bremer, 1998) and items with strong face validity. The pilot results indicated the useful nature of the exercise, suggesting revision and validation. As a pilot project only, the original PFS needed clarification and definition, which allows for statistically meaningful validation and standardization studies. The current design allows for statistical study and use by a wide audience.

Introduction

If we are to effectively place youth who sexually offend, harm others, or use their sexuality as a tool for power and control, we need to respond also to general knowledge about adolescent intervention. The decision about where on a continuum of care effective intervention lies with a particular youth also must consider life factors that influence his/her attention to intervention. Hollin (1991) summarizes the evidence for supporting community-based treatment whenever possible. Removing a youth from the home community, isolating the individual in an artificially structured residential environment, brings its own risks for later life difficulties. Secondly, even in this serious social arena of sexual offenses, we must attend to the three decades of literature on resiliency in order to define support for positive growth. The Search Institute's work on developmental assets is a current example of focusing on skills growth rather than the origins of problems (Benson, Galbraith, & Espeland, 1994).

Risk assessment scales for juveniles are currently in the initial stages of standardization. Juvenile risk assessment protocols are a concise attempt to develop an instrument that has predictive value for sexual recidivists (Epperson, this volume; Prentky, 2000; Worling, 2001). Although this is a valuable approach derived from the adult literature, the adolescent field is better served by defining effective interventions from a holistic position. The PFS provides a means for systematic placement, planning, and progress measurement. There is good reason to develop adequate risk assessment tools. There is also good reason to develop an effective and efficient means of placing a youth where s/he has the best odds for positive change. When do we leave a sibling incest offender in the home? When do we take fairly well-functioning youth and place his/her in a long-term correctional setting? Do we wait too long for residential placement? Does placement out of the community occur solely on the level of the charged offense? All these queries and more are now typically answered idiosyncratically through methods developed in each separate jurisdiction and program.

The focus on "risks" and "needs" is understandable from a safety perspective. However, from the client perspective a problem-saturated approach provides little basis for engagement or motivation to change. Determining placement based on a charged offense often alienates the youth, further discrediting adult guidance in the treatment arena. Legal charges of sexual abuse, which can vary across jurisdictions, do not always accurately reflect the severity of the incidents involved.

Coding Criteria

Coding is based on bringing together the information obtained through interview, historical documentation (such as court records and prior counseling records), and current psychological testing. Coding is ultimately a clinical judgment. The clinician does the coding after obtaining the information necessary for an evaluation. Information sources appear in the outline in Figure B.1.

Critical items are included, as this informs us about a single concern that stands out from the summary information. Since measures of risk and for placement decision are in the research stage, it is important to "red flag" specific notable concerns when most other protective factors appear strong. One of our examples in the item definitions includes a young man who by all appearances would function well at home while attending treatment. However, he expressed his arousal to very young girls and perceived this interest as mutual. This statement would warrant a recommendation for removal from the community.

Three areas of functioning are assessed. These are personal development, sexuality, and environmental support. Data collection will investigate each factor individually and determine whether these summary clusters hold together statistically.

Interviewing is similar in structure across interviews. We use a report format with specific areas to cover within each area of functioning. Interviewing in this manner ensures obtaining the same information from all youth evaluated and that all information is available. The outline for all interviews is shown on the following page in Figure B.1.

INFORMATION RESOURCES

Interviews
Teleconferences
Social Service Reports
Corrections Reports
Court Records
Mental Health Reports

SOCIAL HISTORY

Born & Raised: when, where, etc.
Activities: organized; sports, clubs, religious youth
Community Involvement: volunteer, religious activities; with who? where?
Friends History: best friend (length of time known)
Accidents, Illness, Head Injury
Harm to Others: (animals, fire setting, disregard for rights) separate developmentally expected harm (e.g., bites at 3, fights with siblings)

SCHOOL

Grades
Individualized Education Plan
Truancy
Discipline
Sexual Harassment

EMPLOYMENT

Place of Employment: (reverse chronological order) hours per week, duration of job

FAMILY

Genogram
Dynamics: physical abuse, neglect
Strengths
Weaknesses
Parents' Position on identified sexual behavior

PSYCHOLOGICAL TESTING

Tests Used
Interpreted By
Summary

SUMMARY

Describe Appearance, Attitude, Response Pattern, General Functioning

OFFICIAL VERSION

Take from Court Petition Factual Basis, Police Report.

ADOLESCENT'S VERSION

Summarize Prior Interview
This Interview
Similarities/Discrepancies
Client's Perception of Victim Perspective
Client Attitude, Presentation Style

SEXUAL HISTORY

Where Learned: school, friends, family
Define Terms: (at least three) masturbation, heterosexuality, etc.
Early Peer Body Play: 4-6 yrs. expected
Puberty: when; early, middle, late
Sexual Messages: none, negative, positive
Access to Sexual Materials: phone, internet, magazines, books, movies
Sexual Thoughts
Sexual Preference: describe
Fetishes
Prior Sexual Victimization

DRUG USE

Prior Assessments: if any
Experimentation/Use
Parent Opinion

SOCIAL SERVICE INTERVENTIONS

Child Protection, Family Services

PRIOR PSYCHOLOGICAL/ PSYCHIATRIC INTERVENTIONS

Current Medications
Agency/Therapist/Dates with reason, recommendations, outcome (reverse chronological order)

Figure B.1

Not all components of the definition are coded at any particular rating level. Not every facet of definition will fit every case. Critical items are noted when one specific aspect of the youth's experience overrides all else for rating determination.

Summary Presentation

The evaluation report includes a summary of protective factors. The summary immediately precedes recommendations, allowing easy access for allied professionals to reference the reason for specific recommendations. Factors are listed and key characteristics described for each one. Critical items are described. Since the scale is currently in pilot format, numerical value should not be assigned at this point. Summary examples are presented at the end of the coding manual.

PERSONAL DEVELOPMENT

P1 | GENERAL BEHAVIOR

This factor considers the evidence for a positive social orientation versus an asocial or antisocial orientation. It includes delinquent acts across settings. This factor focuses on behavior rather than the dynamics of relationships. It does include classifications of behavior patterns defined by impulsiveness, compulsiveness, and aggression. Impulsivity, a multidimensional construct, is a pervasive component of entrenched antisocial behavior (Hare, 1991). Compulsivity's key characteristic is the uncontrollable repetition of a behavior that interferes with daily functioning. The ability to make informed and thoughtful decisions that follow mainstream social norms can be a determinant for community-based treatment.

RATING 0: Youth follows rules across situation such as home and school. There is no history of aggressive acts toward people, animals, or objects. There is no record of delinquency. There is evidence that the youth makes decisions using reason and foresight. There are no indications of drug use/abuse.

> *Example: Todd followed rules without any trouble. He had no record of behavioral infractions in school. His parents reported that he generally followed the house rules and asked about mak-*

ing changes when he disagreed. At 16, there was no evidence of drug use or experimentation.

Example: Ward behaved appropriately in all settings. He was helpful at home and talked things out when there was a disagreement. He was active in sports and religious youth activities. He reported no interest in drug use, and his parents confirmed this. He had never been identified as a troublemaker in any setting.

RATING 1: Youth may show situation-specific mild to moderate aggression. There may be peer-influenced or spontaneous incidences of antisocial behavior. There has not been a prior identified need for intervention. There is no evidence of the use of a weapon against persons. There may be a brief delinquent history without significant crimes against persons. Youth may disclose experimental use of illicit drugs and/or alcohol.

Example: Nick believed he was not aggressive. He elaborated by saying he would respond with force to threats against a friend or himself. He talked about hitting or punching rather than carrying a gun or knife for protection. He admitted trying "weed" and alcohol, but felt it was not for him as he has seen the consequences of drug abuse in his family.

RATING 2: Youth shows significant disruption in a specific situation such as school or home, or there is moderate disruption across situations. There is a moderate level of person-oriented aggression. Interventions have taken place, through either social services or mental health. Behavior, although impulsive, makes sense under the life circumstances for the youth.

Example: Tim had been to court for stealing a bike and shoplifting a couple of times. He was not gang-affiliated, yet verbalized antisocial sentiments and associated with delinquent youth. He had not been involved with social service agencies. Tim admitted trying "weed" but felt uncomfortable with regular users because he has seen what can happen in his family. His mother had been in chemical dependency programs in the past and admitted to a lack of consistent parenting.

RATING 3: Youth shows consistent and generalized disruptive behavior across situations. Frequent assaultive events include the use of a weapon. There is a pattern of repeated failed interventions at the community level. Youth has a record of drug abuse and failed chemical dependency treatment. Youth shows a history of impulsive or compulsive behaviors. Youth displays a general and consistent disregard for the rights of others.

> *Example: Tony was in a correctional school while remaining in the community. He had frequent rule violations in that setting. His mom felt he would do what he wants, and she presented as hopeless about gaining control. Tony had a history of property crimes since age 11. Recently, he was charged with a gang-related assault in a neighborhood park.*

> *Example: Ken, charged with statutory rape, had a significant delinquent history. He had spent time at three different community correctional programs. He was on the verge of dismissal from an alternative high school. He believed he deserved to get what he took and refused to take a victim's perspective. His family had requested placement outside the home due to repeated property damage.*

P2 | SCHOOL ATTENDANCE

This factor is a unique item due to the significance of truancy and absenteeism in studies on recidivist delinquents. Consistent school attendance has been strongly associated with higher levels of personal and social assets (Benson, 1993). There is the common sense response as well—that is, if a youth attends school regularly, family and professionals know they are in a structured and monitored situation, increasing the likelihood they can maintain safe behavior while in community-based treatment.

RATING 0: Youth attends school regularly. There is no historical or current concern with attendance in terms of skipping classes, tardiness, truancy, or extended absenteeism.

> *Example: Ward had a perfect attendance record. He was an honor student and planned on attending a top-ten college.*

RATING 1: There is mild concern regarding school attendance. There may be intermittent skipping of classes and truancy. This has not reached the level of juvenile court intervention. It may be historical with no current concern. It may be a recent concern with no history.

Example: Tom's parents had received two notices in the last year regarding class absences. He was tardy often enough to affect his first-hour class grade. Tom had no record of absenteeism through sixth grade (age 12).

RATING 2: There is moderate concern about school attendance. There has been professional involvement or program modification based on absenteeism. Youth is currently responsive to intervention.

Example: Ken entered an alternative school due to a truancy petition at age 14. This placement appeared to meet Ken's school needs and he currently attends regularly.

RATING 3: There is significant concern about prolonged absenteeism. There may have been court involvement or social services notification. School placement may have been determined by truancy concerns. There is no school attendance due to his dropping out.

Example: Charlie dropped out of school with parental permission at age 16. By that time, he was a full 2 years behind in credits. He had numerous interventions designed to help him stay in school and did not respond to any of them.

| P3 | SOCIAL ADJUSTMENT |

This factor focuses on social relationships. It considers external assets that help youth develop and maintain positive, caring, and principled life-styles (Benson, 1993). It takes into account historical and current social orientation and activity. This includes peer group activities such as team sports or youth clubs. It includes religious activities, friendships, and free-time activities. This factor also assesses the youth's evidenced social skills in the interview situation. How does s/he relate to the unknown professional? What are the public expressions of the parent-child relationship like?

RATING 0: Youth demonstrates good social skills during interview. An assertive style is apparent even given the stress and self-protectiveness related to the interview. There is good indication of positive friendships that are age appropriate. The youth maintains friendships unless environmental factors (family moves) intervene. Youth can differentiate between friend and best friend, naming peers in different relationship categories. There is participation in organized activities that may include organized sports, youth clubs, religious groups, or neighborhood organizations. Grooming and appearance during interview are situation appropriate.

Example: Fred was clearly making an effort to answer the interviewer's questions through his embarrassment. He spoke standard English in a clear voice. He named two friends he had known since early childhood. Fred always asked for them to be on his baseball team. He listed the sports teams he played with since second grade and talked about his preferences in high school sports. He volunteers with his religious youth group at a local food shelf.

RATING 1: Youth shows pro-social skills along with some selfish pursuits and/or isolating behavior. Interview style is appropriate for the situation. Peer relationships are superficial. Relationships are all on the same level of meaning. Peer group activities hold little or no significant personal meaning. This youth spends time in group activities with no apparent connection. He may externalize responsibility for involvement.

Example: Tom said he enjoyed fishing with his cousin and a couple other guys. He preferred to play on his computer by himself. Most of his free time involved hanging out with his cousin. He liked his "friends" at school but did not do anything with them after school or on weekends. He goes to the "Y" regularly and plays pickup basketball. He added that he often goes because his mother tells him to get out of the house. He participated in no other youth activities on a regular basis.

RATING 2: Youth is mildly socially awkward or defiant in interview. Social history indicates a tendency to isolate without maintaining friendships. Relationships with others tend to be shallow. This youth may participate in loosely organized activities but makes no commitment to teams or groups on a regular basis. There is a thread of disenchantment or disinterest (asocial) in relationships. Grooming and appearance modified for interview.

Example: Ted looked like he put on clean clothes without considering their appearance. He used street language and changed the subject at will. He couldn't speak to his free-time activities, saying, in essence, he would "hang out." He said he had no interest in organized sports and didn't know of other opportunities to socialize. He couldn't name a best friend. He had known his current friends for less than a year.

RATING 3: Youth is notably unresponsive or defiant in interview. There is a consistent style at either end of the continuum, asocial or antisocial. There is no history or current interest in organized activities with the exception of gang membership. This youth may engage only with notably younger or notably older children. Relationships are not age appropriate. He does not modify his grooming or appearance for the interview. This coding applies to youth with a significant pervasive developmental disorder that precludes socialization.

> *Example: Timmy sat at the table first, looking quite grubby. He made no eye contact and was unresponsive verbally. He did not want to draw or play with anything either. After about 10 minutes of furtive glances and barely comprehensible responses, he went under the table, curled up, and refused to move, speak, or respond in any way.*

> *Example: Josh swaggered in, proudly wearing his gang colors. He responded to inquiry by swearing about "the man." He used street language to describe his friends. He defiantly listed the crimes they've been involved in together.*

P4 | EMOTIONAL ADJUSTMENT

This factor considers the emotional status of the youth. It is coded by considering the immediate affective responses in interview, information provided through psychological testing, and reports of emotional expression. This is the factor with the lowest inter-rater reliability on the pilot PFS version (67% agreement). It continues to be a factor that we need more and better information about to answer the question of affective regulation and behavioral control. Affect measures are included in the ERASOR (Worling & Curwen, 2001) and the JSOAP (Prentky et al., 2000). An individual able to correctly identify and share emotional reactions will likely handle the day-to-day experiences in the open community more effectively. During interviews, the range of affective responsiveness and the fit of the emotion to the situation are noted. Psychometrics, including depression assessment and personality profiles, reflect emotional reaction relative to the peer group.

RATING 0: Youth has a history of emotional stability and appropriate responsiveness to a variety of situations. Youth shows a range of affect in interview that matches the situation under discussion. Responses to psychological testing are in the normal range.

Example: Mike initially appeared somber during interview. As he told his story, he warmed up, shared with sadness difficult experiences, and lighted up when he talked about his favorite activities. Personality assessments showed no indicators of emotional maladjustment.

RATING 1: Youth has a minor history of maladaptive responses. There is a range of affect during interview. Moments during interview may be emotionally incongruent. Concerns are generated through psychological testing, with clinically significant indices of imbalanced mood. Current or historical use of medication such as antianxiety, antidepressant, or attention deficit may be effective.

Example: Tom laughed nervously throughout the interview. He could describe situations accurately, but his affective reactions did not always match the situation. He was taking Ritalin and had been for 3 years. The school diagnosed his attention deficit disorder. Personality measures indicated somewhat elevated anxiety and dependency needs.

RATING 2: Youth has a history of maladaptive responses. Youth displays inappropriate affect to a variety of experiences during interview. Clinically significant issues are raised through the psychometric battery. Medication has not helped moderate difficulties in the youth's life.

Example: Mark has always appeared too quiet and "sad" to his parents. Because he was involved in school, sports, and family activities, they did not intervene. Mark was unable to identify anything in his life he enjoyed at this point. He was clearly upset and often on the verge of tears during interview. Testing suggested significant depression, anxiety, and possibly even diagnosable panic attacks and agoraphobia.

RATING 3: Youth has a notable history of emotional maladjustment. Consistent inappropriate affect takes place during interview. This may appear as "atonality" (lack of affect) or affective expression that does not match the subject matter under discussion. There are multiple prior mental health interventions. There are intermittent unsuccessful attempts to moderate conditions such as bipolar disorder with medication. This youth refuses medication either out of resistance or because he wishes to continue with illicit substance use.

Example: Joe responded throughout interview with no range of affect. He had been under the care of counselors off and on since age 5. Diagnoses were varied, and he had been through trials of antidepressants, antianxiety medication, and stimulants. None of these attempts had affected Joe's lifestyle.

SEXUALITY

S1 | IDENTIFIED SEXUAL BEHAVIOR CHARACTERISTICS

The identified sexual behavior is defined as the behavior on which the referral is based. This may or may not be a legal offense. The baseline definition is an apparently sexual behavior that does harm to others. The offense-related variables may act as a "protective factor." The described behaviors, including frequency and use of power (implied or actual), are a dimension that may be useful in determining the needed structure of treatment. Given the paucity of data in the field, it is important to test the relevance of the known, harmful, sexual behavior for the continuum of treatment settings and success. Research with adolescents who sexually offend is countering some of the myths about "risk" and "safety." For example, older risk checklists such as the *Oregon Matrix* (Smith & Monastersky, 1986) and the *Decision Matrix Guide* (Steen, 1989) consider penetration as indicating higher risk. However, current studies suggest risk may not correlate with penetration (Langstrom & Grann, 2000).

RATING 0: No intentionally harmful, sexual behavior directed toward another. One sexual act of brief duration with no overt coercion or force. There is no notable power differential, and the youth is not in a position of authority.

Example: Joe, age 12, admitted to a sexual incident involving another 12-year-old and a 9-year-old boy. They were playing in a local park and dared each other to drop their pants. Then Joe got the idea of seeing if they could get their penises to touch by standing close together and trying to get erections. The 9-year-old went home and told his mom the other boys played with his penis in the park.

A peer consensual sexual contact reported by an underage (by state statute) girl's parents when she agrees the sexual relationship was consensual.

Example: Sherie, 14 years old, told her parents she feared a pregnancy. Her boyfriend Jon, 16, and she had been dating 7 months. Her parents reported the sexual relationship to the authorities, and Jon was charged with a sexual offense.

RATING 1: Two or three sexual acts, including sexual harassment, which are of short duration within less than 3 months. There is similarity between the acts.

Example: Michael, age 12, told his 7-year-old sister, Susie, she could play with his video games if she let him touch her "boobies" and crotch. She agreed and he touched her over her clothing. About a month later, he asked her to show him her "privates." Susie said "no" and Michael left her alone. A few months later, Susie told her teenage cousin about Michael's interest in her body. He had not approached her again in the intervening time.

One sexual act where there is a notable power differential or position of acknowledged authority. There may be some verbal coercion or bribery without threat of physical harm or actual use of force. There may be an age-based power differential or position of authority.

Example: Jo, age 16, had a regular baby-sitting job with two young children of a neighbor. Their parents were friends. One day when the children wanted to go to the park, Jo said, "We'll go if you play a game with me first." The game involved the children's letting Jo touch their bare genitals.

RATING 2: More than three sexual acts with one or multiple victims or physically forced penetration in a single event. There is a clear power differential and use of verbal bribery or threats. Initiator is in a position of power or authority by age or relationship. There is no escalation of behaviors.

Example: Bob began sexually touching his Down's syndrome sister when she reached puberty. This went on for a few months with increased frequency and differing sexual acts before she talked to a teacher about it.

Example: Jack was walking Judy home one night and took a shortcut through an alley. He stopped and told her to "suck my dick." When she said "no," he grabbed her and forced her head down to his penis. She was crying and trying to escape. He ignored her. Jack held her against the wall, pulled off her skirt, and pushed his erect penis into her vagina.

RATING 3: Multiple offenses over a significant period of time (more than 6 months) which involved multiple sexual acts and/or multiple victims. These appear to escalate. There is use of threats and/or force as a means of control. There may be use of a weapon (critical item).

Example: Tom's 10-year-old cousin talked during counseling about her secret with Tom, age 14. Two years ago, he began following her to the playground and then, during wrestling games, touched her vaginal area. When she told him to stop, he didn't listen. This happened almost every week. When she tried to stay away from him, he would find ways to get her alone. He said if she told she would get in trouble because everyone would know she wanted to do it. He started to touch her in their homes. He would touch her nipples and vaginal area. He began to take out his penis and have her touch him. He sometimes rubbed his penis up against her. After about a year, he began having sexual intercourse with her, stating she would only get into trouble if she told anyone now.

There is a single incident, involving sadistic behavior where the youth admits to feeling pleasure while hurting someone else. There is a predatory pattern culminating in forced victimization. The youth can describe planning process and victim selection.

Example: Sal was burning the stomach of his 2-year-old sister while touching her vaginal area and masturbating.

S2 | PERSONAL BOUNDARIES

Personal boundaries refer to the dynamic attitudes about how relationships are defined. Is there recognition of different social roles such as acquaintance versus close friend? This includes the delegation of responsibility for the offense. It also includes how the individual defines the boundary between the interviewer and him/herself. "Boundaries" is a term in frequent use in the sexual and domestic abuse fields. It is loosely defined in terms relating to physical space (how close someone gets to someone else relative to the depth of their relationship), social perspective (other people are "the same" as me versus other people are "different" from me), and recognition of relational norms (acquaintance, friend, confidante, lover).

Numerous sophisticated psychological and sociological theories are combined in this notion of personal boundaries. The development of these factors is in part an attempt at making meaning and enabling understanding for allied professionals at a day-to-day level of functioning. It also considers the role of admittance, minimization, and denial within a psychosocial rather than a correctional context. For example, the initial pilot study on the PFS (Bremer, 1998) found that denial of a sexual offense did not affect treatment success in a community-based setting. The way a youth tells the story of the harmful sexual behavior also informs us about their personal boundaries. Someone who denies is actually showing recognition of the social boundaries that could help rather than interfere with their ability to respond to treatment.

RATING 0: Youth is able to admit to the identified concern without detail. Responsibility is taken for his own behavior, and he can appropriate responsibility to others accurately. Youth may admit sexual intent and can define the harmful nature of the act. Youth acknowledges the victim with understanding. There is a sense of ego strength; the person recognizes that the interviewer is a stranger and does not immediately divulge meaningful private detail.

> *Example: Joe told the investigator that he and his friends dared each other to take down their pants. He said he got the idea of "waving" their penises right then. He said he felt embarrassed because now it seemed so stupid. He wasn't sure the act had anything to do with sex. He was willing to talk with a counselor to figure that out for himself.*

RATING 1: Youth minimizes or denies the identified concern. There is acknowledgment that it occurred without full admission of sexual intent. The client describes the behavior as notably less harmful than the official records indicate, or apportions responsibility to others or past events. Interaction with the interviewer ranges from a cooperative style to some level of withdrawal or complicity.

Example: Tom initially said he did not ever touch Amy. He changed his story during a second interview, saying he might have touched her "privates" while they were wrestling but it was always accidental. He said he kept doing it to "bug her." He said she was "a pain in the neck." Amy reported Tom fondling her genital area while holding her down. She said he would put his hand down between her pants and underpants.

RATING 2: Youth expresses significant confusion or may feel victimized by being identified as a sexual offender. Evidence for this includes the variability in the story across interviewers or directly in this interview. There is a consistent sense of indignation. There is a lack of understanding of what abuse means. There can be a more accurate story of the sexual concern when the word abuse is not used.

Example: Four different professionals interviewed Ron about his offense. Each time, his story changed, supporting his denial in an inconsistent manner. In one of his stories, he stated that he thought he heard the woman calling him from inside the house. In another telling of the story, Ron said he entered the house to put the cat in because it was so cold (in the middle of June). He was clearly exasperated by the whole evaluation process and said it was a waste of time.

RATING 3: Youth divulges significant personal sexual history in detail or denies corroborated events repeatedly. The history may include the current identified event of concern or not. The details described show a lack of the nature of the relationship with an unknown professional. There is significant externalization of responsibility that includes blaming circumstances and/or the victim. This externalization can occur with both over- and under-disclosure. Interaction with the interviewer is notable for either withdrawal or overcomplicity. Withdrawal includes silence, changing the subject, or defiance. Overcomplicity involves the client's taking an equal stance with the interviewer, often with a conspiratorial tone.

Example: Ward, age 17, on first interview, described one of his sexual contacts with the 2½-year-old girl in detail. He explained that she flirted with him and followed him around. He knew she wanted to be his "girlfriend" because she would lift up her dress in front of him and smile. He looked the interviewer directly in the eye and would look for agreement and understanding with these statements. He never seemed to recognize how unusual his statements were or how unlikely it was that an adult professional would agree with him.

S3 | SEXUAL AROUSAL PREFERENCES

This factor assesses the client's thoughts and feelings related to sexual identity. It considers the client's arousal patterns, sexual preferences, and sexual fantasies. Sexual preferences can determine the needed level of structure and inform effective treatment planning. The connection between fantasy and action in adolescents who act out sexually is unknown, so further investigation of this area is highly relevant. Since community safety and the status of the individual and family contribute to determining the level of intervention, we will err on the side of community safety.

RATING 0: There is no evidence of an arousal pattern related to harmful sexual behavior. There is no evidence of a preference for children or the need for violence in connection with sexual arousal. Fantasies are age appropriate.

> *Example: Michael described his attraction to girls. He liked girls in his class but did not have a girlfriend. He daydreamed about a young female pop star. He was curious about sexual touch with a girlfriend but had only kissed his girlfriends in the past.*

RATING 1: Fantasies and planning are related to the harmful sexual behavior. Client has a sense of control over these urges and recognizes their inappropriateness.

> *Example: Tom said he would think about when he could get his sister Amy (6) alone. He tried to avoid these situations because he felt he would try to touch her sexually if he was alone with her.*

RATING 2: There is an attraction to the abusive element in the sexual event, either in terms of pedophilic interest or in terms of arousal to violence. Client is aware of this as a problem but unsure about personal control. This includes a concern over sexualizing nonsexual interactions or behavior on the part of the potential sexual partner.

> *Example: Bob understood that it was not okay to be sexual with a sister, but also felt his situation was "different." He ignored the meaning of her disability and perceived her as a willing partner.*

RATING 3: Attraction to prepubescent children or a connection between sex and violence are a strong enough component that the client is unaware of the meaning of what they are telling you. Youth demonstrates a lack of control and perceived need for control of sexual preference. There are significant distortions from the social norm.

Example: Sal described the need to burn the skin of his younger siblings while he fondled them. He said he only felt sexually aroused when he knew he was causing fear and physical pain, usually by burning.

Example: Ed could only repeat over and over how these children knew he loved them and he would never harm them. When he was sexually aroused, he was always drawn to images of 6- to 8-year-old children.

ENVIRONMENTAL SUPPORT

E1 | CAREGIVER STABILITY

The presence of multiple caregivers during childhood predicts adolescent delinquent behavior in the literature. Hawkins et al. (1998) review evidence that shows disrupted parent-child relationships are predictive of later violent behavior. Harris et al. (1993), in a study of adult violent recidivists, conclude that some evidence shows that separation from parents prior to age 16 is a predictor. Farrington (1991) shows evidence that separation from parents at age 10 acts as an early predictor of violence. It is of theoretical importance as well that "caretaker" relationships form the basis of social orientation and recognition of the "other" as subject (Rutter, 1972). Thus, caregiver stability can support youth at large in the community.

RATING 0: Youth has stable and active birth parents. The family constellation has not been disrupted by major or repeated trauma.

Example: Wes was the youngest of three boys born to Diane and David. He was raised by his birth parents. They had lived in their current suburban home 23 years. The nuclear family, up until now, had not suffered any notable trauma. Two of four grandparents were deceased. Family members could describe their grief process and coming to terms with these natural deaths.

RATING 1: Youth is raised by either one parent or relative, or consistently in a stepfamily, adoptive family, or foster family. The family constellation has not been disrupted by major or repeated trauma.

> *Example: Matt went to live with his maternal grandmother after the death of his mother. His birth father did not think he could raise him properly. Matt was 3 at the time. He was approaching his 17th birthday and continued to live with his grandmother in the same neighborhood.*

RATING 2: Youth lives with birth family or in a "caretaker-stable" living situation where there is high constant stress or where there has been major trauma.

> *Example: Joe lived with his birth father and stepmother. His dad remarried last year after a divorce 4 years ago. Joe's birth mom moved out of state, sending Joe to live with his father. She has regular but infrequent visitation. His stepmother had three young children, and the family life now focused on them. Joe described himself as a living "Cinderella" and was very angry about his situation.*

RATING 3: An unstable caretaking situation includes those in which there have been changes in caregivers for significant periods of time (more than 6 months at a time), either by movement of the child or movement of the adult (multiple stepparents).

> *Example: Tom was born to Tom Sr. and Joann. They were never married and had a turbulent relationship. Tom stayed with his maternal grandmother for 2 years prior to entering school. His grandmother stated, "Joann dropped him off one day for me to baby-sit and didn't contact me again for 4 days." During childhood, Tom stayed with relatives on both sides of the family for short and long stays. He had moved 11 times in his 14 years.*

E2 | FAMILY STYLE

The ability for a youth to maintain behavioral safety in the community can depend on the availability of structure and support in the family or living situation. Research demonstrates that parental monitoring, standards, and discipline help maintain youth pro-social behavior (Benson et al., 1994). The Search Institute's assets research also shows the importance of family support, communication, and parental involvement in their children's lives. Caretaker versus biological family stability and structure defines the midrange of the continuum of care (Benson et al.).

RATING 0: The family is stable with active and involved parent(s). Family members are able to define and implement consistent discipline. Caretaker and youth interviews match closely. Parent(s) tell their story with a balance of concerns and hopes. There is no history of parental drug abuse or criminality.

> *Example: Joe could list three important rules in his family and the consequences for breaking them. The family used loss of privileges and "time-out" as consequences. Parents' list of rules included these three. Both parents admitted to and described how they handle their anger in relation to child behavior. Joe's stepmother was a youth basketball coach for his team.*

RATING 1: The family strives for stability but has definable skill deficits. There is an understanding of the need for structure and discipline with day-to-day difficulty in maintaining a structure. Portrayal of family life leans toward the overly positive or negative. Parental attention focuses on their own needs rather than their children's needs.

> *Example: Bev, Nick's mom, was aware of the disruptions she had created by partnering with an abusive man and then getting involved with drugs after she left him. She stated how she would like her family to grow and how she worked toward that goal. She was proud of her children and defined their accomplishments without mentioning their difficulties, which were clearly documented in court and social service records.*

RATING 2: The family can speak to structure with little success at achieving it. Children have equal or greater weight in making decisions that impact family life. There may be some history of drug abuse or criminality in the family history. Parents/caretakers support youth denial and/or minimization.

> *Example: Monica described her failure at getting the children to school, remembering appointments, and keeping a job. She said this was not helpful for her or her children, but was unable to break free of disorganization. She successfully kicked a "crack" habit after 18 months in prison. She relies on the older children*

to provide some money, cook, and get the younger two dressed
and on the school bus.

RATING 3: The family has no stability. There is no defined discipline
for children or discipline is inconsistent. There is a history of abusive
relationships within the family constellation. Portrayal of family life is
either chaotic or completely closed (everything can be dealt with
within the family). Caretakers may have a history of significant drug
abuse or criminality.

*Example: Al and his younger sister were raised by their birth par-
ents. This was the first and only marriage for both parents.
Mom and Dad significantly disagreed about child-rearing decisions. They engaged the children in these heated arguments.
They admitted to fighting openly throughout the children's lives.
Al described his relationship with his sister as the only "safe" one
in the family. Parents argued openly in interview, threatening
separation and throwing insults at each other. Dad stated that it
was the kids who were in charge of the family life, which of
course Mom denied.*

*Example: Dad was in prison on a sex offense. This was not the
first time he had served in prison. Relatives caring for the children said they "raised themselves." These relatives insisted that
now they could take care of the children without any involvement
of the "system."*

E3 | COOPERATION

In order for youth to succeed in a community-based program, they
must be willing to cooperate with the basic requirements consistently. Direct contact with service providers is minimal (typically 2 to
4 hours a week).

RATING 0: Youth appears on time for appointment. Legal guardian
(parent or other) appears with youth to sign consents and engage in
program. Youth actively participates in interview. There is a sense of
interaction and accurate information. Youth shows motivation to
change.

*Example: Joe and his parents kept their initial appointment and
were on time. They showed an interest in the program content*

and carefully reviewed issues related to confidentiality. Joe agreed that he could benefit from working with a counselor to better define the meaning of his sexual behavior.

RATING 1: Youth cooperates with the structure of the evaluation but not the intent. The initial appointment occurs, with complaints about it being unnecessary or inconvenient. There is no acknowledgement of a desire for help in problem resolution.

> *Example: Harry came with his parents to their first scheduled appointment. He became resistant to the question of counseling. Parents made it clear that this was the only time Harry could miss school.*

RATING 2: Youth is late to appointment or misses one appointment. There is confusion and resistance about participation by a legal guardian. Youth interview style is reactive. There is a sense of disinterest or inability in providing accurate information. Interest in participation may be dependent on potential court consequences.

> *Example: Nick and his mom came to their first appointment on time. Nick then missed two scheduled appointments without notice. When he appeared after contact by his probation officer, he said he overslept. One of the appointments was for 2:00 p.m. Mom did not return phone calls and did not accompany Nick to his evaluation recommendations session.*

RATING 3: There are repeated missed appointments. Youth is unable or unwilling to participate in interview. There is a sense of "dragging" out responses. There are major inaccuracies between stories of youth's history. Youth is hostile to the notion of a need to change.

> *Example: Trey failed to show for his first appointment. He came 40 minutes late to the second one, stating he "hasn't got time for this." His mom asked that others send the paperwork to her, and stated she was only willing to communicate by phone. Trey said he doesn't need any program, and that the offense was "a load of ****."*

Protective Factors Scale:

Determining the level of intervention for youth with harming sexual behavior.

Client #:

		Rating	Critical Item	Comment
Personal Development				
P1	General Behavior			
P2	School Attendance			
P3	Social Adjustment			
P4	Emotional Adjustment			
Sexuality				
S1	Harming Sexual Behavior			
S2	Personal Boundaries			
S3	Sexual Preferences			
Environmental Support				
E1	Caregiver Stability			
E2	Family Style			
E3	Cooperation			

Report Summary Statement

Ten protective factors are considered when making placement decisions for youth with harming or abusive sexual behavior. It is in the best interests of the youth, family, and community to intervene at the level predictive of success. It is important to keep in mind that underestimates of the need for structure places everyone in a position of risk and that overestimates can backfire and create the same situation.

> **Example #1:** *Nat presented at interview as a well-groomed, physically mature adolescent. He responded to inquiry without elaboration. He was more willing to talk about current positive life stories than his disrupted and disrupting childhood.*
>
> *P1 General Behavior: Nat typically follows rules in the community. He has no delinquent history.*
>
> *P2 School Attendance: There is no record of truancy or absenteeism.*
>
> *P3 Social Adjustment: Nat's childhood was devoid of positive social experiences. This changed 3 years ago, and he now participates in team sports and is on the varsity cheerleading squad. He is maintaining friendships made since adolescence.*
>
> *P4 Emotional Adjustment: Nat's emotional reactions are out of balance. His testing responses are indicative of a clinical depression. He swings from anger and resentment to hopelessness and self-hate.*
>
> *S1 Harming Sexual Behavior: Nat sexually abused a disabled younger sister. The abuse involved multiple acts over an extended period.*
>
> *S2 Personal Boundaries: Nat presents as equal to adults. He admits to the sibling incest but minimizes the sexual acts and blames his sister to some extent for his sexualization of her.*
>
> *S3 Sexual Preferences: Nat would not disclose his fantasies in interview. In testing, his responses indicated confusion about gender identity and concern about arousal to children.*
>
> *E1 Caregiver Stability: Nat experienced the death of his birth father, lived with an abusive stepfather, and only recently experiences the presence of a caring stepfather.*

E2 Family Style: Nat's childhood was chaotic and traumatic. Parents are now striving for stability but remain focused on themselves and the younger children.

E3 Cooperation: There is superficial cooperation with control over the meaning of childhood experiences.

The recommendation for Nat included placement outside of the family or relative home for effective treatment.

Example #2: Jean presented at interview as a reasonably groomed, physically mature adolescent. She responded to inquiry in an open and direct manner. She appears actively involved in the resolution of the concerns that brought her in for evaluation.

P1 General Behavior: Jean typically follows rules in the community, at school, and at home. She has no delinquent history.

P2 School Attendance: There is no record of truancy or absenteeism.

P3 Social Adjustment: Jean's childhood included positive social experiences. She had limited experience with peer-group activities. She maintains relationships and differentiates between levels of relationship.

P4 Emotional Adjustment: Jean's emotional reactions are out of balance. Her testing responses are indicative of a severe clinical depression. She does not, however, respond impulsively to her moods.

S1 Harming Sexual Behavior: Jean self-reported sexually abusing two young boys she baby-sat 3 years previously. She reported two incidents of molestation and three or four occasions when she kissed one of the boys with sexual intent.

S2 Personal Boundaries: Jean takes full responsibility for the sexual offense. She knows the behavior was wrong and wants to resolve the situation. She does not disclose unnecessary detail.

S3 Sexual Preferences: She clearly states her peer heterosexual orientation. She does appear fearful of the power of sexuality in her life.

E1 Caregiver Stability: Jean was raised from birth by her birth parents.

E2 Family Style: Jean, her three older brothers, and her parents present as a "typical" nuclear family. However, the facade is thin, and Jean's report of childhood sexual abuse by her brother is denied by her parents. There is notable disengagement between the parents and between parents and children.

E3 Cooperation: Jean is sincerely cooperative and motivated to resolve her sexually harming behaviors.

The recommendation for Jean was community-based therapy with family involvement if possible.

References

Barbaree, H. E., Marshall, W. L., & Hudson, S. M. (1993). *The juvenile sex offender.* New York: The Guilford Press.

Bengis, S. (1986). *A comprehensive service-delivery system with a continuum of care for adolescent sexual offenders.* Orwell, VT: Safer Society program.

Benson, P. L. (1993). *The troubled journey: A profile of american youth.* Minneapolis, MN: Search Institute Free Spirit Publishing Inc.

Benson, P. L., Galbraith, J., & Espeland, P. (1994). *What kids need to succeed: Proven, practical ways to raise good kids.* Minneapolis, MN: Search Institute and Free Spirit Publishing Inc.

Blum, R. W. & Rinehart, P. M. (Undated). *Reducing the risk: Connections that make a difference in the lives of youth.* Minneapolis, MN: Division of General Pediatrics and Adolescent Health, University of Minnesota.

Bremer, J. F. (1998). Challenges in the assessment and treatment of sexually abusive adolescents. *The Irish Journal of Psychology, 19 (1)*, 82-92.

Coleman, S. (1989). *Violent and chronic juvenile crime.* St. Paul, MN: Criminal Justice Statistical Analysis Center.

Engle, P. L., Castle, S., & Menon, P. (1996). Child development: Vulnerability and resilience. *Social Science and Medicine, 43*, 621-635.

Evens, C. C. & Vender Stoep, A. (1997). Risk factors for juvenile justice system referral among children in a public mental health system. *Journal of Mental Health Administration, 24*, 443-455.

Farrington, D. P. (1991). Childhood aggression and adult violence: Early predictors and later-life outcomes. In D.J. Pepler & K.H. Rubin (Eds.), *The development and treatment of childhood aggression* (pp. 5-29). Mahwah, NJ: Lawrence Erlbaum Associates.

Farrington, D. P., Loeber, R., Elliot, D., Hawkins, J. D., Kandel, D. B., Klein, M. W., et al. (1990). Advancing knowledge about the onset of delinquency and crime. In B. B. Lahey & A. E. Kazdin (Eds.), *Advances in clinical child psychology* (pp. 283-342). New York: Plenum.

Gray, A. S. & Wallace, R. (1992). *Adolescent Sexual Offender Assessment Packet.* Orwell, VT: The Safer Society Press.

Hare, R. D. (1991). *The Hare Psychopathy Checklist–Revised.* Toronto: Multi Health Systems.

Harris, G. T., Rice, M. E., & Quinsey, V. L. (1993). Violent recidivism of mentally disordered offenders: The development of a statistical prediction instrument. *Criminal Justice and Behavior, 20,* 315-335.

Hawkins, J. D., Herrenkohl, T., Farrington, D. P., Brewer, D., Catalano, R. F., & Harachi, T. W. (1998). A review of predictors of youth violence. In R. Loeber & D. P. Farrington (Eds.), *Serious and violent juvenile offenders: Risk factors and successful interventions* (pp. 106-146). Thousand Oaks, CA: Sage.

Hollin, C. R. (1991). Training for residential work with young offenders: Structure and content. *Issues in Criminology and Legal Psychology, 2,* 97-100.

Hunter, J. A. & Lexier, L. J. (1998). Ethical and legal issues in the assessment and treatment of juvenile sex offenders. *Child Maltreatment, 3,* 339-348.

Langstrom, N. & Grann, M. (2000) Risk for criminal recidivism among young sex offenders. *Journal of Interpersonal Violence, 15,* 855-871

Monahan, J. (1982). Childhood predictors of adult criminal behavior. In F. N. Dutile, C. H. Foust, & D. R. Webster (Eds.), *Early childhood intervention and juvenile delinquency* (p. 11-21). Lexington, KY: D.C. Heath.

National Task Force on Juvenile Sexual Offending. (1993). The revised report from the National Task Force on Juvenile Sexual Offending. *Juvenile & Family Court Journal, 44 (4).* Reno, NV: National Council of Juvenile and Family Court Judges.

Patterson, G. R., Reid, J. B., & Dishion, T. J. (1992). *Antisocial boys: A social interactional approach.* Eugene, OR: Castalia.

Prentky, R., Harris, B., Frizzell, K., & Righthand, S. (2000). An actuarial procedure for assessing risk with juvenile sex offenders. *Sexual Abuse: A Journal of Research and Treatment, 12,* 71-93.

Ryan, G. D. & Lane, S. L. (1991). *Juvenile sexual offending: Causes, consequences, and correction.* Lexington, MA: Lexington Books.

Rutter, M. (1972). *Maternal deprivation reassessed.* Middlesex, England: Penguin Books, Ltd.

Rutter, M. & Giller, H. (1984). *Juvenile delinquency: Trends and perspectives.* New York: The Guilford Press.

Smith, W. R. & Monastersky, C. (1986). Assessing juvenile sexual offenders risk for reoffending. *Criminal Justice and Behavior, 13,*115-140.

Steen, C. & Monette, B. (1989). *Treating adolescent sex offenders in the community.* Springfield, IL: Charles C. Thomas.

Williams, K. R., Guerra, N. G., & Elliot, D. S. (1997). *Human development and violence prevention: A focus on youth.* Boulder, CO: Center for the Study and Prevention of Violence, Institute of Behavioral Science, University of Colorado, Boulder.

Worling, J. & Curwen, T. (2001). *Estimate of Risk of Adolescent Sexual Offense Recidivism (ERASOR) Version 2.0.* Ontario, Canada: Thistletown Regional Centre for Children & Adolescents SAFE-T Program.

Juvenile Sexual Offense Recidivism Rate Assessment Tool–II (JSORRAT–II)

Douglas L. Epperson, Christopher A. Ralston,
David Fowers, & John DeWitt

The JSORRAT–II scoring sheet and instructions are provided in the
following pages. Professionals are urged to review the information in
chapter seven around the advantages, limitations, and use of this
instrument. Those interested can contact the authors for further
information. Correspondence regarding the use of this instrument
should be directed to Douglas L. Epperson, College of Liberal Arts and
Sciences, 202 Catt Hall, Iowa State University, Ames, Iowa 50011-1301.
E-mail: dle@iastate.edu.

Juvenile Sexual Offense Recidivism Risk Assessment Tool–II (JSORRAT–II)

Score Recording Sheet

Name: _____ ID # _____

1. Number of adjudications for sex offenses (including current adjudication):

   One...0
   Two...1
   Three...2
   Four or more......................................3

2. Number of different victims in charged sex offenses:

   One...0
   Two...1
   Three...2

3. Length of sexual offending history based on charged sex offenses:

   Only one charge.................................0
   1 day to 5.99 months........................1
   6.00 to 11.99 months........................2
   12.00 months or more.................. 3

4. Under any form of supervision when they committed any sex offense for which they were eventually charged?

   No...0
   Yes..1

5. Was any charged felony-level sex offense committed in a public?

   No...0
   Yes..1

6. Use of deception or grooming in any charged sex offense?

   No...0
   Yes..1

7. Prior sex offender treatment status:

   Never entered...................................0
   No prior treatment failures............1
   At least one prior treatment failure..2

8. Number of officially documented incidents of hands-on sexual abuse in which the offender was the victim:

   None...0
   One to four......................................1
   Five or more....................................2

9. Number of officially documented incidents of physical abuse where the offender was the victim:

   None...0
   One to four......................................1
   Five or more....................................2

10. Any placement in special education?

    No...0
    Yes..1

11. Number of education time periods with discipline problems:

    None or one....................................0
    Two..1
    Three...2

12. Number of adjudications for non-sexual offenses:

    None or one....................................0
    Two or more....................................1

    TOTAL SCORE:

Scorer: _____ Date: _____

Revised 6-3-2005

Scoring Guidelines for the Juvenile Sexual Offense Recidivism Risk Assessment Tool–II (JSORRAT–II) ©

Douglas L. Epperson, Ph.D.
Christopher A. Ralston, M.S.
Iowa State University

David Fowers, LCSW
John DeWitt, Ph.D.
Utah State Juvenile Justice Services

Contact Information: dle@iastate.edu

General Instructions

The JSORRAT–II is a sexual recidivism risk assessment tool designed for juvenile male sexual offenders between the ages 12.0 to 17.99 years at the time of their index (most recent) sexual offense. Juveniles age 16 or older at the time of their index sexual offense who score in the low risk range on the JSORRAT–II may benefit from a secondary screen.

➤ The JSORRAT–II was designed to be scored based on a file review, so it is critical that the entire case file be reviewed before scoring the JSORRAT–II.

➤ Use only official documents in the case file as data sources in scoring the JSORRAT–II. Do not use information that is not documented in the file.

➤ Score all items unless there is insufficient data in the file for even a reasonable approximation. Items that cannot be scored because of missing data should be counted as a zero when computing the total score for the JSORRAT–II.

➤ For items 1 through 6, only sexual offenses for which the person was charged are counted. Sexual offenses are defined as all sexual offenses by statute and include charges for attempted sexual offenses and conspiracy to commit a sexual offense.

- Item 1 additionally requires that the sexual offense be adjudicated.

- Item 5 additionally requires that the sexual offense charge be for a felony-level ("hands-on") sex offense.

Revised 6-3-2005

JSORRAT–II

ITEM 1

Number of adjudications for sexual offenses including the current adjudication:

One 0
Two 1
Three 2
Four or more 3

Scoring Criteria

Count all sexual offense charges that were adjudicated prior to age 18, including the most recent offense. Include all adjudications regardless of level (e.g., misdemeanor, felony). Also, include adjudications for attempted sexual offenses or for conspiracy to commit a sexual offense prior to age 18. This item is based on a simple count of official adjudications for sexual offenses prior to age 18. The number of discrete events or victims is not relevant to this item, just the number of adjudications for sexual offenses.

Examples

1. A juvenile has a record of one misdemeanor-level adjudication for sexually lewd behavior and one felony-level adjudication for sexual abuse of a child less than age 14. *Count as two adjudications, score as 1.*

2. A juvenile was charged with four counts of felony-level sexual abuse of a child, but reached a plea agreement. According to the terms of the plea, he was adjudicated for only two counts. *Count as two adjudications, score as 1.*

3. A juvenile was adjudicated for one felony-level sexual abuse of a child, but during the course of treatment he disclosed three other offenses. None of the additional offenses were charged or adjudicated. *Count as one adjudication, score as 0.*

4. A juvenile has a record of one felony-level adjudication based on the sexual assault of three victims. *Count as one adjudication, score as 0.*

5. A juvenile was adjudicated for two felony-level sexual offenses based on six discrete sexual molestations of the same victim. *Count as two adjudications, score as 1.*

© Douglas L. Epperson, Christopher A. Ralston, David Fowers, John DeWitt

Scoring Criteria

Count the number of different victims in charged sexual offenses perpetrated by the juvenile sex offender (JSO), including the current offense. The number of distinct victims is what is counted for this item; the number of charges, adjudications, or event contacts is not relevant. For "hands-on" charged sexual offenses, count each discrete victim that was offended against. However, if the JSO was charged with a "hands-off" exposure offense (e.g., "mooning") in which a large number of people witnessed the exposure, count as only one victim for each such offense. Do not count self-report or alleged victims if the incidents did not result in an official charge.

Examples

1. A JSO was charged with misdemeanor lewdness after exposing his posterior to several cars passing him by. As many as 10 people witnessed this offense. *Count as one victim, score as 0 (note that the charge was for a "hands-off" exposure offense).*

2. A JSO was charged and adjudicated for an incident in which he fondled two children whom he was babysitting. *Count two victims, score as 1.*

3. A JSO has a record of four charges for "hands-on" sexual offenses against two different victims on multiple occasions. *Count as two victims, score as 1.*

4. During the course of individual, sexual offender specific treatment, a JSO divulged that he had two additional victims for which he was not charged. His only officially charged sexual offense involved one victim. *Count as one victim, score as 0 (note that only victims of officially charged offenses are counted).*

5. A JSO has two charges for exposing himself to a group of children on a playground and for exposing himself to another group of children at the library two months later. *Count as two victims and score as 1 (note that these are two discrete events and charges with only one victim counted for each event because of the offense being a "hands-off" exposure offense).*

© Douglas L. Epperson, Christopher A. Ralston, David Fowers, John DeWitt

---

JSORRAT–II

ITEM 2

Number of different victims in charged sexual offenses:

One 0

Two 1

Three 2

Scoring Criteria

This item reflects the duration of officially charged sexual offending behavior. Determine the dates of the first sexual offense charge and the most recent sexual offense charge. Calculate the number of full months between the two dates. For example, if the difference between the two dates is 8 months and 17 days, this would be counted as 8 months. If the offender only has one official sexual offense charge, score this item as zero. Do not count self-reported or alleged sexual offenses that did not result in an official charge.

Examples

1. A juvenile was charged for his first sexual offense November 6, 2001, and the date of his most recent sexual offense was April 30, 2002. The exact difference is 5 months and 24 days. *Count as 5.0 months, score as 1.*

2. A juvenile was charged for his first sexual offense on June 4, 2002, but that charge did not result in an official adjudication. His only other sexual offense, which is his most recent offense, was charged on January 18, 2005. *Count as 31 months, score as 3 (note that this item does not require a charge be adjudicated).*

3. A juvenile self-reported a sexual offense that occurred in October 2003, but that sexual offense was never charged. His only other sexual offense that resulted in an official charge was his index offense, which was charged on July 17, 2004. *Count as zero months, score as 0 (note that uncharged offenses are not counted in this item, so this JSO only has one charged sex offense).*

JSORRAT–II

ITEM 3

Length of sexual offending history based upon time between the charge date for first sexual offense and the charge date for the last sexual offense:

Zero time (only one charge) ... 0

0.01 to 5.99 months 1

6.00 to 11.99 2

12 or more months 3

JSORRAT–II

ITEM 4

Was the juvenile sexual offender under any form of court-ordered supervision when he committed any sexual offense for which he was subsequently charged?

No 0
Yes 1

Scoring Criteria

Score "Yes" if the JSO committed any sexual offense (for which he was subsequently charged), including the current offense, while under some form of court-ordered supervision. Supervision includes probation, incarceration in a detention center or half-way house, or placement in a treatment facility. Note that the court-ordered supervision does not have to be the result of previous sexual offense adjudications. Only a charge for a sexual offense committed while under supervision is necessary for a score of "Yes" on this item; an adjudication is not required. Do not include self-reported sexual offenses that did not result in a formal charge.

Examples

1. A juvenile committed a misdemeanor-level sexual offense while still on probation for a previous shoplifting offense. He was officially charged for the sexual offense. ***Count as "Yes," score as 1.***

2. While at a residential treatment facility, a juvenile committed a felony-level sexual offense against another resident and was subsequently charged for that offense. ***Count as "Yes," score as 1.***

3. A juvenile was incarcerated in a juvenile detention facility after the adjudication of a felony assault charge. While incarcerated, he sexually assaulted a detention facility worker. ***Count as "Yes," score as 1.***

4. A juvenile self-reported committing sexual offenses while on probation for a previous sexual offense. However, none of these offenses were charged. ***Count as "No," score as 0.***

© Douglas L. Epperson, Christopher A. Ralston, David Fowers, John DeWitt

Scoring Criteria

Score "Yes" if the JSO was charged for any felony-level ("hands-on") sexual offense, including the current offense, where any part of the sexual activity occurred in a public place.

A public place is defined as any area that is built and maintained for the general public, generally accessible by people in the community, or is open to the scrutiny of others. Examples of public places include schools, workplaces, parks, vacant lots, offender's or victim's yards, public restrooms, and vehicles located in public places. Do not score "Yes" if the charged offense was a misdemeanor-level ("hands-off") sexual offense.

Examples

1. A juvenile was charged with felony-level sexual assault that occurred in a restroom at a park. *Count as "Yes," score as 1.*

2. A juvenile was charged with felony-level sexual assault after luring the victim from a playground into his home with the promise of playing video games. The actual assault occurred in the home. *Count as "No," score as 0 (note that all of the sexual activity occurred in the perpetrator's home).*

3. A juvenile was charged with felony-level sexual abuse of a child for an offense that occurred in the yard of a friend's house. *Count as "Yes," score as 1.*

4. A juvenile was charged felony-level sexual assault in the victim's room at a residential treatment unit. *Count as "Yes," score as 1 (note that all areas of a state treatment or correctional facility are considered public places).*

5. A juvenile was charged for a misdemeanor-level exposure offense ("mooning") while at an outdoor public swimming pool. *Count as "No," score as 0 (note that only felony-level ["hands-on"] sexual offenses are counted on this item).*

6. A juvenile was charged with felony-level sexual abuse for an offense occurring in an apartment complex corridor. *Count as "Yes," score as 1 (note that, although an apartment unit itself is a private place, the common corridor is a public place).*

© Douglas L. Epperson, Christopher A. Ralston, David Fowers, John DeWitt

---

JSORRAT–II

ITEM 5

Was any charged felony-level ("hands-on") sexual offense committed in a public place?

No 0
Yes 1

Scoring Criteria

Score "Yes" if the JSO was charged for any sexual offense, including the current offense, that involved deception and/or grooming. Deception may include the JSO misrepresenting his identity, the statements of an authority figure, or his responsibilities vis a vis the victim. Grooming behavior may include efforts to engage the victim through play activities, verbal enticements, or bribery.

Examples

1. A juvenile was charged with sexual abuse of a child after persuading a victim that they had permission from a parent figure to engage in a sexual act. *Count as "Yes," score as 1.*

2. A juvenile was charged with misdemeanor exposure after exposing his genitals to a younger child. The offense occurred after the perpetrator had invited the victim to play video games for several consecutive days in order to establish a relationship. *Count as "Yes," score as 1.*

3. A juvenile was charged with sexual abuse of a child after promising to give his victim some gift in exchange for engaging in sexual acts. *Count as "Yes," score as 1.*

4. A juvenile was charged with sexual assault after forcibly assaulting a stranger at a party. *Count as "No," score as 0 (note that, although this is clearly a forcible assault, there is no indication of deception or grooming).*

© Douglas L. Epperson, Christopher A. Ralston, David Fowers, John DeWitt

---

JSORRAT–II

ITEM 6

Did the offender engage in deception or grooming of the victim prior to any charged sexual offense?

No 0
Yes 1

JSORRAT–II

ITEM 7

What is the JSO's prior sexual offender specific treatment status?

Never entered 0

Entered and had no prior treatment failures 1

Entered and failed at least one prior treatment 2

Scoring Criteria

Determine if the JSO had ever entered sexual offender specific treatment or been mandated to participate in treatment prior to his current sexual offense adjudication. If the JSO has no history of such treatment or treatment mandate, score this item as "Never Entered." If the JSO had entered all mandated sexual offender treatments and any number of additional sexual offender treatments prior to his current offense and did not fail any treatment, score this item as "Entered and had no prior treatment failures." If the JSO entered any number of prior treatments and failed at least one treatment attempt, score this item as "Entered and failed at least one prior treatment." Sexual offender specific treatment may include individual or group outpatient treatment or individual or group inpatient treatment where the primary focus of the treatment was sexual offending desires or behaviors. Treatment failures include refusing to enter mandated treatment, quitting or absconding from treatment, or being removed from treatment by staff. Do not count evaluations as treatment.

Examples

1. A juvenile entered and completed outpatient sexual offender specific treatment prior to the index offense, and that was his only mandated SO treatment. He had no other involvement in sexual offender treatment. **Count as "Entered and completed all prior treatments," score as 1.**

2. A juvenile was mandated to participate in sexual offender treatment as part of a prior sexual offense adjudication, but he refused to enter that treatment. **Count as "Entered and failed at least one prior treatment," score as 2.**

3. A juvenile entered residential sexual offender treatment, but absconded during the course of treatment. **Count as "Entered and failed at least one prior treatment," score as 2.**

4. The file did not document any mandate for sexual offender treatment and there was no evidence of treatment involvement in the file. **Count as "Never entered," score as 0.**

© Douglas L. Epperson, Christopher A. Ralston, David Fowers, John DeWitt

Scoring Criteria

Count all officially documented "hands-on" sexual abuse incidents where the JSO was the victim. Official documentation may include police, court, child protective services, or medical reports. Do not count self-reported victimization incidents that are not officially documented. "Hands-on" sexual abuse includes direct contact with the victim (incidents of exhibitionism would be excluded). Such acts may include fondling of the victim, forcing the victim to fondle the abuser, oral sex performed on the victim, forcing the victim to perform oral sex on the abuser, penetration of the victim's anus, or forcing the victim to penetrate the abuser's vagina or anus.

Examples

1. A JSO was the victim of an officially charged and adjudicated sexual violation by an adult relative. Though the perpetrator was charged with only one count, a police report indicated that the abuse had occurred on two occasions and involved oral sex on the victim. **Count as two incidents and score as 1.**

2. A JSO was the victim of several founded sexual abuse incidents. A child protective services report of the incidents indicated the perpetrator sodomized the JSO at least five times over the course of one year. **Count as five incidents and score as 2.**

3. A JSO was the victim of a single sexual abuse incident at a foster home that was officially reported to child protective services. Though the incident was founded, it did not result in an official charge. **Count as one incident and score as 1 (note that criminal charges are not required for the event to be considered officially documented).**

4. A JSO was the victim of an officially charged sexual abuse incident, in which his uncle exposed his genitalia to the JSO on at least four occasions. **Count as "None," score as 0 (note that all offenses involved non-contact sexual abuse).**

© Douglas L. Epperson, Christopher A. Ralston, David Fowers, John DeWitt

---

JSORRAT–II

ITEM 8

Number of officially documented "hands-on" sexual abuse incidents where the JSO was the victim:

None 0

One to four 1

Five or more 2

ITEM 9

Number of officially documented incidents of physical abuse where the JSO was the victim:

None 0

One to four 1

Five or more 2

Scoring Criteria

Count all officially documented physical abuse incidents where the juvenile sexual offender was the victim. Official documentation may include police, court, child protective services, or medical reports. Do not include self-reported victimization incidents that are not officially documented. Physical abuse must involve direct contact with the victim, but the severity of injury sustained by the JSO is irrelevant.

Examples

1. A JSO was the victim of physical abuse committed by his father for which the father was officially charged. Though the father was charged with only one count, a police report indicated that the abuse had occurred on two occasions and had resulted in several bruises to the JSO's arms and back. ***Count as two incidents and score as 1.***

2. A JSO was the victim of several founded physical abuse incidents. A child protective services report of the incidents indicated the JSO's mother had used a leather belt to severely punish her child on at least one dozen occasions. ***Count as 12 incidents and score as 2.***

3. A JSO was the victim of a single physical abuse incident perpetrated at a foster home that was officially reported to child protective services. Though the incident was founded, it did not result in an official charge. ***Count as one incident and score as 1 (note that criminal charges are not required for the event to be considered officially documented).***

4. There is no mention of child abuse anywhere in the file. ***Count as no incidents and score as 0.***

5. Although the JSO alleged that physical abuse had occurred, such abuse was not documented through official reports in the file. ***Count as no incidents and score as 0.***

© Douglas L. Epperson, Christopher A. Ralston, David Fowers, John DeWitt

Scoring Criteria

Score "Yes" if the JSO was ever officially placed in a special education program. Special education placement may include assistance for educational, mental, or learning disabilities; emotional or behavioral disorders; or for reasons unknown, yet a history of special education was clearly documented.

Examples

1. A JSO was officially placed in a special education classroom for students with learning disabilities involving reading. *Count as "Yes," score as 1.*

2. A JSO received official special education assistance for one hour per week as a result of a mathematical learning disability. *Count as "Yes," score as 1.*

3. A JSO was officially classified as behaviorally disordered. *Count as "Yes," score as 1.*

4. A JSO received additional assistance or tutoring at home or at an external agency, but there was no evidence of special education placement at school. *Count as "No," score as 0.*

© Douglas L. Epperson, Christopher A. Ralston, David Fowers, John DeWitt

JSORRAT–II

ITEM 10

Does the JSO have a history of special education placement?

No 0

Yes 1

JSORRAT–II

ITEM 11

Number of educational time periods with discipline problems (elementary school, middle school/junior high school, high school):

None or one	0
Two	1
Three	2

Scoring Criteria

Count the number of education time periods in which the juvenile sexual offender had received any number of school disciplines for problematic behavior, as documented in the case file. The three educational time periods include elementary school, middle school or junior high, and high school. Behaviors that may have resulted in formal school discipline include non-sexual violence, sexual aggression, property offenses, oppositional behavior, verbal harassment, truancy, and other behavior problems noted but not specified.

Examples

1. In a probation report, the probation officer reported that the JSO had been suspended from high school for participating in a physical assault on another student. In a separate report of education progress provided to the court, a school attendance official reported that the JSO was frequently truant in middle school. *Count as two time periods with disciplines, score as 1.*

2. In an education summary report, a school official reported that the JSO had been sent to the principal's office after verbally harassing another student during his fifth-grade year. The report also indicated that this event was an isolated incident. *Count as one time period with a discipline, score as 0.*

3. In a psychological assessment report, a psychiatrist reported communicating with school officials with regard to behavior problems the JSO had exhibited over the course of his schooling. The psychiatrist reported that school officials had disclosed that the JSO had pervasive oppositional problems that resulted in frequent disciplinary problems starting in the second grade and continuing to the present. At the time of the report, the JSO was in the eleventh grade. *Count as three time periods with disciplines, score as 2.*

4. In a case file, nothing was mentioned about the JSO's school performance or behavior patterns. *Count as no time periods with disciplines, score as 0.*

© Douglas L. Epperson, Christopher A. Ralston, David Fowers, John DeWitt

Scoring Criteria

Count all non-sexual criminal offenses for which the JSO was adjudicated prior to the JSO's current (index) sexual offense adjudication. Non-sexual criminal offenses may include both misdemeanor and felony-level offenses that are not sexual offenses by statute.

Examples

1. A JSO had one petty theft adjudication that occurred six months prior to his current sexual offense adjudication. *Count as one, score as 0.*

2. A JSO was adjudicated for two felony assault charges one year prior to his current sexual offense adjudication. *Count as two, score as 1.*

3. The only adjudications that the JSO has on his record are for sexual offenses. *Count as none, score as 0.*

© Douglas L. Epperson, Christopher A. Ralston, David Fowers, John DeWitt

---

JSORRAT–II

ITEM 12

Number of adjudications for non-sexual offenses prior to the most recent (index) sexual offense:

None or one 0
Two or more 1

Author Biographies

DAVID S. PRESCOTT, PHD, has worked in and around inpatient settings for over 20 years and is currently Treatment Assessment Director at the Sand Ridge Secure Treatment Center in Wisconsin. He is on the Executive Board of Directors of the Association for the Treatment of Sexual Abusers and edits that organization's newsletter. David's primary interests include risk assessment and building collaboration among professionals involved in the assessment and treatment of sexual violence.

JANIS BREMER, PHD, is currently the Clinical Director for Adolescent Services at Project Pathfinder, Inc. She has worked in outpatient, correctional residential, and court assessment arenas. She has published internationally in professional journals and as a book contributor. She gives presentations and workshops on national and international levels. Dr. Bremer participated on the APN National Task Force for Guidelines on Juvenile Sex Offender Treatment. She is a member of the Association for the Treatment of Sexual Abusers and helped found the Minnesota Chapter of this organization. Contact at jbremer@projectpathfinder.org.

PATRICIA COFFEY, PHD, has a forensic psychology private practice based in Madison, Wisconsin. Dr. Coffey obtained her PhD in Clinical Psychology from the University of Vermont in 1994. She has worked in private practice and for the State of Wisconsin since completing her PhD. She has extensive experience conducting sexual and violent offender assessments for adult and juvenile populations. Prior to her current focus on conducting forensic evaluations, Dr. Coffey provided treatment for both victims and offenders. Dr. Coffey has published articles in the area of child sexual abuse, dating violence, and the impact of witnessing domestic violence. Dr. Coffey can be reached at Forensic Psychology Services, P.O. Box 907, Madison, Wisconsin 53701-0907 or patticoffey@charter.net.

DENNIS DOREN, PHD, is the Evaluation Director at the Sand Ridge Secure Treatment Center in Wisconsin. He received his PhD in Clinical Psychology with a subspecialty in Crime and Delinquency Studies from the Florida State University in 1983. Since mid-1994, Dr. Doren has conducted and testified about sex offender civil commitment evaluations, served as a consultant, and/or conducted training on risk assessment of sex offenders in 15 of the 17 states with active sex offender civil commitment laws, as well as other places where civil commitments were not the main issue. His second book, published in 2002, was entitled *Evaluating Sex Offenders: A Manual for Civil Commitments and Beyond.* His other publications concerning sex offender assessments include numerous book chapters and articles in professional periodicals. Dr. Doren has presented at various national and international conferences on topics related to the assessment of sex offenders.

DOUG EPPERSON, PHD, is Professor of Psychology and Associate Dean of the College of Liberal Arts and Sciences at Iowa State University; CHRIS RALSTON, MS, is a doctoral student in counseling psychology at Iowa State University; DAVE FOWERS, LCSW, is a Program Manager for the Utah Division of Juvenile Justice Services, JOHN DEWITT, PHD, is Director of Research, Evaluation, and Planning for the Utah Division of Juvenile Justice Services; and KATE GORE, MS, is a doctoral student in counseling psychology at Iowa State University.

The authors wish to thank the Utah Juvenile Court and the Utah Division of Juvenile Justice Services for their financial and staff support of this research project, which received Institutional Review Board approval from the Utah Department of Human Services and Iowa State University. Particular appreciation is extended to Sandy Nosack, who was primarily responsible for locating and pulling files, and to the many Juvenile Justice Services staff and NOJOS members who redacted files. We are also grateful to the following Iowa State University students who reviewed case files, extracted data into codebooks, and/or entered the codebook data into electronic files: Laurel Garrett, April Moyer, Amanda Pipal, Marnie Rasch, Heather Rynearson, Aaron Scherer, and Janelle Smith.

Correspondence regarding chapter seven and appendix C should be directed to Douglas L. Epperson, College of Liberal Arts and Sciences, 202 Catt Hall, Iowa State University, Ames, Iowa 50011-1301. E-mail: dle@iastate.edu